Jeep
From Bantam to Wrangler

Other Titles in the Crowood AutoClassics Series

JEEP

From Bantam to Wrangler

Bill Munro

First published in 2000 by
The Crowood Press Ltd
Ramsbury, Marlborough
Wiltshire SN8 2HR

British Library Cataloguing-in-Publication Data
A catalogue record for this book is available from the British Library.

ISBN 1 86126 319 8

Photographic Acknowledgements
Air International; *Autocar*; The Automobile Association; BT Archive; British Motor Industry
Heritage Centre; Chrysler Jeep UK; DaimlerChrysler Public Relations; Ford Motor
Company, Brentwood, Essex and Dearborn, Michigan, USA; Andrew Hemsley; Philip
Jarrett; Mahindra & Mahindra Ltd.; Michael MacSems; The National Motor Museum,
Beaulieu; The Royal Marines Museum; Rod Blackaller; Ian McClean; Barry Redman; Tony
Sudds; Pat Willis.

Designed and typeset by Textype Typesetters, Cambridge
Printed and bound by the Bath Press

Contents

Acknowledgements

We are very lucky to have a great wealth of archive material carefully kept by museums all over the country. No motoring book can ever be written without digging deep into these archives, nor can we do the job without the help of the generous and enthusiastic help of car club members and historic vehicle owners. To these people, listed in alphabetical order, I owe a very big 'thank you', and if I have forgotten anyone, please forgive me.

To the companies, museums and institutions:
Air International; J. C. Bamford Sales Ltd.; Chris Bashall of the Surrey Off-Road Centre; Borg-Warner Automotive; Brian Rees of Chrysler Jeep UK Ltd; Eugene Hyderman and Jeffrey Trimmer of Jeep Division, DaimlerChrysler; Essex Constabulary; Ron Staughton and Sandra J. Bialic of the Ford Motor Company; ISO Publications, London; Mahindra & Mahindra Ltd., Bombay, India; The Modern Records Centre, Warwick University; Derek Armitage of the Museum of Army Flying; The Museum of British Road Transport, Coventry; The Museum of Modern Art, New York; The National Motor Museum, Beaulieu; Perkins Engines; Will Turner of Ricardo FFD; Mark Little of the Royal Marines Museum; David Fletcher of the Tank Museum, Bovington; The US Defense Attaché, London; The US Army Quartermaster Museum, Virginia, USA; and Jonathan Webb of West Sussex County Council.

To the car clubs and individual Jeep and classic car enthusiasts:
Tony Beadle of the Society of Automotive Historians; Dave Bone; Ken Broughton; Andy Brown; Andrew Brown of Lighthouse Jeep Spares; George Burls; Dean and Denis Burton; Rod Blackaller of the American Motors Owners Club; John A Bluth; Andy Bush of the All Wheel Drive Club; Rex Cadman of the Invicta Military Preservation Society; Roy D. Chapin Jnr; Pat Curran; Mark Deane; Jack Weisinger and Danny Hartling of the Forward Control Willys Jeep Association; Kit Foster; Tommy Gaule; Max Gregory; Karl Haas; John Hanlon; Bill Hirst; Bruce Hoad; Roy Hopper of the Chislehurst Society; Ken Howell; Philip Jarrett; Gordon and Rod of Jeep South; Roger Jerram; Patrick Kear and Mark Askew of *Jeep World*; Derek Lamb; John Leach; Dave and Rosemary Lee; Ian McClean; Paul Martin-David; John Matthews; George Moreton; Roger Morris; Peter Moynihan; Bob Palma; Mike Parker; Robin Penrice; Bill Pickett; Richard Pickles; Bryan Purves; Barry Redman of the Jeep Club UK; Derek Redmond; Eugene Reynolds; Charlie Rowlands; Dave Sargent; Paul Stevens; Tony Sudds; Jeff Tucker; Saull White; Andy Whitehead; Pat Willis; Mike Wilson; Jeff Wright; Roy Woods; Mark Young; and Ray Young.

Introduction

It might easily have been a recipe for disaster: a committee comprised of soldiers and bureaucrats sitting down to design a completely new light army truck from scratch, at first not even knowing exactly what they wanted. But it wasn't a disaster: the jeep was an outstanding success, not only in its army role but as a whole new type of vehicle that the world would buy and, more often than not, copy.

But do we need another book about the Jeep? If one were to write a book that collated every piece of information written about the Jeep that included every available picture, every technical detail, and the name of every prominent individual responsible for its development and use, the volume would be bigger than several telephone directories. Thus each new book on the Jeep can only add to the whole story, and this is what I have attempted to do here, as well as trying to explain, through analysis of its history, why Jeep has remained at the top of its class.

The evolution of the jeep is collated to include input from all three of the manufacturers involved: Bantam, Willys-Overland and Ford. The jeep's World War II military service has been comprehensively written in many other volumes, so it would be wasteful to recycle such learned and well researched detail simply for its own sake. However, some mention of the procurement, distribution and use of jeeps by the British Armed Forces is made, as well as covering attempts to get jeeps airborne.

Our story, however, concentrates on the civilian Jeep, its concept and development under Willys, Kaiser Industries, the American Motors Corporation, the Chrysler Corporation and now DaimlerChrysler. Export and overseas production are a vital part of Jeep history, and some of these developments are explored here as well.

There is a British angle, too, much of which has been not been covered in any detail in any book – indeed the first pilot model from Bantam could trace an ancestry back to England's Austin Seven. Pre-standardized and standard production jeeps were supplied to British armed forces, who were among the first to put them into active service. The viscous coupling in the more sophisticated four-wheel-drive systems was a product of British inventiveness, and the Perkins 4.192 diesel engine that was such an important powerplant in overseas models was designed by an English company. There have been unsuccessful attempts to licence-build Jeeps in the UK, by Standard, Perkins, Rover and excavator makers J. C. Bamford. In sales, AMC set up their own UK distribution network in the 1970s, and in recent times Chrysler Jeep UK has established itself as the Chrysler Corporation's most successful European dealer. There is a strong following for modern and historic Jeeps in the British Isles too, and some mention is made of how those enthusiasts use and enjoy their Jeeps.

The story comes right up to date with the introduction of the latest Jeep, the WJ Grand Cherokee, and with details of the most recent Icon, Dakar, Jeepster and Commander concept vehicles. There are details of the formation of DaimlerChrysler in 1998 by the merger of Chrysler and Daimler-Benz: this mighty combine is the third largest car maker in the world, with the power to fund the now astronomical costs of developing new models, and to reduce manufacturing expenses across the board.

'JEEP' IS A TRADEMARK

DaimlerChrysler are very keen to ensure proper use of the Jeep name. The United States Trademark Registration registered the name 'Jeep' to Willys-Overland in 1950, and from that time only the owners of the trademark have been allowed to use it. Thus, throughout this story, only vehicles carrying the brand name will be referred to in this way. Early military vehicles built within the US Army's procurement programme will be referred to as 'jeeps', with a small first letter. Other manufacturers' vehicles built to a similar format will be referred to by their own make and model name.

Evolution

1937 The American Bantam Car Company sell the US Army three Bantam chassis for evaluation as light reconnaissance vehicles. At Fort Benning, Georgia, Colonel Robert G. Howie builds a light weapons carrier, the 'Belly Flopper'.

1940 The US government introduce the Rearmament Program. The two concepts of a light weapons carrier and a light reconnaissance vehicle are combined into one single vehicle, the 'Truck, 4x4, Light'. Specifications are sent out to 135 manufacturers: American Bantam and Willys-Overland alone respond. American Bantam provide a single prototype, which is tested at the US Army Quartermaster Corps' depot at Camp Holabird, Baltimore. Bantam's plans are given to Willys-Overland and the Ford Motor Company, who provide pilot vehicles for evaluation.

1941 Production vehicles from Bantam, Willys and Ford go into service with Allied Forces. The Willys MB, the first standardized 'jeep', is developed and goes into production. Ford are asked to build an identical model to help supply enough to meet demand, and agree to do so. The US Navy base at Pearl Harbour, Hawaii, is attacked by Japan on 7 December, and the USA are brought into World War II.

1942 Ford's version of the Willys MB, the GPW, goes into production at Dearborn and four other plants in the US.

1944 Willys-Overland begin development of a civilian jeep.

1945 At the end of World War II, production of the Ford GPW ends and Willys introduce the first civilian Jeep, the CJ-2A.

1946 Willys-Overland introduce the new all-steel Station Wagon and light truck.

1952 Willys-Overland introduce a new military Jeep, the M38A1.

1953 Willys-Overland are bought by Kaiser Automotive. The new company is named Willys Motors Inc.

1954 A new generation of civilian Jeep, the CJ-5, is introduced, based on the M38A1.

1963 The J-Series station wagons and trucks, the Wagoneer and the Gladiator, are introduced. Willys Motors Inc. is renamed the Kaiser-Jeep Corporation.

1966 The Buick V6 engine is installed in the CJ-5, and the American Motors Corporation six-cylinder and V8 engines are introduced into the J-Series.

1970 Kaiser-Jeep Corporation is bought by the American Motors Corporation. Two new divisions, the Jeep Corporation and the AM General, are formed.

1972 The entire Jeep range is reconfigured to accept AMC components and meet new market demands.

1976	Jeep Corporation introduces the new CJ-7.
1979	Renault buy a significant stake in AMC. Renault vehicles are assembled in the USA, and Jeep vehicles are sold via Renault dealers in France and Belgium.
1984	The new 'Uniframe' construction XJ Cherokee and Wagoneer are introduced, and become top selling lines.
1986	A new generation of 'traditional' Jeep, the YJ Wrangler, is introduced to replace the CJ-7.
1987	Chrysler Corporation buy American Motors Corporation, including Renault's share.
1993	The new ZJ Grand Cherokee range is introduced.
1996	The revised TJ Wrangler, with coil-spring suspension, is introduced.
1998	Chrysler Corporation merge with Daimler-Benz AG to form DaimlerChrysler.
1998	The new WJ Grand Cherokee is introduced.

1 Evolution, not Invention

'The jeep is an evolution, not an invention.' This observation was made by Brigadier-General J. S. Barzynski, the commanding officer of the US Army's Quartermaster Depot in 1942, and his words sum up the Jeep's life story almost before it began, for no one person sat down with a clean sheet of paper and invented the jeep. It grew from a number of different requirements and technological advancements, all brought together by the right people, at the right time, and in the right places. Those people had the foresight and determination to get the job done under great pressure and in an astonishingly short time, without losing sight of what they were trying to create. As some fairly astute individual once said: 'There is nothing so strong as an idea whose time has come.'

THE SEARCH FOR A LIGHT RECONNAISSANCE VEHICLE

At first the US Army were looking for two vehicles to fulfil two tasks: they needed a fast, light, highly manoeuvrable reconnaissance vehicle, and they also wanted a vehicle to provide light armed support for the infantry. Motorcycles were tested with a view to replacing the horses of the army's scouts, but the hostile countryside of many US overseas territories was difficult for the crude machines of the day, and so the army began to consider the acquisition of a suitable light reconnaissance vehicle – an LRV.

The search began in 1910 when the US Army Quartermaster Corps assessed a number of production automobiles. Those that came out best were the Ford Model T and the 20hp Hupmobile, but no single model proved itself to be ideal. The army stuck to its horses and motorcycles, but when the USA entered the war in Europe in 1917, 70,000 Harley Davidson motorcycles, many of them fitted with sidecars and light machine guns, went into service.

The procurement of army vehicles

The Great War taught the US Army a hard lesson. The number of motor vehicle makes they were using was an astonishingly high 216, and this was nothing short of a nightmare for those who had to keep them serviceable on the Western Front. Standardization to a small number of basic types was imperative, but after attempts to make trucks of its own, in 1933 the War Department made a significant decision: to purchase only 'complete vehicles from the automotive industry'.

Between the wars, the procurement of vehicles for the US Army was the responsibility of two separate corps: combat vehicles such as tanks and armoured cars came under the Ordnance Department, whilst the Quartermaster Corps – the QMC – were responsible for general purpose types. The QMC further classified theirs into administrative types, which could be regular civilian vehicles modified as necessary, and specifically designed tactical types, for combat support. The US Army already knew of the usefulness of four-wheel drive even before 1917, as trucks with this feature from the pioneering makers Jefferey and FWD had already made a name for themselves, and it would not be too long before 4WD (four-wheel drive) would be mandatory for all tactical vehicles.

The search for an LRV continued with the testing of light tracked vehicles. This came to nothing, as did another review, in 1923, of the Model T Ford. A stripped-out version performed well, but the equipment demanded by the diverse needs of the infantry, the cavalry and the artillery weighed the Ford down too much, and the project was abandoned.

The British army had been using ver-sions of the Austin Seven since 1928, and the German army were using the Bavarian-made Dixi version even earlier. In November 1932 the Infantry Board recommended that an Austin Seven roadster, built under licence by the American Austin company of Butler, Pennsylvania, be acquired and sent to Fort Benning, Georgia, for testing as a possible replacement for motorcycles. This vehicle, a special version known as the Bantam-Overland, was fitted with minimal bodywork and balloon tyres, and at one point light armaments were fitted. Although they did find it satisfactory, the US army did not purchase any more: in depres-

---

The Austin Seven in America

As production methods improved after the Great War, car prices began to fall steadily in Britain, but even so, most were still beyond the means of the working man. There had been a post-war boom in the manufacture of rather crude cyclecars, but when Sir Herbert Austin introduced his new Seven in 1922, he caused a sensation. Here was a modern motor car in perfect miniature, with a four-cylinder water-cooled engine, three-speed gearbox and a four-seat tourer body with full weather protection. Its chassis, with a 'top hat' cross-section, was light but very strong. Also, the 'Baby Austin' proved to be extremely economical: 'Motoring at Tram Fare', said a 1923 poster. It was reliable and serviceable, and within a few short years had attracted huge sales.

The success of the Seven also attracted attention from abroad: in 1927 the German motorcycle manufacturers Dixi negotiated a licence to make a left-hand-drive version, and the following year in France, component manufacturer Lucien Rosengart followed suit. America, however, was a market that Sir Herbert intended to tackle himself. Thus in 1929 he set up the American Austin Car Company in Butler, Pennsylvania, and the cars were launched in New York in January 1930. America thought that the Bantam, as the tiny Seven was called in advertising material, was cute, but although it was promoted as an economy car, it failed to attract enough sales, even in the depression: its novelty and nickel-and-dime running costs were not enough, at a purchase price of $445 – higher than a Model A Ford – to ensure success.

In 1932 the factory closed with debts exceeding $1 million. The whole concern was bought by one of American Austin's dealers, Roy C. Evans, who envisaged the Austin as a town car, and under the new regime the factory began to show a profit. However, in 1937 the company was again in trouble, due to underhand dealings by a small group of shareholders. Evans managed to get a rescue package together and he resumed business, renaming it the American Bantam Car Company. A restyled range was offered, which included the Boulevard delivery van with its open driver's compartment, aimed at the smart shops in America's major cities. By June 1940, with losses mounting, Bantam seemed to be in terminal trouble. Even the Hollywood coupe designed by a young stylist, Alex Tremulis, failed to revive the company. Evans' real hope for survival would be a contract from the US Army . . .

sion-ridden America, they just didn't have the money.

A light weapons carrier

The previous year Colonel Robert G. Howie began investigating the possibility of building a light four-wheeled weapons carrier to replace the army's Harley Davidson outfits. An infantryman in the Great War, Howie had been connected with motor vehicles for much of his life, and he knew that it was vital to bring up light machine weapons quickly to hold and consolidate ground won in action. In seeking to find what sort of vehicle could carry these weapons, he bought an old Dodge tourer and modified it at his own expense: lack of resources ended the project, however.

In the summer of 1934 Colonel Howie moved to Fort Benning to take up a post as an instructor in the tank section. He resumed work on his project, and by April 1937 he and his assistant, Master Sergeant Melvin C. Wiley, had designed and built a vehicle with a rear-mounted Austin Seven engine. Its official name was the 'Howie machine-gun carrier', but because it was driven from a prone position, it quickly earned the nickname of 'Belly Flopper'. In tests this highly unconventional vehicle carried a light mortar and a machine gun, and towed a light anti-aircraft gun.

Bantam and the army begin to do business

In 1937 Roy Evans saw a chance to save his struggling American Bantam Car Company by securing a lucrative government contract. He had representatives in Europe studying light military vehicle types, and mindful of the previous tests with the Austin Seven, sold to the Quartermaster Corps three Bantam chassis for experimen-

tal purposes. Under tests they did not do well, however, and when, in September, Evans offered to supply more chassis for tests, he learned that 'there appeared to be no further military requirements for the type of vehicle that they built'.

But Evans did not give up. In early 1940 he employed Charles H. (Harry) Payne in Washington to try to sell the Bantam to the military. Payne was in the right place at the right time, for in mid-1940 the US government released its 'Rearmament Program' to the auto makers. In charge was former General Motors' president William S. 'Big Bill' Knudsen, who had been drafted into the army as the head of the National Defense Advisory Committee. The big, soft-spoken Knudsen had little interest in the military side of army life – he never even learned to salute – but it didn't matter, because he had a job to do: to supply the army with as many of the right type of motor vehicles that he could get made, including the ethereal LRV. The QMC decided that the Bantam should be examined for the role, and began serious discussions regarding their requirements for a 'Truck, 4x4, Light'. With this definition the LRV began to take on some sort of real identity.

On 19 June 1940 Col Howie was told to go to the American Bantam factory, and to take the plans of his machine-gun carrier with him. There he met representatives from the Ordnance and Quartermaster Committee, who told Bantam's president, Frank Fenn, that the needs of an LRV and a light machine-gun carrier should be met by one vehicle; they also expressed their intention to procure a number of specific prototypes. Seventy vehicles were to be ordered: forty of these would go to the infantry for testing, twenty to the cavalry, and the remaining ten to the field artillery. At the request of the cavalry, eight of the total were to have four-wheel steering.

The Ordnance and Quartermaster Committee remained at Butler for one day, talking to Frank Fenn, Harry Payne and their new chief engineer, Karl Probst. The owner of the independent PSM Design Studio in Detroit, Probst had been persuaded by Bill Knudsen to take up the job at Bantam. As the latter were effectively broke, Probst accepted the post with the understanding that he wouldn't get paid until Bantam did.

Bantam wanted to base the vehicle on as many of their standard components as possible, but Howie told them that it should be completely new. Moreover Probst had been advised that the vehicle must have four-wheel drive, which by this time was mandatory for tactical vehicles. On his way to Bantam, Probst called at the axle makers Spicer in Toledo, Ohio, and gave a layout drawing of the proposed drive-train to Bob Lewis, Spicer's chief engineer.

Howie stayed at Bantam for nine more days, writing the specifications along with Bantam's plant manager, the engineer and former racing driver Harold Crist. With them was Robert F. Brown, the civilian engineer from Camp Holabird, the Quartermaster Corps' depot at Baltimore, Maryland.

Howie's participation in the project ended in July 1940, when he was transferred to Fort Knox, but when at Butler he had been asked by the Ordnance and Quartermaster Committee if he thought Bantam had the capacity to build the new vehicle. It was a crucial question, and what Howie had to report could not have been favourable: at that time the factory was not operating, and had not made a profit in nearly four years. Military contracts would offer a lifeline for American Bantam.

'TRUCK, 4X4, LIGHT': THE ORIGINAL SPECIFICATION

The Ordnance Technical Committee met on 27 June 1940 to agree specifications for the 'Truck, 4x4, Light'. It would have been fascinating to have sat in on the meeting, for once the definition had been laid down, the jeep seems almost to have designed itself. The Bantam's size was almost right: the 80in (2,032mm) wheelbase and 47in (1,194mm) track chosen were only 5in (127mm) greater. A rectangular body was simple enough to arrive at, and so were four seats, but less obvious were the reasons for the specified height of 40in (1,016mm): in fact it was the height of the average shrubbery found in and around the eastern USA, which meant that a truck's driver would be able to drive behind bushes to avoid enemy fire. The folding windscreen was a simple, practical feature, as was a towing hitch of the standard army pintle type; and the built-in 30-calibre machine-gun mount was necessary for the light weapons carrier role.

To save wear and tear on the transmission, it was stipulated that the mandatory four-wheel drive should have provision for disengaging the drive to the front axle via a two-speed transfer case. Full floating axles were demanded, and the hydraulic brakes were to be modern industry standard. As regards performance, the truck was required to achieve a good highway cruising speed, and have off-road ability: namely a minimum 50mph (80kmph) top speed on a hard surface, and a 3mph (5kmph) crawling speed. It had to be able to climb hills with a maximum 60 degree grade climbing limit, and with gradient approach and departure angles of at least 45 and 40 degrees respectively. A 6½in (165mm) minimum ground clearance made

The evolution of the Jeep's four-wheel drive: the early years

Four-wheel drive trucks from FWD and Jeffery, both of Wisconsin, had been in use in the USA from the first decade of the twentieth century, and had proved themselves tough and able performers in the winter mud of mid-western America. However, for their time they were big trucks, and four-wheel drive had not been developed for lighter trucks or cars. The Model T Ford, with its high ground clearance, buggy springs, light weight and strong engine, just didn't need four-wheel drive to cope with rural American dirt roads.

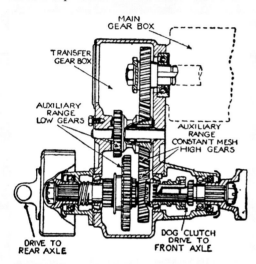

The first Spicer transfer case. Simple, compact and above all tough, it was common to all pilot and production World War II jeeps.

Most cars and trucks by the 1930s had the engine in the front, with a driveline to the rear axle. There were exceptions, like Citroen's brilliant 11cv 'Traction Avant', the Alvis 4/75, and the exotic but temperamental Cords. The problem of transmitting power smoothly and without excess wear to wheels that steer was overcome by Rzeppa's invention of constant-velocity joints in the 1920s. The Marmon-Herrington Company had, after many years of experience in building huge all-terrain vehicles for the construction industry, supplied a four-wheel drive conversion for light and medium trucks in the USA by fitting a transfer gearbox to the back of the gearbox, and taking a second propshaft to a driven front axle. Spicer used exactly the same principle for the jeep axle sets – though nothing in life is ever as simple.

As a four-wheeled vehicle drives around a turn, each wheel rotates at a different speed. On a driven axle, a differential allows each wheel to do this whilst still supplying drive to at least one of the wheels. A simple transfer case like Spicer's links the front and back axles precisely together, but in a turn the front wheels want to rotate at speeds different from the rear ones. This causes 'wind-up', where the driveshafts are actually twisted as a result of being driven at conflicting speeds. On loose ground this does not matter, as the wind-up can be scrubbed out harmlessly, but the friction of the tyres on a hard road prevents this, and eventually this will result in driveshaft breakage. For permanent four-wheel drive to be acceptable for use on hard roads, a form of centre differential that would allow all wheels to rotate at different speeds had to be developed.

sure it didn't bottom out too readily.

To give it adequate power, the engine was required to have at least four cylinders and to develop at least 85lb/ft of torque. An oil-bath air cleaner was mandatory, and it should have provision for adequate cooling for low speed work. Aluminium cylinder heads were troublesome in service, so they were ruled out. The cavalry continued to insist that a four-wheel steer version be supplied. Critically, all this would have to be in a package weighing no more than 1,275lb (578kg) dry, because the cavalry wanted troopers to be able to manhandle the truck out of tight spots.

On 2 July, in accordance with procure-

Willys-Overland

John North Willys was a natural salesman. He was born in New York State in 1873; as a sixteen-year-old he took the profits of the laundry business he ran, and went into selling and repairing bicycles. In 1899 he saw his first car, and was hooked. In 1906 he started a dealership company, the American Motor Car Sales Company, to sell American and Overland cars.

The Toledo, Ohio-based Overland company failed to deliver the automobiles ordered, for it was on the brink of bankruptcy. Willys took control of the company, renaming it Willys-Overland, and by the end of 1908 it was the world's second-largest car maker. John North Willys had a talent for organizing the financial structure of his companies, although he often ventured near to insolvency. This proved near-disastrous in 1921, so Willys mortgaged his own house and estate, and took over as general manager of Willys-Overland: by 1923 the car maker was back into the black.

John North Willys sold his holdings in the company in 1929 and took up a position as the US Ambassador to Poland. Willys-Overland collapsed in the depression, and Willys returned in 1932, once again to invest his own money to revive the company. The following February, after the Detroit bank crisis, Willys went into receivership. But Willys was to have a guardian angel in George Ritter, an Ohio lawyer, who worked out a complicated deal to reorganize the company and raise cash to get it back into business. The deal was ready by early 1935, but John North Willys was not to see the results of Ritter's work: he had a heart attack in the spring of that year, and died the following August. He was sixty-two.

Ward Canaday, a one-time advertising manager of Willys-Overland, immediately pushed his way into John Willys's place. Canaday had left to help form the United States Advertising Corporation, moving the Willys account over with him, but now he was back. Ritter and Canaday invited John North Willys's first wife and C. O. Miniger to form Empire Securities: this was to own Willys-Overland plus Canaday's advertising company, renamed Canaday, Ewell and Thurber Incorporated. Willys-Overland was split into two divisions: Willys-Overland Motors Inc., and the Willys Real Estate Corporation, which would sell off surplus property to raise cash and pay off creditors. Thus Willys-Overland Motors Inc. could face the late 1930s poor, but debt free.

---

ment regulations, the specification was sent out to 135 prospective suppliers, offering a $175,000 contract for delivery of a running pilot vehicle, and a further sixty-nine vehicles for testing. The list did not contain anything of a particularly advanced or unusual nature (four-wheel steering excepted!) but the time-scale – the pilot vehicle had to be delivered within forty-nine days, in time for testing during late summer manoeuvres – meant that only two companies responded. Naturally, one was American Bantam.

Enter Willys-Overland. . .

The other was Willys-Overland, a medium-sized organization based at Toledo, Ohio who, like Bantam, had survived a period of receivership. They, too, specialized in cars that were compact by US standards, the latest of these being the Americar. The chairman of Willys, Ward M. Canaday, had tried to sell to the US Army its own idea of an LRV, named the 'Mosquito', and in late 1939 sent outline drawings to the Planning Section of the General Staff. After receiving advice of the Howie machine-gun carrier's existence by Marmon-Herrington's Col Herrington, top executives of Willys-Overland Motors – namely Joseph W. Frazer, the president, and the vice president of engineering, Delmar G. ('Barney') Roos – went to Fort Benning on 15 March 1940 to see it demonstrated.

Frazer dismissed the 'Belly Flopper' out

The pre-war Willys sedan had some pretty up-to-date styling in a compact package: 'Half the price, half the mileage', said the slogan.

of hand, but it fascinated Roos. He agreed with Benning's General Walter G. Short when they discussed it and the 'Mosquito', that the LRV should be much stronger and heavier, and conventional in its layout. Willys-Overland thus had as much of an interest in the LRV project as Bantam, but there was already a third concern involved: the Ford Motor Company.

...and Ford

According to Dale Roeder of Ford's truck division, and Clarence F. Kramer, chief engineer of the body engineering department, Bill Knudsen brought Ford into the LRV project in the summer of 1940 when he announced the Rearmament Program. Knudsen worked for Ford until 1921, when he joined General

Motors. Besides knowing Ford's engineering capabilities, he was good friends with Henry Ford, Henry's son Edsel, and production wizard Charles Sorensen. He also knew of Henry's hatred of war and his intense dislike of US President Franklin D. Roosevelt.

Although Edsel was the president of the Ford Motor Company, Henry was the largest stockholder and his final word was law. He had already refused point blank to make Rolls-Royce Merlin aero engines because they were for a foreign nation at war, and would only consent to building Consolidated B-24 Liberator bombers if he made the whole plane and not just components, as Knudsen had first wanted. From that point, according to Charles Sorensen in his autobiography *My Forty Years with Ford*, Henry was kept right out of the Rearmament Program.

BANTAM GET BUSY

At Bantam, Karl Probst began work on the prototype even before the specifications were sent out. He built a chassis with the Bantam's 'top hat' section; longitudinal semi-elliptic front springs located the front and rear axles; and narrowed versions of Spicer's hypoid axle – developed for Studebaker's new compact Champion model – were chosen, fitting constant-velocity joints on the front one. Both were connected to the Spicer transfer box. The Bantam engine was too small for the specification, so a 112ci (1.82 litre) Continental industrial side-valve four-cylinder unit, model BY4112, was sourced: its 45 BHP was more than double that of the Bantam engine, and comfortably met the required torque figure.

The vehicle was completed in forty-eight days. On one point the Bantam vehicle did not meet the requirements: at 1,300lb

(590kg) its weight was higher than specified. Probst and his engineering team had found it impossible to meet the maximum weight and build a vehicle that would be strong enough to take the punishment of combat duty, despite the cavalry's insistence that the vehicle should be light enough to be manhandled over rough ground.

After a quick test the new vehicle was driven over the Appalachian Mountains to Camp Holabird. Apparently Probst took some little time to test the car on certain mountain tracks – maybe he developed a liking for off-roading, for he made the 5pm, 21 September deadline by just half an hour. The trip gave Bantam a chance to run the engine in and assess its fuel consumption, too. For three weeks Holabird's staff tested it to its fullest extent, and despite some shortcomings, behaved up to expectations. It was clear to all that the basic idea was right.

THE FIGHT FOR CONTRACTS

The Quartermaster Corps Subcommittee had met on 18 October 1940, and recommended that Ford, Willys and Bantam should be asked to build 500 vehicles each, even though pilot vehicles from the other two makers had not yet been seen, let alone tested. The bid from Willys, despite being the cheapest, had been rejected because they could not meet the deadline, and Ford had not even attempted to bid. Bantam protested strongly, maintaining that they had developed the vehicle for the army, and that *they* had the wherewithal to fulfil any and all future contracts for it.

Clarence Kramer from Ford and Gene Rice from Willys went to view the Bantam pilot vehicle at Holabird, and were allowed to inspect its every detail. They were impressed by its performance, and took plenty of ideas from it for their own pilot vehicles. Bantam were outraged when they saw that their rivals were given complete access to what, under civilian industrial practice, was a secret vehicle; but the objection was met by a curt response from the army, who insisted that it was their vehicle, and that by the terms of military procurement they would allow whom they liked to examine it. To reinforce the point the

army then delivered Bantam's blueprints to Ford and Willys.

The QMC's course of action was in fact correct government procedure; it was also vital. The US government knew it was heading for war, despite intense lobbying in Washington by a strong and vociferous pacifist movement. After years of non-intervention, the US was getting tough on the Japanese who had occupied much of the South East Asian mainland, and their sym-

Bantam's sixty-nine day wonder, complete with junk-yard front wings, one-piece windscreen and Bantam Roadster scuttle. The civilian vehicle ancestry of the Bantam pilot can easily be seen, as the finish of the scuttle and bonnet, taken from a production car, are much better than the simple rear tub.

pathy was growing for European countries occupied by Nazi forces. The implementation of the Rearmament Program was therefore becoming more pressing. On 29 December 1940, in one of his famous 'fire-side chat' radio broadcasts, US President Franklin D Roosevelt told his people: 'We must be the great arsenal of democracy'.

This chilling New Year message served to prepare the minds of the American people for war, because in the following January, Roosevelt was about to present the Lend-Lease scheme for approval by Congress. Winston Churchill had known of this well in advance when, in a radio broadcast in February 1941, he said, 'Give us the tools, and we'll finish the job'. Neutrality Acts passed in the 1930s had prevented America from supplying arms to warring nations, but a new Neutrality Act, the so-called 'Cash and Carry' Act, already pushed through by Roosevelt in September 1940, allowed America to sell arms to any country, provided they collected them in their own ships.

Lend-Lease did not have overwhelming support in Congress – one politician described it as 'like lending someone your chewing gum – you don't want it back!' – but it was the shot in the arm that Britain really wanted, in that US industrial might and military hardware would be shipped to Allied forces fighting in Europe and the Far East. It was anticipated that over 11,000 examples of the 'Truck, 4x4, Light' – already being referred to as a 'jeep' at Camp Holabird – would be needed by the summer of 1941.

The urgent need to get the new vehicle into production over-rode all other concerns. It was decided to order 500 vehicles each from Bantam, Ford and Willys, subject to the suitability of the as yet unseen pilot vehicles from the other two makers. Besides, orders for large quantities of axle sets would substantially lower the unit costs.

Ford, recognizing the army's needs, stepped in at this point. To Ford, the manufacture of a complete vehicle in quantity would present no problem; not only was there the colossal River Rouge plant at Dearborn, Michigan, but several other assembly plants all over the US. They bid for a contract for sole manufacturing rights, the price of which included tooling costs. For this, Ford wanted the vehicle 'for free' to develop how they liked when peace broke out. In the face of Ford's problems – the US operation had made losses throughout the 1930s – the lure of a ready-made vehicle, with a guaranteed government contract and the distinct possibility of having it to themselves when peace eventually returned, was huge. But the bid was overruled by the NDAC, who were compelled to diversify their sources of supply.

The chief of staff General Moore had to make a decision as to how many vehicles to order, and from whom. He had been under pressure from Bill Knudsen at the NDAC, who had told the QMG's office '. . .to get a big supply of jeeps and trucks rolling, and rolling fast!' A major bottleneck in jeep production was the axle sets, as Spicer were the only manufacturers. But the Ford Motor Company could easily replicate Spicer's axle manufacturing tools, and make them in quantity; they offered to loan Spicer tooling equipment for the axle sets, and agreed to make large quantities themselves. As a result, not 1,500 vehicles in total were to be purchased, but 1,500 each from Bantam, Ford and Willys.

THE QUAD AND THE PYGMY

Willys sent two Quads, as their pilot vehicles were named, to Holabird on 13 November 1940: a four-wheel-steer version, thus complying with the cavalry's specific demand, and a two-wheel-steer version. Both, however, failed to comply with one crucial specification, weighing in at an obese 2,520lb (1,143kg); Roos had built the Quad as tough as possible, and the powerful 134ci (2.18 litre) Go-Devil engine was heavy. The Quads underwent the same testing as the original Bantam, and hit problems: there were chassis fractures, steering and transmission failures, and overheating problems. Following a breakage of its air-cleaner mounting, one engine swallowed a quantity of mud and dirt and gave out.

Ford made two prototypes: one with a body they built themselves, and the other with a body by pressed-steel body pioneers Budd. The Budd model had its headlights mounted on the front wings, but the Ford-bodied vehicle was innovative in that the headlights were mounted behind the grille, fitted on a swivelling bracket and locked by a wing nut. This offered two advantages: first, the lights were protected from accidental damage such as would risk either removing the light altogether or deflecting the beam upwards so as to give the crew's position away to the enemy; it would also allow a headlight to light up the engine bay at night, which was useful for emergency repairs in the field. Also, Ford engineers had seen that the Bantam's one-piece windscreen was breaking under stress, so they fitted a split windscreen, and two pads were screwed to the front of the bonnet to cushion the frame from jolts when it was folded down.

A Bantam BRC, one of the seventy vehicles due under the first contract. This is actually one of the eight four-wheel-steer versions.

The Ford pilot vehicles – at Dearborn the prototype had been named the Pygmy – arrived at Holabird a couple of weeks after the Willys Quad, and they underwent similar testing. Both had Ford's own body design, one with four-wheel steer. An interesting aside, here, on a more personal level, is that Edsel Ford had brought his two eldest sons, Henry II and Benson, into the family firm, where they were 'getting their hands dirty' on the production lines, learning the auto business from the bottom up. After a spell at the Willow Run bomber plant they were both sent to the engineering department, where they worked on the pilot LRVs. Edsel was delighted to see the two young Fords driving a pygmy in a special demonstration on some brushland off Rotunda Drive, before the vehicles were delivered to Holabird.

The 45bhp, 119ci (1.95 litre) tractor engine in the Pygmy could not match the Willys, and its crash gearbox was inferior

in operation to the Warner synchromesh box fitted to the Willys and the Bantam. The Pygmy performed without any trouble, but it, too, was substantially overweight, and both Ford and Willys moved to get the army to increase the weight limit.

Willys were told to put the problems of the Quad right and to get its weight below a new, raised limit of 2,160lb (980kg). The Technical Committee reported that '. . .there was nothing to indicate that the Willys design ultimately would not prove completely satisfactory' – so Barney Roos put the Quad on a strict diet, paring ounces from every possible component: the chassis was made of a lighter steel; each nut, bolt and split pin was trimmed; and even the weight of the paint was taken into account. The new version was the MA, and with it the company would fulfil its contract for 1,500 vehicles.

Ford's initial production vehicle was the GP, a modification of the Pygmy. Bantam's was the BRC 40, the lightest of the three, but

The front of the Budd-bodied Ford pilot vehicle, with its headlights atop the front wings. The rest of the body, although different in its actual dimensions, follows the same basic outline as the Ford-bodied Pygmy. Ford nicknamed the vehicles 'Blitz Buggies'.

the army had, under protest from both Bantam and the using arms, raised the specified weight again, to a minimum 2,268lb (1,051kg). Barney Roos had stuck to his first instincts and the advice he had been given at Holabird. The insistence of the infantry, that the vehicle should be light enough to be manhandled over rough ground, was obviated by the results of the tests, in which the heavier, sturdier Willys MA and Ford GP had proved themselves to be a much better concept than Bantam's lightweight, and far superior to the Army's original idea. With torquey four-pot engines and low-range gearing, they didn't need to be manhandled because they were tough enough to be driven over or through just about anything the test drivers could

point them at. Thus the army agreed to a weight limit of almost double its original.

TIME FOR TOUGH DECISIONS

Delivery of the 4,500 jeeps began in early 1941, and although progress was hampered by a strike at Spicer, it was largely completed by late summer. In May 1941 a contract was awarded to Bantam for a further 1,000 jeeps. Because Ford was able to deliver on time, they were given further orders for over 2,500 vehicles; most of these were delivered to Allied troops.

There remained the question of standardization, and comparative tests of the three

The Pygmy put to the 'washboard' at Camp Holabird. This track of concrete pillars is designed to shake anything loose that might fall off in battle. Note the bracing for the front wings, which is an extension of the brush-guard grille. The headlights are mounted on truck door hinges, which enabled them to be swivelled over to light up the engine bay.

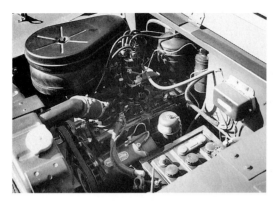

The Bantam BRC 40's Continental engine, much more compact than the other two power units.

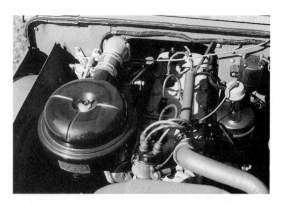

The GP's weak point, the tractor-derived engine, was physically big and heavy, and underpowered for its job in the 'Blitz Buggy'.

production models were held in June 1941. The new jeep was to be built by Willys, but it would be an amalgam of the best features of all three pilots. Thus the chassis would be developed from the MA, the engine would be the Go-Devil, by far the most flexible and powerful unit, and it would be coupled to the Warner gearbox and the Spicer axle set. From the Ford came the floor-mounted gear lever, but most significantly the body design would be largely Ford's own, with the Willys MA front wings; it would also have Ford's split windscreen and the brush-guard grille

Ford put the GP's fuel tank under the driver's seat, a design feature that was adopted for the MB and the GPW.

with its swing-over headlights. The new, standardized production jeep would be numbered by Willys as the MB, and 16,000 were to be ordered.

Bantam's almost moribund state ruled them out as manufacturers. They had been in debt to the government's Reconstruction Finance Corporation since 1938, and could not produce any quantity of vehicles without a further massive loan of government capital. Willys, although not awash with money, was debt free, but it was still small compared to Ford, and not thought by the QMC to be capable of producing enough to meet the demand.

The QMC were determined that Ford should make the jeep exclusively, not least because of Ford's prompt delivery – both Bantam and Willys had been late with orders – but they were over-ruled by Bill Knudsen's Office of Production Management (OPM – the renamed National Defense Advisory Commission) who still insisted that using just one supplier was contrary to policy. To further complicate matters, the QMC proceeded to put out tenders to make the new standardized vehicle. There was also a fourth bid, from the Checker Cab Company of Kalamazoo,

*She may have been
the first pretty girl
to be taken for a
ride in a jeep, but
she was certainly
not the last. . . The
Willys MA poses
outside the
magnificent
frontage of the
Toledo plant for
waiting pressmen.*

*The Willys MA under test at
Holabird. The rear-seat
passengers have rather more to
smile about than the man in
the front, who could be in for a
somewhat messy, if soft,
landing if the MA tipped over
too much. Note the column-
mounted gear lever.*

Four-wheel steer

The US cavalry were very keen to have four-wheel-steer jeeps in service. They were still in the process of mechanization, and envisaged that the turning circle of such a vehicle – some 11ft (3m) shorter than the two-wheel steer – could emulate the cavalryman's ability to wheel and turn fast on his enemy.

Whilst the eight Bantam four-wheel-steer BRCs were undergoing trials with the cavalry, the Quartermaster Corps began questioning the need for such a feature. The manufacture of a limited number of rear-wheel-steer axles would aggravate the supply problem already existing with normal axle sets. Furthermore, the QMC's motor transport division was also opposed to the idea: they were the poor souls who had to keep them running and, already anticipating an easier life with just one standard jeep, didn't fancy the extra work of a four-wheel steer. Nor did the vehicles perform as well as expected, the short wheelbase making them too manoeuvrable to be entirely safe in the turmoil of battle.

A four-wheel-steer GP at the River Rouge plant at Dearborn. Ford's four-wheel-steer mechanism was described as 'delayed rear-wheel-steer action', and the engineers viewed the facility as useful for dodging land obstacles as much as for manoeuvring on the enemy.

The infantry and artillery supported the cavalry's wish for four-wheel-steer jeeps. An order for 6,000 was pending, but by March 1941 General Frink, head of the QMC's motor transport division, put forward the view that '. . .the cavalry cannot definitely state that their mission cannot be performed without the use of this type of vehicle.' This wonderful double negative got the QMC its way. The considerations of cost and practicability overrode what dubious advantages there were to four-wheel steer, and no more than the original eight Bantams, fifty BRC 40s, a handful of Ford GPs and the sole Willys Quad were made.

Michigan. Although they were the cheapest, Checker offered the worst delivery time, and of course had no previous involvement in the programme; they were rejected. Willys were the most expensive bidders. Ford looked to be the favourite, but Knudsen still insisted that Willys be part of the deal, and in the end awarded them the contract – and not for 16,000, but for 18,600 vehicles.

The attack by the Japanese on the US Navy base at Pearl Harbour on 2 December 1941, and the almost immediate declaration of war on the US by Germany, meant that every ounce of Uncle Sam's industrial and military muscle went behind the war effort. The QMC had never abandoned their intent to use Ford as a manufacturer of the jeep, and decided to invite them, with the OPM's consent, to manufacture jeeps to the Willys design. Now Ward Canaday played a master stroke: although the army owned the design of the jeep, the rights to the Go-Devil engine belonged to Willys alone, and only they could say who else, if anybody, could make it. This engine was by far the best of the three, and was crucial to the jeep's serviceability and performance. At the earlier request of

Ford GPs on board a streamlined Ford 'Haul-Away' trailer transporter. The contrast between the stark utility of the 'Blitz Buggies' and the Art Deco truck is little short of amazing.

Holabird's contracting officer, Canaday agreed to provide complete assistance with any other manufacturer in the production of Willys jeeps, including the manufacture of the Go-Devil engine. However, Canaday insisted that those outside makers would build jeeps solely for the US government, and that Willys would have the right, when hostilities ended, to be the exclusive maker of a civilian jeep. It was perhaps the most important event in the jeep's story since the army drew up its original specification.

But how would the army bring Ford back? General Gregory, the Quartermaster General, who had conceived the idea of industrial collaboration for war production, heard that Edsel Ford was visiting Washington, and together with General H. J. Lawes and Colonel E. S. Van Deusen, sought him out in the social security building. Obviously expecting some opposition to his proposal, General Gregory had thought out carefully what he was going to say, and proceeded with these words: 'Mr Ford, the army wants to standardize this vehicle. You and your company can do the US an immeasurable service in this war if you will agree to manufacture it according to the Willys design with the Willys motor and every part interchangeable.' Edsel Ford's reply came swiftly, and must have surprised the waiting soldiers: he simply said, 'Gentlemen, the answer is "yes".' It was a wise move on Edsel's part as the first contract was for

The slat grille on a late-December 1941 MB. This was quickly discarded in favour of Ford's one-piece pressing. The headlight covers were standard issue to American forces.

15,000 standardized jeeps, and this alone would be worth more than $14.6 million.

The QMC decided that the combined pro-

duction capacity of Ford and Willys alone was adequate for the needs of all service users. They also felt that Bantam did not have any economic muscle, Bantam having already demanded 30 per cent of the money payable on the contract for the seventy test vehicles up-front. For the production company this was bad news: after eight years' involvement in the programme, Bantam had believed that they would be the major, if not the sole producers of the army's LRV, and had lobbied the army intensely to this end. But in the final outcome, all they were to get out of the episode, after one last-ditch attempt to re-enter the programme in March 1942 with a bid for 6,000 four-wheel steer jeeps, were two contracts for a total of 1,570 vehicles, and a compensation order for 5,000 two-wheeled trailers for use behind jeeps.

Willys MB, Ford GPW (1941–45)	
Engine	
Type	Willys Go-Devil 4-cylinder sidevalve
Bore x stroke	3.25 x 4.125in
Capacity	134.2cu in (2.2ltr)
Main bearings	3
Max. power	60bhp @ 4000rpm
Max. torque	105lb/ft @ 2000rpm
Chassis	
Transmission	Warner 3-speed manual, synchromesh on 2nd & top
Transfer case	2-speed, part-time four-wheel drive
Suspension	Semi-elliptic leaf springs front and rear
Brakes	4-wheel hydraulic, 9in drums front and rear
Dimensions	
Wheelbase	80in
Track (front and rear)	48.25in
Overall length	132.25in
Overall width	62in
Overall height (top up)	69.75in
Curb weight	2,315lb

2   The War Years: The Jeep's Proving

Lend-Lease was a lifeline to the Allies. British Army missions were sent to Washington to liaise with the Americans and the British Purchasing Commission back home, to ensure that the right equipment in the right quantities came over in time. Even so, early deliveries of military aid were slow: the strike at Spicer held up supplies, and jeeps were stockpiled in American docks, largely because the Atlantic convoys that carried the military aid needed to be increased dramatically. They were, thanks to the innovation of the Liberty Ships and greater success in combating the attacks on the convoys by Nazi U-boats.

The Russians, struggling to hold back the invading German army, fared better, receiving over 2,000 jeeps. It was vital to supply them first, because if Russia fell, a most significant and powerful ally would be lost: the Germans could then move south to occupy Iraq and Persia, cutting off a land route to India and enabling them to link up with the Japanese. By the end of the year, more than 80,000 military vehicles of all types had been shipped to Russia, largely through Iraq and Persia by the monumental efforts of Paiforce (Persia and Iraq Force). Supplies in preparation for a fight back in North Africa and Western Europe were also building steadily. Assessment vehicles were sent to England in the spring of 1941, although the first fifty-six for active service only reached British hands by June. The Ministry of Supply were initially reluctant to accept these new jeeps, still referred to as 'Blitz Buggies' in official documents, preferring motorcycles for reconnaissance work; but

---

Henry J. Kaiser's Liberty Ships

Millionaire Henry J. Kaiser made his money from involvement in major civil engineering projects such as the Boulder Dam and the Golden Gate Bridge, but it was Kaiser's industrial muscle that gave the British and Commonwealth forces perhaps the greatest aid to victory prior to the USA entering the war, namely in the Liberty Ships.

Aid through the Lend-Lease agreement was despatched from the US across the North Atlantic, but Nazi U-boats were sinking the convoy ships faster than they could be put into service. Henry J. Kaiser had never built ships – he knew next to nothing about them, and even referred to the 'front end' and the 'back end' – but his engineers revolutionized shipbuilding: the ships were welded rather than being riveted, the traditional method of construction, and the reduction in building time was dramatic. The first ship, the *Patrick Henry*, was launched on 27 September 1941, having been built in 245 days, and by 1943 the time had come down to an astonishing ten days. The losses in shipping were reversed, and with determined offensives against the U-boats by the Royal Navy and RAF Coastal Command, a 'bridge of ships' continued to supply Allied forces for the duration.

The jeep became a symbol of the GI as soon as it went into service. This is an envelope for use by soldiers' families. Its age can be determined by three things: first, the slat grille on the jeep; second, the GI's uniform; and third, the officer is sitting in the back seat!

A Bantam BRC40 fully kitted out for command and reconnaissance duties, pictured at Oakwood, the wartime home of the Chief Inspector of Mechanization in Chislehurst, Kent. The Express Dairy premises off nearby Willow Grove were used as a supply depot, where jeeps, motorcycles and light trucks were stored and maintained. The 'mailed fist' emblem belongs to the 6th Armoured Division, who would see duty in Tunisia in 1942 and 1943.

the Mechanical Warfare Experimental Establishment (MWEE) tested them for themselves, and found them to be up to the job. In army units they were welcomed immediately, and their versatility was quickly discovered; indeed, the Ministry of Supply would soon be ordering far more jeeps than the US were willing or able to send.

Initially jeeps were transported fully assembled, but further shipments of all military vehicles were sent in CKD form, and by mid-January 1941 contracts were issued from the Ministry of Supply to several factories in the UK to assemble them. These included Northern Counties Coachworks, Nash of Cardiff, Dawnays of Swansea and William Alexander of Edinburgh. Of the 3,650 Ford GPs made, a mere 144 were sent to Britain, and were assembled either at the Bristol Bus Company's works or at Ford's at Dagenham.

Of the pre-standardization models, the BRC 40 was the most plentiful, but it was not the most robust. Its build quality did not match that of the Ford GP – of the early

A Ford GP under test with the British Army at Derwentwater in the Lake District.

models, only Bantams and Ford GPs were sent over, and the Willys MA was not listed as a British Army vehicle – and many were sold off by the British Army to selected dealers as MBs and GPWs came into service. For British armed forces, jeeps were initially modified to comply with the Motor Vehicles (Construction and Use) Acts. These were detail changes and involved mounting the blackout lights on the front wings, moving the driving mirror to the British offside, removing the offside headlight and covering the hole with a blanking plate, and fitting the nearside headlight with a blackout mask. For some time, all military vehicles would carry the current road tax and a civilian-type number plate.

'ONE OF THE TOOLS THAT WON THE WAR'

Not only did the jeep fulfil to the utmost its original roles of reconnaissance, light transport and armed support, but the ingenuity of the troops in the battlefield found uses for it in just about every other conceivable job, both on the front line and behind the lines. It was tough, easily mended, agile and speedy. All manner of light guns were fitted to it, proving its capability as a weapons carrier, one of its original intended purposes. It was an officers' front-line staff car, and most importantly it became a symbol to the people of occupied Europe of the liberating Allies.

Jeeps were used in agriculture in the UK, pulling ploughs and harrows. Furthermore, it was discovered that if the front of the jeep were jacked up and a front wheel removed, a drive belt could be wrapped around the brake drum and attached to a hay baler or a circular saw. The jeep found a ready use as a bus for refugees. It also became a makeshift ambulance, and so use-

Jeeps in the air: lightweight jeeps

Airborne troops came very much into their own in World War II, and their effectiveness was proved beyond doubt when the Germans invaded Crete in May 1941. As early as 1940 Winston Churchill had ordered the formation of a British airborne force, and in 1942 the Glider Pilot Regiment and the Parachute Regiment were formed. The 'Paras' were, and still are, a lightly armed infantry unit. An army division is an amalgamation of many different support units: signals, ordnance, sappers, medics, administration, catering and transport. A fighting force dropped behind enemy lines must have enough vehicles and support to make it function successfully.

The largest land-based aircraft in service with the RAF at the outbreak of war were twin-engined bombers, so any vehicle carried and dropped by parachute had to be very small. To that end research was carried out by the Standard Motor Company and SS Cars, amongst others, to produce a small, troop-carrying 'buggy'. Willys made their own lightweight version of the MB – with typical American humour, this was christened the 'Gipsy Rose Lee' after the famous striptease dancer of the day – and Nuffield Mechanizations produced an experimental short wheel-base lightweight two-seat jeep with drastically cut down body; however, neither entered production.

Fortunately larger, four-engined aircraft soon came into service, and these could tow gliders such as the new Airspeed Horsa and the American-designed Hadrian. Both could carry a full-size jeep plus crew, and the larger Horsa Mk II could take either an equipment trailer or light gun as well. But by 1943 the Germans had been halted, and the planned Allied invasion of Europe meant that many specialist projects, including the expensive miniature vehicles, would be cancelled: instead there was an urgent requirement for as many proven vehicles as could be manufactured.

The standard jeep was adapted in the UK to fit into Mk I Horsa gliders by cutting off the ends of the front bumper and the steps on the front wings so it could be manoeuvred around the Horsa's side door. Also the steering wheel had to be quickly removable, as it was just too tall to fit under the glider's wing spar. Jeeps carried in the front-loading Hadrian did not need these modifications, nor were they neces-

This photograph depicts HQ Group, Royal Artillery landing at Arnhem on 17 September 1944. The jeep and trailer have been unloaded from the Horsa glider, and the equipment is being transferred to the trailer. On the right of the picture the detachable tail of the Horsa can be seen, as well as the damaged wing of another. The soldiers seem unhurried. They were unaware that the Germans were so close. . .

A jeep modified for airborne transport. The ends of the bumpers and the steps behind the front wings have been removed so it can be manoeuvred into a Mk I Horsa glider. The folding pushbike was an added piece of kit supplied to the Paras. . .

sary for the Mk II Horsa. Although most airborne jeeps were carried by glider, a number were dropped for SAS operations from the bomb-bay of specially adapted Halifax bombers.

THE ROTABUGGY

One of the most revolutionary ideas to supply airborne troops with transport involved making jeeps fly. With hindsight the idea seems crazy, but at the time it was treated very seriously. Two series of experiments were conducted simultaneously along this train of thought, one in England and the other in Australia. Each of the projects was begun for different reasons, and although the two research teams were aware of the other, there was, remarkably, no communication between them.

The English project was the Rotabuggy, and the man behind it was Raoul Hafner, an

You'll believe a jeep can fly! The Rotabuggy takes to the air behind a tug aircraft. The fuselage, tailplane, tall windscreen and the rotor can all be clearly seen. What is not visible is the expression on the pilot's face . . . A replica Rotabuggy was built by John May of the Wessex Aviation Society, and is in the Hafner Collection at the Museum of Army Flying at Middle Wallop, Hampshire. Grateful thanks are due to the museum for information on the Rotabuggy, and on airborne operations in general.

Jeeps in the air: lightweight jeeps *(continued)*

Austrian who had laid down the principles of helicopter design in Vienna as early as 1928. The Rotabuggy began life in the spring of 1942 at the Airborne Forces Experimental Establishment at Ringway, in Manchester. Cost was an important consideration in its concept: it was estimated that the Rotabuggy would be about one-eighth of the price of a Horsa glider. It was made by fitting a lightweight aircraft cockpit, fuselage and tail to a Willys MB, with a twin-blade rotor mounted on a frame fixed to the chassis between the pilot and the driver. It made a test run in November 1943, but the towing lorry was not fast enough to get it airborne. Subsequently the Rotabuggy's pilot, Squadron Leader I. M. D. Little, found a 4½ litre blower Bentley which got it into the air.

Tested behind a twin-engined Whitley bomber, the Rotabuggy proved unstable in flight and difficult to land. The problems were tackled systematically, but as larger tug planes and the Mk II Horsa glider came into service, and most importantly, as it became increasingly urgent to get the invasions of mainland Europe under way, any further development had to be abandoned. The Rotabuggy's flying components were stripped off – with the exception of the tall Perspex windscreen and aircraft instruments – and it was returned to service as a normal jeep at the AFEE's depot at Beaulieu, Hampshire. Visitors who mentioned the windscreen and instruments were told that the jeep was occasionally taken for a flight around the airfield circuit!

THE 'FLEEP'

The Australians built a flying jeep when they were facing some very dangerous circumstances. The Japanese had invaded New Guinea, not more than 120 miles (200km) from the northernmost point of Queensland, and it was imperative that the Australian armed forces stopped the enemy right there, and turned them back, by invading the island themselves. The mountainous island had no proper beach-heads so an airborne invasion was the only real option, but the extremely difficult terrain of the island and the absence of flat ground made landings by glider impossible. Lawrence J. Hartnett, president of General Motors' Holden Division, had been appointed as the chairman of Australia's Army Inventors Directorate, and he suggested using a rotary-wing craft because of its short landing capabilities. From this suggestion Project *Skywards* began, namely the fitting of a jeep with a rotary wing to make it fly.

Rotors were taken from a Cierva C.30A Autogyro and fitted to a jeep, with the rotor drive needed for take-off powered from an amphibious jeep's propeller drive, and the vehicle was given a fully enclosing, lightweight, aerodynamic fuselage which could be quickly jettisoned immediately after landing. It was christened the 'Fleep'. However, flight problems were envisaged literally before it even got off the ground, because the Autogyro – and thus any aircraft fitted with its rotor – was unstable at airspeeds over 115mph (180kmph) – and tug aircraft such as the Douglas C-47 cruised at nearly 200mph (320kmph).

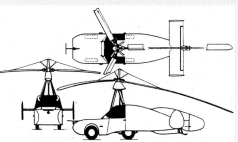

The huge but light superstructure of the Fleep.

Preliminary tests towing an Autogyro behind a C-47 were hair-raising, but despite some mishaps – including landing upside down, and the pilot getting the Autogyro's downward-pointing joystick caught up his trouser leg! – there were no serious injuries. Wind-tunnel tests were carried out on the fuselage designs, and a full vehicle was built. However, by 1944 the campaign against the Japanese was successful enough to obviate the need for an airborne invasion of New Guinea, and the Fleep was abandoned.

A posed shot of British soldiers discussing tactics over a map. The jeep's flat bonnet was useful as a table, and on many occasions it served as an altar, too. These soldiers were part of a detachment of the Royal Artillery sent to North Carolina in 1944 to teach the US Army about anti-aircraft gunnery. The US was never bombed during this war, but skill in AA gunnery was needed to defend the Pacific islands recaptured from the Japanese.

British industry was totally geared up for the war effort, and some firms in the motor industry found themselves converting military vehicles for specific purposes. The jeep's lack of weather protection was a handicap for radio operators. This wood body, specially designed for use on radio vehicles, was made by Carbodies of Coventry. They had once supplied MG with sports-car bodies, and would go on to be makers of London taxis.

ful was it in this role that conversions were made in the UK, in Canada and in Australia by General Motors' Holden subsidiary. There were railway versions with flanged wheels that could pull a 25-ton train. Tracked and half-track versions were made for use in snow, such as the aptly named 'Penguin' from Allis-Chalmers, and Marmon-Herrington's 'Jeep-Tank'. Whatever the job, and whatever the theatre of war, someone with a bit of initiative could adapt a jeep do it.

Some jeeps fell into enemy hands, and the German Army command encouraged its troops to use them. There seems, curiously, to have been no attempt by either the Germans or the Italians to make a copy of the jeep; despite their considerable expertise in the automotive field, both stuck to either the Kubelwagen or motorcycles. The Japanese made a light four-wheel drive, a Datsun, with an air-cooled twin-cylinder engine and a car-type tourer body. To borrow a famous line, Datsun adopted and adapted – but certainly didn't improve upon the original. There was a Toyota which was believed to be superior to the jeep, but it came too late to go into service.

There was no doubt in the mind of any

GPWs on the production lines at Ford's River Rouge plant at Dearborn, Michigan. Production began on 16 October 1941. GPWs were also built at Chester, Pennsylvania; Dallas, Texas; Louisville, Kentucky; and Richmond, California.

The Amphibious Jeep

At the same time as the US Army were working on the design of the LRV, the Chief of Infantry declared that, if it were feasible, an amphibious version should be developed in parallel. However, because the most urgent priority was to get a single basic vehicle into service as quickly as possible, the amphibian project was put on 'hold' until March 1941.

The special requirements envisaged for the amphibian were that in water it should be steered either by the wheels or through a movable power take-off. Its maximum speed in water should be 5mph (8kmph), and the changeover from land to water should be carried out, if not necessarily 'on the fly', with the minimum possible delay.

The project involved the addition of a marine hull to the basic jeep chassis. The first two pilot vehicles, one built by Ford and the other by Marmon-Herrington, were presented to the Army by the National Defense Research Committee in February 1942. The Ford was the preferred model, and following tests on two more pilot vehicles, the head of the Quartermaster Corps' Motor Transport Division, General Frink, ordered 5,000 amphibious jeeps, to be codenamed GP-A (A for amphibian). The amphibious jeep was also called the 'sea-going jeep', abbreviated somewhat unfortunately to 'Seep'.

With the entry of the USA into the war, a production programme was pushed through, with the view to using the Seep in sea-borne landings in North Africa. Delays, particularly in the develop-

A cushy number? Royal Marines enjoy a quiet 'boat' ride off the North Devon coast in May sunshine. It's 1943, and this GP-A, along with a whole range of landing craft and amphibious vehicles, are undergoing sea trials prior to the Allied invasion of Sicily.

The Schwimmwagen. Ferdinand Porsche's principle of making an amphibious vehicle by putting wheels on a boat worked very well. Ford's idea of putting a boat hull on a truck – the GP-A – didn't. The Schwimm has four-wheel drive, which it shared with some military issue KdF saloons.

ment of the dies for the hull, meant that it would be too late for this campaign, and also for the US attack on the Japanese-held Pacific island of Guadalcanal.

The GP-A was tested, along with DUKWs and a variety of landing craft, at the Co-operative Experimental Establishment (COXE) at Instow, North Devon in May 1943. COXE's test results did not find the GP-A a very good vehicle. It was a poor performer in rough water, it could not negotiate hummocky ground nor could it ford ditches, and its load capacity was minimal. The testers assessed it as a reasonable runabout, but not much more. The only favourable thing seemed to be that the turning circle was tighter in water than on land! Nevertheless, the GP-A would go into action in the invasion of Sicily and Italy in the summer of 1943, and in the Normandy landings on D-Day, 1944.

Only 12,778 Seeps were built. Despite the great things that were hoped for it, the Seep was something of a failure, perhaps because Ford had addressed the problem in the wrong way. Just as the jeep was a superior vehicle to its German counterpart, the Kubelwagen, so the amphibious version of the Kubel, the Schwimmwagen, was far better than the GP-A. The GP-A was a truck chassis with a boat hull attached to it. Ferdinand Porsche's Schwimm was a pressed-steel 'clam-shell' boat with wheels. Despite having only a 1.1 litre engine, the Schwimm's light weight enabled it to perform better in the water, and with four-wheel drive and good ground clearance it was good on land, too. The Seep, on the other hand, was heavy to drive, and with a shallow freeboard it was dangerously unstable in rough water. Further production of the GP-A was halted when the legendary DUKW, itself in effect a boat hull bolted to a truck chassis, was considered to be far superior.

serving soldier that the jeep was one of the best military vehicles ever produced. General Dwight D. Eisenhower has often been quoted as saying that, along with the landing craft and the Douglas C47 'Dakota' transport plane, it was one of the three tools that won the war. 'Ike' was a logistics man probably before the term was even invented, and his understanding of the way a modern army operates undoubtedly brought his appreciation of the jeep into full focus: his judgement was as perceptive as Napoleon's observation that 'an army marches on its stomach'.

MEANWHILE, ON THE HOME FRONT...

Whilst war raged in Europe, significant events were unfolding at Ford and at Willys. On 10 February 1942, the last private car rolled off the production line at Ford's giant River Rouge plant at Dearborn, Michigan; immediately behind it was the first GPW. A report in *Ford Times* in England said, 'The ugliest motor vehicle in the world is undeniably the "Blitz Buggy", or "Jeep" (*sic*); but it is also, according to US Army authorities, the most useful

This jeep is fitted with experimental infra-red lights and special binoculars; the Allies were way ahead of the Germans in this field. This installation shows just how versatile the jeep was, being completely at home as a testbed for all manner of new gear. Notice also the lighting arrangement for jeeps in the British armed forces: the standard headlights are completely removed, the right-hand space is covered with a blanking plate, the main blackout light is moved to the nearside position, and the small blackout lights have been moved from the lower position in the grille to the tops of the front wings.

motor vehicle they have.' In a later *Ford Times* a US Army expert on light vehicles, Lt Col I. M. Oseth, agreed on the jeep's usefulness with the words: 'The "Jeep" has stepped up the American Army's transport facilities by 50 percent.'

A publicity row

Ward Canaday was an advertising man. He had already ensured that the jeep would be his company's own at the end of the war, and using his own advertising agency he went all out with a publicity campaign that would associate the names of Willys and jeep inseparably in the minds of the public. He commissioned a series of posters showing the jeep in action on the battlefield: 'Giving 'em Hell at Guadalcanal', and

'Brave Officers Dare Death for Men', said just two. But some of these earlier posters caused not a little controversy, and there were two main points of contention.

Many posters said 'Willys build the mighty Jeep', and the Americar sedan was described in adverts as 'The Jeep in Civvies', and as 'designed by the same engineers, built by the same hands, and powered by the same Go-Devil engine as in the rugged "jeeps"'. Truthful enough, and acceptable – but Minneapolis-Moline built a heavy gun tractor that had been given the name 'jeep' by GIs. Both they and Bantam

A main production jeep in the extremes of the Western Desert of North Africa. It was here that the jeep played one of its first decisive roles, in Field Marshal Montgomery's victory over the German army at El Alamein. Tanks were in their element in desert warfare, and the British already enjoyed an advantage over Rommel in terms of both numbers and quality. Monty decided to improve on that advantage. A British squadron, using armed jeeps, went behind the German lines, and ambushed a fuel convoy. The crews of the jeeps unleashed a barrage of incendiary shells, and made off in the confusion. This effectively put the whole of the German tank force out of action. The jeep's manoeuvrability and speed were undoubtedly a crucial factor in ensuring that the operation was accomplished, and that the task force got away safely.

Over there. . . in a nicely set up publicity shot. Some local lads in Burton Bradstock, Dorset, help GIs fill up a jeep at the local garage, no doubt on the promise of a Hershey Bar or some chewing gum.

claimed that they had prior use to the name, and that Willys-Overland should not use it exclusively.

In a 1942 advert Willys claimed that: 'In close collaboration with the Quartermaster Corps of the US Army, they created and perfected the dependable jeep that is being used as the pattern for all command and reconnaissance cars of this type.' This incensed Ford and Bantam. They, together with Minneapolis-Moline, complained to the Federal Trade Commission, who subsequently brought Ward Canaday, Joseph Frazer, Barney Roos and others before them. Engineering blueprints distributed by the Quartermaster Corps in 1940 were presented by Clarence F. Kramer, the chief

body engineer of the Ford Motor Company to the Detroit Division FTC.

Other documents submitted included patents for the windscreen, seat and headlamp design granted to Ford for the design of the GP, and filed in May and June 1941. These showed clearly the shape of the body, including the front end with the headlights behind the grille and the folding windscreen design. It was shown on Ford's blueprints that the Ford design pre-dated the blueprints handed out by the Quartermaster Corps for competitive bidding; as a result the Federal Trade Commission ruled that the design of the jeep as accepted for standard production had not come from Willys. Ford, the Commission accepted, had made a significant contribution on their own, and Ford's body design was the basis of the main production jeep. Ford also pleaded that because the Pygmy was the only one to pass its trial without breakage, *it* was the one that was adopted as the final production design – and this contention was also accepted by the Commission.

As regards the name 'jeep', part of Willys's defence was that their chief test driver, Irving 'Red' Hausmann, began using the name at the trials of the Quad at Holabird to avoid confusing his vehicle with the others. He also claims credit for giving the name to the world. This dates from the time he was demonstrating the Quad in 1940 and, before an astonished press, drove up the steps of the Capitol building in Washington; somebody asked the Quad's name, and Hausmann replied, 'It's a jeep'. Katharine Hillyer's subsequent feature on the Quad in the *Washington Daily News* said 'Jeep Climbs Capitol Steps'. Thus Willys-Overland could justly claim that they had been using the name 'jeep' since 1940, and to further this, filed an application with the US Trademarks Registration in 13 June 1943 for the name 'Jeep'.

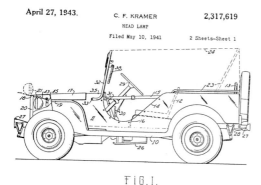

April 27, 1943.

C. F. KRAMER   2,317,619
HEAD LAMP
Filed May 10, 1941   2 Sheets—Sheet 1

FIG.1.

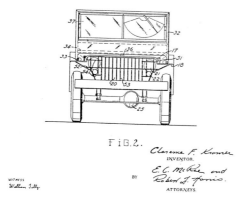

FIG.2.

Ford filed three patent applications in relation to the GP, and these were crucial in the suit that brought Willys before the Federal Trade Commission. Here is No. 2,317,619, the headlight design. The other two were 2,319,869 for the folding windscreen frame, which was adopted for the MB, and 2,317,620 for a design of folding seat, which wasn't. The date, 27 April 1943, is the date the patent was granted, not the application date.

Unbelievably, the hearing was to run for some six years, such was the importance of the future of the jeep to all concerned. But in the meantime Willys toned down the wording of their advertisements, only going so far as to state that they had 'assisted in the jeep's development'. Further advertisements of 1943 and early 1944, as the tide of war turned in the Allies' favour, related true battle stories. Willys continued to sail

a little close to the wind with the slogan 'Willys and Jeep – linked together in the minds of millions'; but then in August 1944 the thrust of Willys-Overland's advertising took a completely new direction: 'Will the jeep speed up farming?', it said. Mere weeks after D-Day, Ward Canaday was working on a civilian market for the jeep.

The civilian Jeep begins to take shape

Throughout the duration of the war, the US War Department received mail from Americans in all walks of life asking if the jeep would be available for public sale after the war had been won, either from ex-government stock or from the manufacturers. The US Department of Agriculture began serious studies of the jeep's uses in industry and agriculture, or – even at this early stage – as a sporting vehicle for hunters and fishermen. Their Farm Tillage Machinery Laboratory in Auburn, Alabama, carried out tests in April 1942 on two jeeps, a GPW and an MB, putting them to ploughs, seed drills and harrows. The jeeps' pulling power was compared to that of a four-horse team, and they could plough twice as fast. Fitted with mud tyres they performed well over the land, even mowing a crop of rye, and they made very good general farm utility vehicles, being used as pick-up trucks and for towing. In short, they were used like a farm horse and a Model T Ford combined.

In general the department was pleased with the way the jeeps performed, though noted that a lower gear ratio and a lower draw-bar would be needed. Furthermore, over at Washington State College's Agricultural Experimental Station, other experiments were conducted, trying out jeeps in forestry, mining and general industry work. To summarize their findings, L. J. Smith and O. J. Trenary produced a document

In the bleak mid-winter. . . When the miserably cold GI driving this Ford GPW was detailed for agricultural duty he probably thought he would be helping young Land Army girls rather than a British soldier! Nevertheless, work on English farms was another wartime job the jeep took in its stride, demonstrating just how useful it would be in peacetime.

called 'The Jeep as a Farm Truck-Tractor for the Post-War Period'.

FOCUSING ON A CIVILIAN JEEP'S SPECIFICATIONS

Just before Christmas in 1943, Congressman Manasco of Alabama invited George W. Ritter, the then vice president and attorney at Willys, to offer his prognosis for peacetime applications for the jeep. Ritter agreed with the Department of Agriculture in saying that the jeep needed different gearing, adding that it would also need a bigger clutch, and that a power take-off would be useful, too. Ritter had to concede that the Willys dealer network would have to be much larger than the present set-up to cope with customer service – but all in all it was conceded that the principle of the jeep being a suitable agricultural-cum-utility vehicle for civilian use was well founded.

Ward Canaday was, no doubt, pleased with the Department of Agriculture's find-

ings: after all, his condition for allowing Ford to manufacture the jeep precluded the Dearborn giant from continuing when government contracts ceased. However, Willys' vice-president, Joseph W. Frazer, had difficulty working with the irascible, domineering Canaday – as did most people, it seems: but as there could only be one man at the top, and because Canaday was president and the largest stockholder of Willys-Overland's holding company, Empire Securities, it was bound to be him. In 1943 Frazer left Willys, subsequently to join forces with Henry J. Kaiser in forming the Kaiser-Frazer car-making concern.

Brooks Stevens comes aboard

Brooks Stevens was one of a pioneering band of people known today as industrial designers, the sort of people who can blend style and function in any item you can name. He formed his own consultancy in 1935, and designed everything from meat packaging to tractors. But most of all

Stevens wanted to design cars that were smaller than the American norm – in fact, just like Willys used to build. Barney Roos considered that he and Stevens were on the same wavelength, and invited him to Toledo for an interview; and it did indeed appear that the two men saw the same future for the auto industry. As a result Stevens was engaged by Willys as from October 1943.

Willys were not going to get the Americar out of mothballs at the end of the war like the rest of the auto industry would do with their 1942 models: they wanted something completely new, and Brooks Stevens' first brief was to style it. He produced a neat two-door sedan with a pleasant, curvaceous shape and plenty of room for six adults, all in a 104in (2,642mm) wheelbase. The new car was known as the 6/66: it had full independent suspension, and except for its side-valve engine, was quite unlike anything Detroit had ever produced before – if it had carried an Auto Union or a Lancia badge, no one would have been surprised. Its compact new engine, under development by Barney Roos, was a step forward in itself, and at 148ci, it was small by US standards. The 6/66 was the kind of car that not only Brooks Stevens and Barney Roos wanted, but what Ward Canaday wanted, too.

CRISIS AT FORD

Danish-born Charles Sorensen had been a faithful servant to Henry Ford: he had joined the Ford Motor Company in its very early years, and had soon become head of the pattern shop. His skill in foundry work earned from Henry the nickname 'Cast-Iron Charlie', and he showed his talent for production engineering in the development of the moving assembly line.

In the late 1930s, and in all good faith, Sorensen recruited Harry Bennett, a former seaman and ex-boxer, to deal with the Union of Auto Workers who were attempting to unionize the company, an attempt that Henry Ford saw as a threat. Undoubtedly Sorensen probably soon wished he hadn't, because Bennett turned out to be extremely manipulative – and Henry loved him, making him head of Ford's security department, the Service Corps. Notorious for keeping the workforce under a reign of terror, Bennett was careful that Henry saw none of his evil, and the old man took him under his wing as the 'tough guy' son that he had always wanted the gentlemanly Edsel to be. Much to the frustration of both Edsel and Sorensen, Bennett was able to use Henry's patronage and capricious mind to take undue control within the company.

In 1941 Henry Ford suffered a debilitating stroke, and in 1943 Edsel Ford died after a battle against stomach cancer. Charles Sorensen was very busy running Ford's massive new Willow Run aircraft factory, and so was not keeping up with events at River Rouge. Bennett took this opportunity to turn Henry against Sorensen, apparently the only obstruction in his path to complete control. However, after Edsel's death, Sorensen saw to it that Henry Ford II was mustered out of the US Navy, considering it his duty to hold the company together until the young man could take over. Young Henry blamed Bennett for his father's death, and harboured a fierce desire to rid the Ford Motor Company of him. This he would do – but not before another head would roll.

When Sorensen realized he no longer had old Henry's ear, he offered his resignation, deciding then to take a vacation in Florida. Henry's parting remark was, 'Well, I guess there's something in life besides work' – heartless words in view of how

'Edsel Ford was a gentleman in the finest, fullest meaning of the word. He was gentle, considerate of others, unsparing of himself – and he was a man.' *Those words are from Charles Sorensen's book* My Forty Years With Ford. *No finer epitaph could have been written for Edsel, who died in 1943. Edsel's active part in Ford's jeep programme, and his agreement to build jeeps to a Willys design, contributed much to the war effort.*

much Sorensen had done for the company. Sorensen was then sixty-two, and when asked about his resignation, tapped his chest and said, 'It hurts here. I've never met anything of this sort before.'

Sorensen goes to Toledo

Ford's loss was to be Willys's gain. Following his vacation, Charles Sorensen was recruited by Canaday and Ritter to replace Joseph W. Frazer as vice-president. He was tempted from semi-retirement by an extremely attractive ten-year contract that guaranteed him a $52,000-a-year salary whether he worked or not. When he took up this post in the spring of 1944, the value of Willys shares more than doubled, such was the esteem in which business held 'Cast-Iron Charlie'. And indeed Sorensen brought to Willys the knowledge of all of Ford's operations, including the GPW, plus a lot more. Unfortunately for those associated with the 6/66, however, as a production expert he had plenty of reason to doubt the commercial wisdom of Willys wanting to build small cars again.

Retaining Brooks Stevens at a much higher salary, Sorensen told him openly that he did not like the 6/66: with materials and labour costs at an unforeseen high, he knew that it could not be as cheap as the Americar (their slogan was that you could buy two Americars for the price of a standard-sized car), and he was also worried that Willys would not be able to find anyone to build the complex body (Willys themselves having only basic body-stamping facilities). Ford, Chevrolet and Chrysler, on the other hand, had a great deal of clout with component suppliers and body makers, and Sorensen feared that the big, steel body-making firms would not entertain contracts from small companies like Willys-Overland, who were about to make what might end up a loser. He was absolutely sure that Willys-Overland should be making specialist utility vehicles, not passenger cars, and as far as he was concerned, the jeep was the very best thing to happen to the company.

THE AGRIJEEP

Charlie Sorensen put his Michigan farm at the disposal of the development engineers to test jeeps for agricultural work, and Willys began work on the CJ-1 (the 'civilian jeep type 1') from early 1944. It was aimed at the farm and the construction site, the forests and the prairies, and much of the assessment that George Ritter had presented to the government guided its development.

The military jeep had been hustled into production in an astonishingly quick time. Not surprisingly it had had some shortcomings, but the government had not allowed any delays in order to amend the faults – so far as the top brass then were concerned, it was working just fine, especially as its life expectancy was measured in weeks rather than in years. Barney Roos's engineering improvements, including modifications to the steering and a toughening of the chassis, were made on the initial pilot vehicle, and naturally this led on to the CJ-2. This vehicle was dubbed the 'Agrijeep', and an application to register it as such was made on 18 May 1944. Under this name, current advertising aimed the jeep at America's, and eventually the world's farmers. Some forty-five CJ-2s were made, and went on test around the US. The production model, the CJ-2A, was demonstrated to the press on 18 July 1945. Barely a fortnight later, on 31 July, Ford's contract to produce the GPW ended: Willys had the jeep to themselves.

3 America's Most Useful Vehicles

Willys had done well out of the war. Besides grabbing the Jeep, they had made a whole lot of other military hardware, which earned them money to spend on new vehicle development. In 1944 the company was worth $73 million, and that year's profits of $4 million went towards what Ward Canaday had planned for the post-war years. But there was a clash of minds as regards what it should be spent on.

Canaday wanted an all-new passenger car, but Charles Sorensen didn't. He knew that the much higher labour costs meant that they would not be able to sell it anywhere near as cheaply as the Americar. He wanted to specialize in building utility vehicles, and most importantly, to modernize the creaking Toledo factory. But the powerful Canaday opposed him. He believed that Willys could not survive on utility vehicles alone, and preferred to spend money in developing the dealership network, widening the base from which the passenger car would be sold. Canaday was the biggest shareholder in the company, so he won.

Charles Sorensen had accepted his job on the understanding that he would move aside when he felt that it might be best for another man to take over. In January 1946 Sorensen, now sixty-six, resigned from his position of president and took on the newly created role of vice-chairman. As president, Sorensen spent a fair proportion of his time at his Florida holiday home. This did not go unnoticed, but it must be said that at Dearborn Sorensen had seen too many of Edsel Ford's excellent ideas crushed into oblivion by 'crazy' Henry Ford for no sound business reasons. 'Cast-Iron Charlie' already knew what it was like to work for an autocrat.

The new president, and chairman, was James D. Mooney. A former General Motors engineer and salesman, he had considerable knowledge in the export field. With him, he brought Arthur J. Wieland and Robert Theiss, both with export experience. Mooney's aim was the export of some 25 percent of future production. The tough little Jeep was ideal for developing countries, and exports would even out the seasonal nature of the home market, and smooth out the production flow at Toledo.

Speaking in a magazine interview, Jim Mooney was candid about the immediate future. He expressed his intention to build a lightweight passenger car, but said that four years of war meant that the public's money would be tight: taxes would be high and new cars would be expensive, and in short supply. Eventually, he predicted, the improvement in the US economy and the increase in production by all the car makers would turn the seller's market into a buyer's one, but in the interim period Mooney believed there would be 'a broad opening for this company with its appealing utility line.'

Willys had worked in a 'make do and mend' way for years, but the new passenger car needed vastly improved production facilities. Mooney intended to build the

The Automobile Association's Jeeps and Caravans

In 1947 the Automobile Association began a national promotional tour. It bought three Car Cruiser caravans, examples of a rather heavy and plain 1946 model that had not sold at all well. Car Cruiser were no doubt pleased to convert the three to mobile office-cum-information centres, as it would serve to promote the caravans as well as the AA. To tow them, the AA bought three ex-WD MBs. One, DJB 425, went into service local to the AA's Guildford headquarters in north-west Surrey. The second, KLR 338 went to North Wales; and the third, FP 4429, saw duty in the Lake District.

One of the AA's three ex-WD jeeps and the three Car Cruiser caravans in a suitably posed picture outside the Guildford HQ.

new 6/71 passenger car, and so got the money for upgrading the Toledo plant. Sorensen hadn't, and didn't. The improvements were paid for by raising a stock option. The Wilson Foundry in Pontiac, Michigan, was bought to build Barney Roos's new lightweight sidevalve six engine for the 6/71. Another purchase essential for the new passenger car was that of modern body presses. 6/71 pilot models had been built and tested, and Mooney made several references about the passenger-car programme. But that was for the future: the Jeep was a reality, and it took priority.

THE CJ-2A

The first production civilian jeep, the CJ-2A, was introduced in August 1945. Willys had been quick to see the Jeep's role as a far wider one than simply as an agricultural tool; Agrijeep would therefore be too constricting a name. The CJ-2A would be an all-round industrial workhorse, and so it hit the markets as the 'Universal'. Priced at just under $1,100, it shared the MB's 80in (2,032mm) wheelbase and many of its body pressings, but the choice of four colours – light tan, grey, light blue and brown – made it look different from a military jeep.

The technical modifications outlined to the Congress committee by George Ritter were adopted in this model. Thus the gear ratios were altered so that they would cope with the slow speed necessary for ploughing, yet still be able to produce a reasonable 60mph (100kmph) cruising speed. The Go-

Devil engine underwent a mild reworking of its combustion chambers so it could produce a flatter torque curve better suited to domestic and farm work. The gear-driven cam-drive, carried over from the last of the MBs, was to Willys's pre-war specification.

Several refinements were added to make the CJ-2A more practical for civilian use, amongst them powered windscreen wipers, an outside fuel filler cap and a tailgate. A taller windscreen allowed for a higher hood, and full sidescreens and a heater were available. Most importantly, the transfer box was adapted for a power take-off (PTO) to drive farm machinery. The driveshaft for this ran centrally and came out at the rear, so it could be connected to a towed, driven implement. The PTO also had a belt drive, accessible from behind the front seats, and a whole range of farm implements were made available for the optional Monroe three-point linkage.

A 'JEEP' ON THE PAYROLL SAVES MONEY FOR YOU

Willys'
4-FUNCTION VEHICLE

The CJ-2A in its first form: this is a very early picture, in which it can be seen that the pressings for the pioneer tools are still left in. The electric windscreen-wiper motor, the fixed headlights, column change and outside filler can also be seen. On the CJ, the windscreen is held down by a clip attached to the grille, rather than by the two spring-clips of the MB.

WILLYS MAKE THE JEEP ALL THEIR OWN

Ward Canaday had wrested exclusive manufacturing rights to the jeep in 1941. Despite the legal action brought by Ford in 1944, Willys had decided that 'Jeep' was to be theirs alone, and that they would hold their ground, no matter what the opposition. Colonel Herrington, the pioneer in the field of four-wheel drive, had written to Willys saying that the jeep was '. . .an invaluable asset to any individual or firm who can claim credit for it.'

Credit for the design could not be given to any one individual or company, but there was still the matter of the ownership of the name. Willys wanted that as badly as they did the vehicle: as far back as 1942 some Go-Devil cylinder heads had 'Jeep' cast into them, and even whilst the Federal Trade Commission hearing was going on, they stamped the Jeep name on the tailgate, bonnet and windscreen frame of very early CJ-2As (though they soon replaced it with 'Willys'). However, it was significant that in

advertising, the name 'Jeep' was written in inverted commas because it was still not a registered title. Moreover on 2 February 1948, the Federal Trade Commission issued a 'cease and desist' order to Willys, preventing them from claiming again in their advertising material that they were the originators of the jeep. But Willys would eventually win the day, and on 13 June 1950 they were granted United States Trademark Registration number 526175 for the name 'Jeep'. At last the brand was theirs exclusively, in name as well as in metal.

THE ALL-STEEL STATION WAGON

The Universal was outstandingly versatile, but it was too small for every application. There was a big market for utility vehicles that would help in the country's concerted effort to develop peacetime production, and the first all-new post-war vehicle from Willys went further to address that need.

The CJ-2A was never intended to be a military vehicle, but the Swiss Air Force bought some in the 1940s for general airfield utility work. This is a restored 1948 example, although because the Swiss authorities were somewhat uncooperative, the restorer cannot guarantee the accuracy of the markings.

'You've never owned a car so useful, so practical. . .' This poster says it all about the Jeep Station Wagon. This is the 463 of 1947. Unlike so much auto artwork of the period, the proportions of the vehicle are not distorted to give an impression of size and speed: they didn't need to be.

You've never owned a car so useful, so practical

No sedan matches a station wagon for all-around usefulness. And no other station wagon is so practical for every use as the "Jeep" Station Wagon—the first with an all-steel body and top for greater safety and longer service. It's a roomy, comfortable family car. When you need extra big load space, all except the driver's seat are removable. Let your Willys-Overland dealer show you how fully the "Jeep" Station Wagon meets your family's needs.

LOTS OF ROOM inside the "Jeep" Station Wagon's all-steel body for passengers—space, too, for things you want to take along. When there's a bulky load to haul, such as a chair or washing machine to be repaired, removing the seats gives 96 cubic feet of cargo space.

WONDERFULLY SMOOTH RIDING on country roads or city streets. Independent front-wheel suspension absorbs road bumps, keeping the car level and steady. It's a thrifty car to drive — the world-famous "Jeep" Engine with overdrive delivers mileage to brag about.

LET IT SNOW or rain or the sun beat down—the "Jeep" Station Wagon's all-steel body and top can take it. Even more important, you drive a "Jeep" Station Wagon with the secure feeling of sturdy steel around and above you.

'Jeep' Station Wagon
WITH ALL STEEL BODY AND TOP

WILLYS-OVERLAND MOTORS, TOLEDO, OHIO
MAKERS OF AMERICA'S MOST USEFUL VEHICLES

Introduced in September 1946, it was the 463 Station Wagon. All previous station wagons were conversions of existing sedans with heavy and expensive wood bodies, but the new Jeep was purpose-built, with an all-steel, seven-seat body. The 463's Jeep-style slatted grille and flat front wings were used to deliberate effect, readily identifying its makers, and its heritage was proudly displayed in script on the glove-box door in the words 'Jeep Station Wagon'.

The 104in (2,642mm) wheelbase chassis had just two-wheel drive, with transverse leaf 'Planadyne' independent front suspension and a conventional live rear axle on longitudinal leaf springs. The 463's Go-Devil engine, coupled to a Warner three-speed manual box, was a little small for the job, but it was the only one available, and the thrust of Willys's advertising was prac-

The first model Jeep truck. The stake truck and stepside body were the original factory body options.

ticality, utility, and above all economy. Alongside the Station Wagon was the 'Panel Delivery': this was simply the Station Wagon's body but with no side windows and no rear seats, and the drop tail-gate replaced by two side-opening doors.

Willys claimed the 463 as the world's first steel-bodied station wagon. Certainly at $1,495 it was the cheapest, and it was simple in its construction. But there was a fundamental reason for its simplicity, as I shall explain: Charles Sorensen was in charge at its inception, when Jim Mooney's new body presses were not even a pipe-dream. Sorensen knew that the big body makers would not be interested in small fry like Willys, so he solved the problem by going to Avco, a supplier to the domestic appliance business, whose presses would

only draw to a depth of around 6in (152mm). Brooks Stevens was then instructed to design body panels that had very simple, shallow curves, and his brilliant work made a virtue of necessity: this was because at speed, a large flat panel will flex and produce a drumming noise unless some shaping is pressed in. The shaping not only gave the Station Wagon a 'woody' appearance, it also endowed the body sides with strength. Its big, square interior was designed to take an 8 x 4ft (2.4 x 1.2m) sheet of board, not only flat on the deck, but upright too, if need be. And the floor was simple to clean: a hosepipe could easily wash off mud, salt and sand.

The truck followed a year later. It, like the Panel Delivery, had an I-beam front axle on longitudinal leaf springs at the front. The truck, with its longer, 118in (2,997mm) wheelbase and stepside body, could be had in two payloads: the 2T was rated at a half-ton, and the 4T could haul a full ton. Given the Jeep name for its own in 1948, the truck was also given four-wheel drive. This made an already useful vehicle even more versatile – yet it only increased the ground clearance by 4in (100mm). By comparison, other four-wheel drive trucks were much higher off the ground.

The Station Wagon had become popular with the well-to-do country-club set who bought it for fishing and hunting expeditions, so a new, smarter version, the 663 Station Sedan, was announced. Identified by a basket-weave decal along its side panels, it had just two-wheel drive – but under the bonnet was the 72bhp 'Lightning Six' 148ci sidevalve engine from the elusive passenger car. The most fascinating announcement for 1948, however, was the Jeepster.

The VJ-2 Jeepster. Brooks Stevens managed to give excellent proportions to the Jeepster's lines, whilst allowing plenty of space for the six passengers. four-wheel drive was never offered on the Jeepster: the concept did not call for it, and besides, with an open body the chassis needed a strong X-brace which did not allow room for the transfer case.

THE JEEPSTER

The Jeepster was the brainchild of Brooks Stevens. Built on a modified Station Wagon chassis, the six-seat steel body had just two doors; access to the rear seats was either by folding down part of the front split bench seat or, if you were young and athletic, by climbing on a step on the side of the body. As a vehicle it was difficult to categorize: for instance, could it be called a sports car? Under the bonnet of the first version, the VJ-2, was the Go-Devil engine, but although the light body and low gearing allowed the Jeepster adequate acceleration, it never had much speed, and thanks to a truck chassis, its handling never made it a real sports car.

If not a sports car, was it a convertible? Certainly the hood could be erected easily, but there were sidescreens instead of wind-up windows. In fact it was a modern version of the pre-war phaeton, a style

Because the Jeepster has no boot, the spare wheel is mounted on the back, using what the Americans refer to as a 'Continental' kit. The term actually comes from the Lincoln Continental of the late 1930s, one of the first cars to reintroduce this method of carrying the spare wheel on the outside.

The CJ-3A in its intended role as a working vehicle. This picture was used in a poster, the caption of which said, 'There is a place in every business where "Jeep" can work'. Other illustrations depicted a man painting structures outdoors using a spray gun, and another using a pneumatic drill, both powered by compressors driven from the Jeep's power take-off. The 'J' logo in the bottom left-hand corner was an early trademark.

Willys CJ-2A (1945–49) and CJ-3A (1948–53)	
Engine	
Type	Willys Go-Devil 4-cylinder sidevalve
Bore x stroke	3.25 x 4.125in
Capacity	134.2cu in (2.2ltr)
Main bearings	3
Max. power	63bhp @ 4000rpm
Max. torque	105lb/ft @ 2000rpm
Chassis	
Transmission	Warner 3-speed manual, synchromesh on 2nd & top
Turning circle	36ft
Transfer case	2-speed, part-time four-wheel drive
Suspension	Semi-elliptic leaf springs front and rear
Brakes	4-wheel hydraulic, 9in drums front and rear
Dimensions	
Wheelbase	80in
Track (front and rear)	48.25in
Overall length	123.125in
Overall width	57.125in (excluding spare wheel)
Overall height (top up)	CJ-2A 69.75in, CJ-3A 66.5in
Curb weight	2,240lb

generally superseded in the mid-1930s by full four-door convertibles. The Lightning engine was put in the Jeepster for 1949, giving this new version, the VJ-3, better performance. Truly the Jeepster was an anachronism, both behind its time and in some ways ahead of it. Still, it attracted something of a cult following.

THE CJ-3A

The CJ-2A had caught on in a big way in America: in its first three full years of production, take-up was over 200,000. But although this was a good total, it was not as high as Willys had hoped. However, its replacement, the CJ-3A, was already on its way. Introduced in late 1948, there was revised seating to give the front passengers a little more leg-room, and a taller one-piece windscreen. Underneath was a stronger transmission and transfer case. It was undeniably better all round than the CJ-2A, but a slump in agriculture and a shortage of raw materials would prevent it from being a far bigger seller. 131,000 were made in a slightly longer production run, from 1948 to 1953.

Willys were also well aware that in the light of modern engine developments, the old Go-Devil was no longer powerful enough.

FOUR-WHEEL DRIVE AND MORE POWER FOR THE STATION WAGON

Four-wheel drive came along in 1949 for the Station Wagon. Numbered as the 4x463, its only engine was the Go-Devil, for Willys did not have the money to re-engineer the chassis to accommodate both it and the physically larger Lightning.

The F-head Hurricane engine made its debut in the new two-wheel-drive 473 Station Wagon for the 1950 model year. The F-4 Hurricane was advertised as 'The most economical and powerful standard engine to use regular gasoline'. The F-head design put the inlet valves in the head, but left the exhaust valves in the block. This meant that the inlet valves could be much bigger and so handle a greater volume of the fuel/air mixture, thus producing more power. When the spark plug is placed right in the centre of the combustion chamber as in the Hurricane, it allows the most efficient combustion, which produces the best

power and fuel consumption. Both compact power units, the F-4 Hurricane and the F-6 Super Hurricane engines, were more than a compromise evolved of necessity and a very tight budget, and much more than the sum of their components.

The truck, the Panel Delivery and the VJ-2 Jeepster would also have the Hurricane, and all would be identified by a new V-shaped grille with six horizontal chrome bars. As it was derived from the Go-Devil block, the Hurricane fitted straight into the four-wheel drive 4x473 series, without any need for chassis re-engineering. It produced more power than the Lightning, so for the 673 Station Wagon and the VJ-3 Jeepster, the little six was bored out to 161ci, making it a 90bhp unit.

The Jeepster would not be around after 1951. After just three years only 19,132 had been made, and many hung on in the dealers' showrooms. The Station Sedan also ended its run in 1951. The Super Hurricane was offered in the two-wheel-drive Station Wagon models, and the Panel Delivery was given a new name, the Sedan Delivery. The Go-Devil was dropped from the Station Wagon and Truck range, leaving the Hurricane as the base engine.

The simple and functional lines of the all-steel Station Wagon have an elegance of their own. The hubcaps, the absence of a 'Four-Wheel Drive' badge on the bonnet side, and lastly the colour scheme, identify this as a 1950 two-wheel-drive model.

Station Wagon, Panel Delivery & Sedan Delivery (1946–65), and Jeepster (1948–50)

Engines

Go Devil

Type	4-cylinder sidevalve
Bore x stroke	3.25 x 4.125in
Capacity	134.2cu in (2.2ltr)
Main bearings	3
Max. power	63bhp @ 4000rpm
Max. torque	105lb/ft @ 2000rpm

Hurricane

Type	In-line 4-cylinder, inlet over exhaust
Bore x stroke	3.25 x 4.125in
Capacity	134.2cu in (2.2ltr)
Main bearings	3
Max. power	75bhp @ 4000rpm
Max. torque	114lb/ft @ 2000rpm

Lightning Six

Type	In-line 6-cylinder sidevalve
Bore x stroke	3.25 x 4.125in/3.125 x 3.55in
Capacity	148cu in/161cu in (2.4ltr/2.6ltr)
Main bearings	4
Max. power	72bhp @ 4000rpm/75bhp @ 4000rpm
Max. torque	117lb/ft @ 1600rpm/120lb/ft @ 2000rpm

Chassis

Transmission	Warner 3-speed manual, synchromesh on 2nd & top, optional overdrive
Turning circle	35ft
Transfer case	2-speed part time four-wheel drive
Suspension (front)	Planadyne transverse leaf independent with 2WD, or solid axle with semi-elliptic leaf springs with four-wheel drive
Suspension (rear)	Solid axle with semi-elliptic leaf springs
Brakes	4-wheel hydraulic, 9.9in drums front and rear

Dimensions

Wheelbase	104in
Track	55.25in front, 57in rear
Overall length	175in
Overall width	68in
Overall height (top up)	71in
Curb weight	2,898lb (Station Wagon)

A 1951 four-wheel drive Station Wagon. The single colour, heavier duty tyres and higher ground clearance give it a purposeful look. The V-grille with five chrome strips was fitted from 1950.

INTERIM MILITARY MODELS

The V35-U

The US Marine Corps wanted a Jeep that could ford deep water. The service manual's method of waterproofing for wartime jeeps was to slap a liberal coating of asbestos grease on the distributor, coil and plugs, and to fit some elaborate plumbing to the exhaust and carburettor. In battle this took far too long to be a realistic option, and clearly some more research was needed. During the 1940s work progressed on complete engine water-

Willys Jeep Truck (1947–65)	
Engine	
Type	Willys Go-Devil, Hurricane or Lightning according to year (*see* Station Wagon specifications)
Chassis	
Transmission	Warner 3-speed manual, synchromesh on 2nd & top
Transfer case	2WD or 2-speed, part time four-wheel drive
Suspension	Semi-elliptic leaf springs front and rear
Brakes	4-wheel hydraulic, 11in drums front and rear
Dimensions	
Wheelbase	114in
Track	55.5in front, 57in rear
Overall length	183.75in
Overall width	66.7in (excluding spare wheel)
Overall height (top up)	78.5in

Post Office Telephones (now British Telecommunications, or BT) ran a radio station in Criggion, on the Welsh borders. The area has always been prone to severe flooding in the spring, and in 1947 the local telephone engineers, prompted by the need to gain access to equipment at all times, bought a surplus GP-A from the Royal Marines. It undoubtedly had its uses, for it was kept in service until February 1968. The vehicle is now in the BT Museum.

proofing, with vehicles tested at the Army's tank proving grounds at Aberdeen, Maryland. The new Navy Jeep, with the identification number V35-U, used a fundamentally unaltered CJ-3A tub: the stampings were not even changed to take out details like the holes where a heater pipe would run. At least some models, if not all, carried a power take-off. This model did not receive full engine waterproofing, but there was a snorkel for the carburettor, and an exhaust that rose high above the rear of the vehicle.

The MC-M38. The pioneer tools are on the reverse side to the MB, because of its outside filler cap. This preserved model has nonstandard indicator lights fitted, for safety reasons.

The V35-U was perhaps the rarest military Jeep, with just 1,000 built.

The MC-M38

As in 1941, fate would step in to accelerate Jeep's development. Communists controlled North Korea, and they believed that neither the US nor the new United Nations would interfere when they invaded South Korea in the summer of 1950. They were wrong. The US Army had been in South Korea since 1949, and under the sanction of the UN, assisted the government in driving back the invaders.

The MBs and GPWs were struggling to cope with the mountainous going and the extremes of cold and wet, or hot and humid weather in Korea – although it must be said that the experience gained in service in those few months was invaluable, albeit hard-won, for the team under Miguel Ordorica who were working on new Jeep programmes. But the urgency of the Korean war demanded more capable Jeeps before a Hurricane-powered model could be developed, so a stop-gap, the MC-M38 (MC was the Army's old notation, M38 the new), was pushed into production. Early M38s were shipped out and tried in combat conditions, then brought back to Toledo and modified, and tested in the Army's facilities at Fort Eustis, Virginia.

The whole improvement package consisted of a stronger transmission, transfer gears, axles, springs and frame, and a heavier-gauge body. Fixed 7in (178mm) headlights were fitted, and electric windscreen wipers. The pioneer tools were moved to the other side of the body because of the outside fuel filler. The 24v electrics were fully waterproofed to NATO standards, as was the engine waterproofing, complete with a snorkel for the carburettor. All this enabled the M38 to run fully submerged. Over 45,000 M38s were supplied between 1950 and 1952 – in fact by the end of 1950, Willys already had a back order for M38s worth $100,000. Once commissioned, some were to stay in service until the early 1960s.

The 'CJ-4'

Willys needed a more powerful civilian Jeep, but the Hurricane was too tall to fit in the CJ-3A. In the late summer of 1949 Willys experimented – as was the practice of motor manufacturers, to take what they'd got and play around with it to see what they needed – by fitting a CJ-3A with a much higher bonnet so that it could take a Hurricane engine. But the big problem at Willys had always been a lack of money. Although Jim Mooney had raised a lot of capital for plant improvements, model development demanded a strong cash flow, and this was not as plentiful as it was with the Big Three, despite good utility vehicle sales in the late 1940s.

In 1949, against a background of production stoppages caused by material shortage, Jim Mooney resigned his position as chairman and president of Willys. The buyer's market that he had predicted had come about, but before the new passenger car had materialized. The next year Charles Sorensen, by now in his late sixties, retired from Willys. Ward Canaday immediately took up the two posts vacated by Mooney, and he now had to make some important decisions. One was to progress a new Hurricane-powered Jeep: begun in March 1950, it was at first identified at Toledo as the 'CJ-4', but a little later was given a new code, 474CJ. This vehicle was something of a hybrid, with a taller bonnet to accommodate the Hurricane engine and rounded front wings, grafted onto a CJ-3A chassis and tub.

The Jeep at the Museum of Modern Art

Barney Roos had said, back in the early 1940s, that, 'the jeep is not the forerunner of a new type of automobile. . . it makes no concession to art, and damn little to comfort!' But there were others who thought that the Jeep was a work of art in its own right. The Museum of Modern Art in New York chose a Jeep to go on show alongside seven other examples of the auto world's finest designs.

The exhibition was arranged by Philip Johnson, the director of the museum's Department of Architecture and Design, and it ran from August to November 1951. All eight cars were placed on an elevated runway in the museum's ground floor gallery and garden. Alongside them, large photographs of other notable cars were displayed, including a current model Ford Tudor and a Lincoln Zephyr. There was also a Jeepster, described in the catalogue as a '. . . sharply rational vehicle', and '. . .an extraordinarily clear-sighted demonstration of esthetic (*sic*) appeal derived from a closely reasoned design program.' This was a fancy way of saying that Willys had crossed a jeep with a truck and come up with a sports car.

The eight cars present were selected to show three visually pleasing ways of combining the essential parts of a motor car. The first was by putting the passengers in an open box separate from the chassis. Second was the 'single envelope' method, meaning the new slab-sided or pontoon style; and lastly was the 'separate envelope', a closed body divided from the engine compartment. Naturally the Jeep – an MC loaned by Willys – came into the first category, alongside a 1931 Mercedes SS and a 1948 MG TC. Cars in the other two categories included a 1949 Cisitalia, a 1939 Bentley with a James Young razor-edged Sports Saloon body, a 1937 Talbot with an exceptional Figoni & Falaschi fixed-head body, a 1937 Cord 810 sedan, and a 1941 Lincoln Continental.

Whilst eulogizing on the beauty of the other exhibits, the catalogue took a more 'cutesy' attitude to the Jeep, saying that it combined '. . .the appeal of an intelligent dog with a gadget', and compared its body to '. . .a sturdy sardine can on wheels' with '. . .the top. . .cut open and folded up, to serve as a windshield'. But the catalogue's author took a more respectful note in outlining the jeep's abilities in relation to its appearance. Summing up, he said, 'The Jeep substitutes for a deliberate esthetic program the formative principles of construction; its design is unified by the economy (disdaining the merely decorative) with which each part is fitted for its purpose. It is one of the few genuine expressions of machine art.'

Canaday's second decision was to scrap the 6/71 and order the design of a new passenger car, the Aero, and this would have a serious knock-on effect on the 474CJ programme because it meant that the cash available for the new Jeep would be seriously squeezed, particularly when the effects of the Korean war were also taken into account. The feared halt in total passenger-car production which happened in World War II was not repeated, but there was a serious drop in supplies of materials, and the public's spending power was badly hit. The 474CJ programme was stopped, and the initial work on building a modified CJ-3A was restarted.

The Army wanted an advanced type of quarter-ton truck, and in 1951 Ford alone were invited to set up a development programme to tender for it. In October 1950 Willys had also begun, quite independently, an Advanced Jeep (AJ) programme; but with no definite commission likely, this was scrapped. Ford's own vehicle would materialize later as the M151 MUTT.

In December 1950 Willys began work on a more modern, conventional Jeep for the Army, using the CJ-4 as its starting point. Tagged the 'CJ-4M' at Toledo and the M38E1 by the Army, it had the original tub and flat-fronted front wings of the 'CJ-4'.

Now Ward Canaday restarted the 'CJ-4' on the back of the Army programme. In January 1951 the military jeep concept began to gel with the new MD-M38A1. This overlapped the CJ-4 and CJ-4MP programme, but work on these two would cease by 21 June. The M38A1 would be the one the Army needed quickly, as the M38 was struggling in the atrocious conditions of Korea.

The MD-M38A1

The MD-M38A1 was introduced on 28 January 1952. Everything was stronger and bigger, with an 81in (2,057mm) wheelbase, a width of 71.75in (1,822mm) and an overall length, spare wheel not included, of 135.5in (3,442mm). There was a downward curve added to the front wings to prevent mud from flying up and back into the occupants' faces. The pioneer tools, once prone to damage and to collecting bits of tree, were tucked inside the back. The Hurricane engine was fully waterproofed, including complete seal-ing for the crankcase ventilation. The MC's running gear was carried over, as was the 24v auxiliary electrical system. The M38A1 was tough enough to handle the atrocious conditions in Korea, and it took the Jeep's reputation even higher.

Running parallel with the CJ-4M programme was the CJ-4MP, the 'front line personnel carrier'. This programme was closed along with the CJ-4M, but the concept was re-opened in September 1951 alongside the M38A1, and materialized as the M170. It found use as a field ambulance, as well as for personnel-carrying duties.

Because the M38A1 was commissioned by the Army, the rights to the chassis and body design were US government property, so they could choose whom they liked to build it. Reminiscent of 1940, a three-way agreement was signed in early 1952 by the US government, Willys and the Ford Motor Company for Ford to build the M38A1 in Canada. These would be for Canadian armed forces only, and would at first be assembled

The MD-M38A1. The cut-out for a snorkel can be seen on the side of the bonnet. The plug on the side of the scuttle is for a power charger, as MDs had a habit of losing battery charge if left for any length of time.

Willys CJ-3B (1952–68)

Engine
Type	Willys Hurricane 4-cylinder, inlet over exhaust
Bore x stroke	3.25 x 4.125in
Capacity	134.2cu in (2.2ltr)
Main bearings	3
Max. power	75bhp @ 4000rpm
Max. torque	114lb/ft @ 2000rpm

Chassis
Transmission	Warner 3-speed manual, synchromesh on 2nd & top
Turning circle	35.5ft (left) 33.8ft (right)
Transfer case	2-speed
Suspension	Semi-elliptic leaf springs front and rear
Brakes	4-wheel hydraulic, 9in drums front and rear

Dimensions
Wheelbase	81in
Track (front and rear)	48.5in
Overall length	129.88in
Overall width	57.125in (excluding spare wheel)
Overall height (top up)	68.88in
Curb weight	2,243lb

from components produced at Toledo until Ford made their own tooling to the Willys design.

If Ward Canaday had pinned his hopes on introducing the 'CJ-4' at the same time as the MD, he was in for a let-down. Canaday had to have permission from the Army to use the body and frame. Back in 1941 Canaday had held a very strong hand when the Army asked him if he would give permission for Ford to build the then new jeep to Willys design. He agreed, on the condition that Willys alone would have the rights to the jeep in peacetime. His ace was permission for Ford to make the Go-Devil engine, which was the property of Willys. At that time the Army were in a tight spot and had to accede, but now circumstances were much different: now, the Army would not give Canaday permission.

THE CJ-3B

Less than three weeks prior to the M38A1's announcement, Willys therefore had to cancel the new Universal model. What were they to do? Here was a super new vehicle, more powerful and tougher than its predecessors, and every inch a Jeep. Willys owned the Hurricane engine and had issue of the transmission and axles, but because they did not have the rights to the body press tools, they could not build a civilian version of the M38A1.

Much of the company's available cash had gone into the passenger car programme, and the slump in sales meant that Willys did not have enough money to build a completely new body for a new Hurricane-powered CJ. A compromise had to be found, and that was the CJ-3B. Initially called the CJ-4A, it was a mix-and-

British Jeep conversions

Although a huge number of jeeps were abandoned in Europe by the Allies after the end of World War II, the British Army had many still in service, either supplied directly or 'inherited' from American forces who had gone home. Some jeeps were sold off piecemeal, but in 1952, in the first of two major dispersal sales, the older ones were auctioned off, to be replaced by the new Austin Champ. The British government directed motor manufacturers to 'export or die', and they were allocated steel according to their export potential. New cars, if they could be found, were at a premium; so much so that, to prevent profiteering, the government made all new car purchasers sign a declaration, a covenant, to say that they would not sell their new car for a fixed period of time. There was a ready market for anything on wheels, new or old, and ex-army jeeps provided a useful, if somewhat Spartan means of transport; quite a few were bought up by enterprising companies who converted them into various forms of station wagon, van and pick-up truck.

Metamet, of Belsize Lane in north-west London, extended jeep chassis for their conversions, which included a station wagon, a light truck and the open-bodied caravanner. They also modified standard jeeps by fitting doors. Some mechanical modifications available for UK jeeps were an elbow to adapt an SU carburettor, and a conversion to a Lucas distributor and 12v electrics.

Two of Farmcraft's conversion of ex-Army jeeps: the truck, left, and the Adventurer estate car.

Farmcraft offered a basic, ex-army, road-registered jeep 'in good running order' for £125. For £300, the 'Standard' jeep, resprayed in the customer's choice of colour, would come with a reconditioned engine, a new hood and seats, and a full tool kit. A truck conversion was available for up to £478 10s. The 'Burleigh' estate car was £525, whilst the more luxurious 'Adventurer', with a seasoned hardwood body, carpets, wood dash surround and sliding windows, was £650. Although the wood estate-car body must have added a lot of weight to the jeep, Farmcraft guaranteed 22mpg (12.9l/100km)! Farmcraft could supply an aluminium skinned wood-framed hard top for a basic jeep, and a full range of spares and manuals. Universal Car Distributors of Chiswick, West London; Jeep International of Dymchurch, Kent; and Eurotech were also suppliers of spare parts.

match of existing and new body, chassis and engine components. On an 81in (2,057mm) wheelbase, the tub was from the CJ-3A, but the scuttle and bonnet were taller so as to clear the engine, and this new front end gave it an ungainly look in comparison to the clean, simple lines of the early flat-fenders. It is said that compromises are rarely satisfactory, but the new Jeep was undoubtedly a better performer and that was what truly mattered. The ugly duckling CJ-3B went on sale in the US in 1952, with production overlapping its predecessor by some months. Toledo had no

The CJ-3B. Its high bonnet may spoil an otherwise elegant line, but it performed better, and that is what mattered.

love for its new baby, but they could have foreseen that it would be the most enduring of all flat-fender Jeep models, and be the basis of many export variations. It was a case of 'handsome is as handsome does', and sales held up well in the home market.

The one-millionth civilian Jeep vehicle, a truck, came off the production line on 19 March 1952. This was cheering news for Willys, but the Korean War had proved a double-edged sword. Material allocations for passenger cars were restricted, although there was some compensation for all auto makers, with in excess of $6.5 billion worth of orders for military hardware. Nevertheless the war caused a serious drop in the US economy. Sales of all Willys models fell by a half in 1952, including those of the new Aero. A fifty-three-day national steel strike in the summer, and a slump in agriculture, ate into production and sales alike, and in the whole auto industry some 1,200 workers were laid off during the course of the year. The 1953 Jeep line-up did not therefore see any innovations, although that year – Willys's fiftieth birthday – would see a major change.

THE STANDARD CONNECTION

Already export markets had been sought by the Willys-Overland Export Corporation.

Jeep four-wheel-drive systems: free-wheel hubs

Disengaging the front axle on a four-wheel drive vehicle with a basic transfer box prevents drive-line wind-up. However, running in 2WD still caused wear on the differential and its bearings, and the drag in the axle adversely affects fuel consumption. A simple way of reducing that drag is to fit free-wheel hubs.

The Warn free-wheel hub. The centre of the hub had to be turned to either lock or unlock the hub.

The automatic Cutlass 'Powerlock' hub.

One type, the Warn Lockomatic, has to be engaged or disengaged manually. Getting out of the vehicle to do this could be a bit of an inconvenience in bad weather, when encountering the kind of going that demands four-wheel drive. The Cutlass Power-Lock hub freewheels automatically in 2WD, and locks when the drive is provided in four-wheel drive.

FWD of Kingston-on-Thames, Surrey, became the first legitimate Jeep agent in the UK, and Olding and Company were listed in the early 1950s. They had a hard time selling Jeeps, as import duties added some 30 per cent to the price, and there was still a fair number of wartime models around. But the demand for Land Rovers world-wide was far greater than Solihull could keep up with, and so there was plenty of room for the Jeep. The best way for Willys, and the one they took to readily, was to license production to overseas companies. One such attempt was with the smallest of Britain's 'big six' makers, the Standard Motor Company of Coventry.

Captain Sir John Black, the chairman of the Standard Motor Company, was a forceful and ambitious man. In 1933, as Captain Black, he became joint managing director with Standard's founder, Reginald Maudslay. Following Maudslay's retirement, Black brought the little Coventry company up to sixth place in the league table of

British motor manufacturers.

In 1945 Standard built the ungainly two-wheel-drive FGPV, or 'farmers' general purpose vehicle'. This was soon abandoned, but in 1946 Standard began manufacture of Ferguson tractors. Besides his tractor work, Harry Ferguson was involved with Rolt-Dixon Developments, a company working on four-wheel drive systems. With Ferguson's money, Rolt-Dixon became Harry Ferguson Research Ltd.

Sir John had a voracious attitude to competition. He wanted a slice of the Land Rover market, and a prototype four-wheel drive utility vehicle, the 'Languard', had already been built with that intention. But the chance of a more beneficial arrangement presented itself. In December 1952 Sir John sailed to the USA, taking with him his new prototype sports car, the 20TS, which was designed to be an export rival to the MG T-series.

Sir John spent some time at Toledo with Ward Canaday, and a memorandum was drawn up, dated 24 February 1953, between Willys and Standard for an agreement that would last an expected five to ten years. It would be a two-way deal: Standard would provide the tooling to produce the CJ-3B in Coventry at a rate of fifty per day, buying in Hurricane engines for the first year until the plant to manufacture them in Coventry was in place. Coventry-made CJ-3Bs would be sold as the Standard-Willys Jeep in the UK, and as the Willys Jeep in the Commonwealth. Now, Standard would be able to attack Land Rover on their own ground with a proven brand. Export sales of Jeeps would make a major contribution to Britain's balance of payments, and Willys would have an entry into the otherwise sterling area. Standard were also lined up make the M38A1, for which Canaday had grand plans. He saw it selling not only to British and Commonwealth armed forces, but as the standard quarter-ton truck for NATO.

During and before Sir John's transatlantic trip, the 20TS was being developed

The Languard was Standard's attempt to cash in on the Land Rover and Jeep markets, prior to Sir John Black's negotiations with Willys-Overland. Standard were very serious about the Languard, registering its name in dozens of countries around the world. Power is from the 2.1 litre Vanguard engine. Six slats in the grille give a nod to Jeep, and although it appears to have many Land Rover body components, close comparison shows that the Languard is a different vehicle.

into a new sports car, the Triumph TR2, and it would soon be ready for production. For their part in the agreement, Willys would market the TR2 as the Willys-Triumph Sports through their own dealerships. However, the memorandum did not tell the whole story. Willys needed a business partner if they were to prosper, and rumours had been around for some months about a take-over of Willys by Kaiser-Frazer – rumours that had a solid base of truth. In the event of a take-over, the agreement between Willys and Standard was to be binding upon Kaiser-Frazer – yet Sir John Black claimed to be unaware of such a deal. In fact he was sent news of the take-over during his return flight to London on 6 March, and when he read the message, he went white with rage. He spent the rest of the flight cutting up and re-pasting the press handouts, earning himself a reprimand from the stewardess for marking the seat-back table with his razor blade!

On 15 April Sir John wrote to Ward Canaday, breaking off his negotiations. He stated that he had '. . .come to the conclusion that it would not be possible for my company to proceed with the tentative arrangement we made with you to manufacture the Willys-Overland Jeep in this country, and for you to sell our sports car in the United States of America. . .You will recollect, at the time of negotiations, I was under the impression that there was no contemplation of an amalgamation, and that I was dealing with you [Canaday] as President and Chairman of your board. . .'

Sir John continued, 'It is. . .apparent that whoever acquires the financial control is bound to have the final say, and as we are not acquainted with any of the Kaiser-Frazer directorate or management, I feel that we could not proceed.' Sir John also alluded to a four-wheel drive vehicle under development by Harry Ferguson, that he,

Ferguson, had discussed with Canaday. This in part, Sir John claimed, compromised the deal, and also 'altered his [Ferguson's] outlook in this regard,' as Ferguson was attempting to sell his Harry Ferguson Research Company to Willys.

But why should Kaiser's financial control upset Sir John Black? Surely the new owner's money would have been welcome news, for it would have underpinned the investment that Standard were about to make? And as the Jeep belonged to Willys, Sir John would have to accept any changes made to it without any real arguments. Furthermore, Kaiser's principally urban dealers would likely augment TR2 sales. There had to be another reason for Sir John Black's withdrawal.

Standard had already begun to build overseas assembly plants of their own, in places such as Belgium, Australia and India, and the assembly of Standard cars in the USA would be a logical step. Not mentioned in any correspondence was a plan for Willys to make the TR2 at Toledo, but Sir John had taken the 20TS there to evaluate just that possibility. As financial controllers, Kaiser's 'final say' could theoretically compromise anything to do with the manufacture of Standard cars in the US. That, to Sir John, would be unacceptable. If he was to have control over the manufacture of his cars at Toledo, he would have to buy a significant share-holding in Willys, or at least have an influential position on Willys's board. Kaiser's take-over stopped any such ideas immediately.

The fortunes of the already successful Standard Motor Company were to rise still further over the following fifteen years, but Standard and Triumph marques would eventually die, the latter suffocated by British Leyland. On the other hand, Jeep's lot would grow, and the success would be much longer lasting.

4 Willys Motors Inc: Under Kaiser's Banner

Willys-Overland had been doing business with Kaiser Industries since 1951. There had also been some interchange of engineering staff, as Willys were supplying Go-Devil and Lightning engines for Kaiser's sub-compact 'Henry J' two-door sedan. But the Henry J was the same price as a basic two-door Chevy, so not surprisingly it was never commercially successful on a large scale. In fact Kaiser's automotive side began to lose out all round, the sales high of nearly 154,000 large models in 1951 dropping to just over 32,000 the following year.

In the spring of 1952 Edgar Kaiser approached Ward Canaday with the offer of a take-over. Joining forces would benefit both companies, for customers valued an identifiable heritage. Some shied away from Kaiser because they felt that it would not survive as an auto maker – and these fears were not without foundation, as Kaiser had already been to the government for money. On the other hand, Willys was celebrating its fiftieth anniversary, but they needed a powerful partner if they were to expand as Ward Canaday wanted – and Kaiser Industries had assets in excess of $800 million.

Working out the details of the take-over lasted three months, but finally in April 1953 Kaiser Industries bought Willys-Overland for $62.3 million cash, raised from outside the Kaiser Automobile concern. Henry J. Kaiser's son Edgar took his seat on the Willys board as president of the renamed Willys Motors Inc., and Ward Canaday finally retired; Barney Roos also departed, to set up his own consultancy business.

The companies' model lines would layer well, with the Henry J at the bottom, the Aero in the middle, the big Kaisers at the top and Jeeps adding the icing on the cake. The engineering facilities complemented each other, too: Kaiser had no forging plant and would be able to use the excellent facilities at Toledo; and at Willys's disposal would be Kaiser's new $3 million body plant in Shadyside, Ohio.

Kaiser's huge Willow Run plant had become a white elephant: Toledo had far more usable space for car production, and Willow Run was sold in November 1953 to General Motors for £9.28 million. Kaiser had experienced labour problems at Willow Run, and no doubt Edgar Kaiser anticipated a fight from the Union of Auto Workers when he announced the transfer of production to Toledo. However, the auto industry was in recession due to the Korean War, and the UAW co-operated with the move. Workers on the tracks at Toledo would take an average 10 per cent pay cut, and would work on Kaiser sedans, Willys Station Wagons, trucks, Aeros and Universals, all mixed up on the same track, at a rate of twenty-five vehicles an hour. For the next seventeen years Kaiser would develop some of the most innovative designs ever to carry the Jeep name, usually employing the ingenuity of Brooks Stevens to do so.

Henry J. Kaiser's automobiles

In the aftermath of World War II, the American auto industry quickly re-established itself in business by revamping its 1941 designs. This was not the policy of Henry J. Kaiser, however: in 1945 he signed a deal with ex-Willys vice president Joseph. A. Frazer, who had bought defunct car maker Graham in 1941. Ford's huge Willow Run bomber plant was acquired, and by late 1946 the first models, with ultra-modern 'slab-sided' styling, were on sale. They were badged as two separate lines: the Kaiser and the more expensive Frazer.

The 1947 Kaiser and Frazer cars with the proud entrepreneurs: left, a Kaiser with Joseph Frazer; and right, a Frazer with Henry J. Kaiser.

A 5 per cent market share against nearly twenty other brands was the reward for their efforts, although sales dropped off as other manufacturers' new models came out. In 1949 Kaiser raised $44 million from the Reconstruction Finance Corporation, a government organization created in the Depression year of 1932, to design a new model. 1951 was the last year for the Frazer line: Joseph Frazer left the company, and from then on there would be just Kaisers.

Although elegant, Kaisers were expensive and mechanically conservative. The 1953 Kaiser Dragon was a whopping $3,924 – the sort of money that would get you a Cadillac – but where V8 engines were becoming the norm, Kaisers still used a sidevalve six. Since 1947 new OHV four-and six-cylinder engines were under development, and an aluminium V8 which would 'show the industry what horsepower really means'; for the Kaiser, however, these engines never materialized, nor could the company afford to style further new models, and as a result Kaiser automobiles went into terminal decline in the home market.

TRUCK AND STATION WAGON UPGRADES

If the Jeep truck and Station Wagon lacked anything it was real power, and for the 1954 model year Willys engineers installed Kaiser's standard 226ci (3.67 litre) sidevalve engine as an option for the whole range. The new engine, christened the Super Lightning in its Willys application, replaced the 161ci Lightning, but left the Hurricane as the base option, and right from the beginning it was available on four-wheel drive – but only four-wheel drive. This was one immediate benefit of Kaiser's investment. Truck sales increased by around 2,000 in the first year, most of which had the new engine.

FOREIGN EXPANSION

Kaiser Industries' overseas automotive operations would be helped greatly by Jeep, largely because it was an ideal vehicle for developing or agricultural countries. The assembly of Willys commercial vehi-

cles was started in the Netherlands by Nederlandssche Kaiser-Frazer (Nekaf), in the old Kaiser plant established in 1948. In late 1953 a deal was made with Mitsubishi Heavy Industries in Nagoya, Japan, to license the manufacture of CJ-3B-based Jeeps. After World War II, Japan was held responsible for a huge amount of war reparations, and the Jeep contract was one way in which their industry could be kick-started to help cover those liabilities. The range included a four-door, six-seat, all-steel station wagon similar to the 463, and production of all models grew to some eight to ten thousand vehicles annually.

Willys-Overland do Brasil SA was set up at Sao Paolo in 1954. By the end of the year the tooling for the Willys Aero was shipped out to Brazil, and was joined by a locally made CJ-3B. Before his deposition in 1955, President Peron of Argentina had offered incentives to foreign industrial investors, including car makers, as a way of bringing in hard currency to stabilize the raging inflation of the previous three years. On 5 October 1955 Henry J. and Edgar Kaiser

Simple, tough and effective; the one-ton Jeep truck with a stepside body. The three horizontal chrome bars on the grille date this as a product of the early Kaiser years.

signed a contract to construct a car- and truck-building complex: involving a large local financial input, Industrias Kaiser Argentina (IKA) was set up in Cordoba, 500 miles (800km) north-west of Buenos Aires. Besides passenger cars, the huge new concern would also make Jeep Station Wagons and trucks and the CJ-3B.

AN END TO PASSENGER CARS

As one consequence of this move Kaiser ran down the production of passenger cars in the US. The price of the Willys Aero, powered now only by the 226ci Kaiser six, was cut drastically to try and shift it off the dealers' forecourts. The bulk of Kaiser's big sedan production went to Argentina, and only 9,000 1955 Kaisers, all McCulloch supercharged Manhattans, were sold on the home market. Gone were the promised new engines. The Latin American operations and the switch at home to commercial vehicle manufacture were wise moves – 1954's commercial vehicle sales at home

were up by 70,000 on the previous year – but Henry J. Kaiser was finally forced to admit that the Big Three had licked him in the home market for passenger cars. He was used to dealing in multi-million dollar sums, but his auto-making business was small fry compared to the giants in the industry. Talking of his original 1940s investment, Henry J. said, 'We were not surprised that we had to toss $50 million in the automotive pool. We were surprised that it disappeared without a ripple.'

Stillborn lightweight

An experimental lightweight version of the MD-M38A1 was developed by Willys in 1953 for the Army and Marine Corps. Dubbed the 'Aero Jeep' or the 'Bobcat', it was a two-seater with a very short wheelbase, and was for airborne use. An aluminium body was tried, though it proved unsuitable. The project was dropped when the military opted for the Hudson-designed M422 'Mighty Mite'.

The Kaiser Manhattan (top) and the Willys Aero (bottom). Both these 1954 models featured Kaiser's 226cu in Kaiser six-cylinder engine. Neither, however, would see production in the US beyond 1955.

THE CJ-5

Kaiser needed a modern Universal, and since Willys had put so much work into the M38A1, it was decided that a civilian version of this military model would be the best thing to have. After some negotiation, they eventually acquired the rights from the US government for the M38A1 body tooling and the chassis, and October 1954 saw the introduction of the CJ-5. Its military heritage was very clear. The new Jeep shared the basic body shape of the M38A1 but had chrome-trimmed headlights and 6v electrics. The rounded front wings and a full-width scuttle not only brought the Universal up to date in its styling but, like the military version, gave more room inside both in the front and on the rear bench seat.

Although many of the body panels were shared with the M38A1, the CJ-5 had a separate tail-gate and a side-mounted spare wheel; the 6v battery was stowed in a box in the scuttle. The snorkel hole in the side of the bonnet was left, covered with a blanking plate. The Hurricane engine – the main reason for starting the whole project – was under the bonnet. Softer springs gave a kinder ride, but the driver and passengers were as open to the weather as before without the optional top and side-screens. Still there were no metal doors, but this was because of the Jeep's chassis and body design: the chassis was flexible, and the steel tub body was designed to give strength to the vehicle as a whole, and to flex with it – a full-depth aperture would therefore weaken the body tub and, over rough ground, hinged metal doors would bang against the door shuts.

The CJ-5: all-new, but still all-Jeep, as this publicity shot shows. A one-piece windscreen was standard for the US market, but export models had a split screen.

Meyer snow ploughs were an option for all Jeep vehicles. This CJ-5 has the optional hard top, and a wrecker attachment on the rear. The flat-bladed snow plough could be set to push snow to the left, right or straight ahead.

The CJ-5 arrives in the UK

Steele Griffiths of Camberwell, South London – Kaiser dealers since 1946 – replaced Olding and Company as the new British Jeep concessionaires. They supplied a CJ-5 to *Commercial Motor* magazine for a road test, and it was taken to the REME testing ground at Bagshot Heath, Surrey, for some tough off-road work. The writer was pleased with its overall performance – even though when trying to produce some of the airborne shots for the photographer it burst a tyre when it landed at a bad angle. However, good as the CJ-5 showed itself to be, four things would deter the British buyer. First there was the lack of weather protection in comparison to the Land Rover; second, it was available in left-hand drive only; third, the Land Rover dealership and spares network was far greater than those for Jeep; and last, import duties put the price up to very high £875.

THE CJ-6

The CJ-5 was a tough worker but it lacked a decent-sized pickup bed, and so to make more cargo space or rear seating room, the CJ-5's wheelbase was stretched by 20in (500mm). Introduced in late 1955, this new version was called the CJ-6. Mechanically it was identical to the CJ-5, but the body design allowed more room: in this version the tops of the rear wheel arches were squared off inside, and up to four passengers could be carried on two sideways-mounted bench seats. In contemporary road tests it was found that the CJ-6 could do everything its shorter brother could do, but it had more load space and greater straight-line stability under heavy braking.

WAGON AND TRUCK IMPROVEMENTS

The new policy of concentrating on commercial vehicles led to significant changes

Willys CJ-5 & CJ-6 (1954–72)

Engine

Type	Willys Hurricane 4-cylinder, inlet over exhaust
Bore x stroke	3.25 x 4.125in
Capacity	134.2cu in (2.2ltr)
Main bearings	3
Max. power	75bhp @ 4000rpm
Max. torque	114lb/ft @ 2000rpm

Chassis

Transmission	Warner 3-speed manual, synchromesh on 2nd & top
Turning circle	CJ-5, 36ft, CJ-6, 39ft
Transfer case	2-speed, part time four-wheel drive
Suspension	Semi-elliptic leaf springs front and rear
Brakes	4-wheel hydraulic, 9in drums front and rear

Dimensions

Wheelbase	CJ-5, 81in, CJ-6, 101in
Track (front and rear)	48.5in
Overall length	CJ-5, 135.5in, CJ-6, 155.5in
Overall width	71.75in (including spare wheel)
Overall height (top up)	69.5in
Curb weight	2,413lb

The CJ-6. The extra length behind the front seats is clear to see, as is the join in the body panels behind the fuel filler.

Willys Jeep Utility Wagon and Truck (1954–65)

Engine

Hurricane

Type	Willys 4-cylinder, inlet over exhaust
Bore x stroke	3.25 x 4.125in
Capacity	134.2cu in (2.2ltr)
Main bearings	3
Max. power	75bhp @ 4000rpm
Max. torque	114lb/ft @ 2000rpm

Super Lightning

Type	6-cylinder, sidevalve
Bore x stroke	3.94 x 4.375in
Capacity	226cu in (3.67ltr)
Main bearings	4
Max. power	105bhp @ 3600rpm
Max. torque	190lb/ft @ 1400rpm

Chassis

Transmission:	Warner 3-speed manual, synchromesh 2nd & top, optional overdrive
Turning circle	Utility Wagon & Delivery 37.7ft, Truck 36.6ft
Transfer case	2-speed, part time four-wheel drive
Suspension	Solid axles with semi elliptical leaf springs front and rear
Overall height	74.5in
Brakes	4-wheel hydraulic. Utility Wagon & Delivery, 9.9in drums front and rear, Truck 11in drums front and rear

Dimensions

Wheelbase	Utility Wagon & Utility Delivery, 104in, Truck, 118in
Track	Front, 56in, rear, 63.5in
Overall length	Utility Wagon & Utility Delivery, 174.75in, Truck 183.75in
Overall width	66.625in
Overall height	74.5in
Curb weight	Utility Wagon 3,000lb, Truck 3,500lb

in the truck and Station Wagon vehicles. In 1954 they were given a change in name, henceforth being known as the Utility Wagon, the Utility Delivery and the Utility Truck, and the range would undergo a series of improvements over the next four years. For 1955 Planadyne front suspension or an I-beam axle were offered as options on the two-wheel drive Utility Wagon and Delivery, though this choice was dropped for 1956 as the I-beam axle was standardized.

A special edition of the Utility Wagon known as 'the Maverick' came out for 1956: Willys Motors Inc. were sponsors of the light-hearted TV Western *Maverick*, starring James Garner, and the model was a merchandizing spin-off. With two-wheel drive and the Hurricane engine, it was carried over to 1957, and for this year, in common with the rest of the Wagon and Delivery models, had the option of a one-piece windscreen and a low-line ribbed roof. In 1958, all models gained 12-volt electrics and a fresh-air heater, and although the truck retained its high roof and split windscreen to the end, the new roof and windscreen were standardized for the Wagon and the Delivery.

THE DJ-3A DISPATCHER

Production of the CJ-3A was abandoned in 1953, but a new flat-fender model, the two-wheel drive DJ-3A Dispatcher, came along in 1955. The notion of a two-wheel drive Jeep was not new even then: in Argentina there had been an experiment to produce such a vehicle, although this had failed; also

---

Hotchkiss

The French motor company Hotchkiss dates back to 1903, and their record is one of making quality cars. By the 1930s they had established a sporting pedigree that included three outright wins in the Monte Carlo rally. Despite two post-war Monte wins, sales of the 3.5-litre 2050 model were crippled by the French government's heavy post-war taxation on large cars. Peugeot took a controlling interest in 1950, and when in 1954 Hotchkiss absorbed Delage and Delahaye, these prestige names, along with Hotchkiss, would no longer be seen on private cars.

Following the end of the war, many jeeps were left in France. However, the French government would not sell off its stock of jeep spares to private owners. On the recommendation of Englishman Henry Ainsworth, a Hotchkiss board member, the company took a concession from Willys-Overland to sell CJ-2A Universals and spares in France. By 1952 the company had secured a licence from Willys-Overland to manufacture a version of the CJ-3A.

At this time the French government, under a re-arming programme, began looking for its own home-made light reconnaissance vehicle. Peugeot and Delahaye built examples, but although the Delahaye was adopted, it was found to be sub-standard, and the models in service were soon sold off. Seeing that Hotchkiss were making the 'real thing', the French government decided they would buy

A Hotchkiss M201, in the colours of a French desert regiment. The French referred to an off-road vehicle as a VLTT, or 'Véhicule de Liaison Tout Terrain'.

them. The model made was the M201, an updated Willys MB, with a stronger chassis and improved steering; there was also full engine waterproofing, 12v electrics for the lighting and ignition, a 24v radio system, a speedometer calibrated in km/h, electric windscreen wipers and a Solex carburettor.

For civilian buyers the JH101 was introduced in 1954, with bodywork identical to the CJ-3B. It retained the Go-Devil engine and an MB gearbox, but had a unique transfer case to make its gear ratios suitable for civilian applications. It was superseded in 1961 by the JH102, which offered the option of diesel power, better steering and a bigger fuel tank. A longer wheelbase version, the HWL, offered an extra half metre of pickup bed. In 1969 the company – by then called Hotchkiss-Brandt SA – had built around 40,000 Jeeps; however, production was moved to Spain where the JH102 and HWL continued under the VIASA name.

'Jeep' DISPATCHER · SURREY GALA · FLEETVAN

'JEEP' DISPATCHER, DJ-3A
Lightweight, highly manoeuvrable—turns in a radius of 17½ ft.—the Dispatcher has a cargo capacity of 40 cu. ft., an ample gate opening 35¹¹⁄₁₆ in. high by 35 in. wide and an easy-to-load platform height of just 23¾ inches. Open body or optional Soft Top, Half Top and Hardtop models with ten standard body colors to choose from. All models have optional vented, folding windshields.

DISPATCHER DJ-3A

'JEEP' SURREY GALA, DJ-3A
Colorful choice of smart shops, small businesses, resort motels and hotels throughout the world, the Surrey Gala with the fringe on top is economical to buy and operate. Washable curtains, tops and seat coverings made of sturdy weather-resistant fabrics. Three two-tone paint options.

SURREY GALA DJ-3A

'JEEP' FLEETVAN, MODEL FJ-3A
Specifically designed for light-duty, multi-stop operation, the 'Jeep' Fleetvan is efficient, rugged, highly manoeuvrable and economical. Carries 1,000 lbs. of payload on 81 inches of wheelbase and supports a cargo capacity of 170 cu. ft. Only 154 in. long and 64.7 in. wide, the Fleetvan turns in a radius of 17 ft., important in traffic and the loading area. The driver of the Fleetvan can see an object only three feet high 12 in. from the front bumper. Side door height is 70 in. for easy walk-through.

FLEETVAN FJ-3A

Three two-wheel-drive Jeep vehicles: the DJ-3A Dispatcher, top; the DJ-3A Surrey Gala, which could be had in pink with a pink and white candy-striped top; and the FJ-3A Fleetvan.

the running gear was used in the Piero Duiso-designed Autoar, although this did not go into long-term production. The DJ-3A was intended to be the lowest-priced delivery vehicle on the US market – a 'bargain basement' truck – and this it certainly was. Based on the CJ-3A Universal with its original low bonnet, the Dispatcher used the Go-Devil engine and a column gear change for its three-speed gearbox. As there was no transfer case, the rear axle had a centrally placed differential. This Jeep was for street use, and all Dispatchers carried cheaper-to-make four-bolt wheels and street tyres. Body options offered were a hard top, with sliding doors if you wanted them, or a soft top. You could also have a tail-gate or, with the hard top, a single back door. Another version was the Surrey Gala, a dressed-up model with a candy-stripe top and seats, for use in resort hotels and golf clubs.

THE FC: A 'CABOVER' JEEP

In 1955 Willys built a two-wheel drive, forward-control van for the US Postal Service. This was the FJ-3, a manoeuvrable little van with an 80in (203mm) wheelbase chassis. It was derived from the CJ-3A and was powered by a Go-Devil engine, and it would lead to a new Jeep, the FC series.

Tough as the CJs were, they had precious little cargo-carrying space – even the new, longer wheelbase CJ-6 was limited. For the commercial user, there was little point in having a Jeep to get you up the side of a mountain if you couldn't carry your tools or materials to the job; nor was there any lightweight four-wheel drive truck on the home market from any other maker. To plug the gap, Willys developed the FC-150 'forward control' Jeep. Announced to public at the US Auto Show in December 1956, it was based upon an adapted CJ-5 chassis. The steering column was mounted almost upright at the extreme front of the chassis, and the pedals moved up front too, with the driving cab placed over the front wheels. A Hurricane engine sat behind and between the driver and passenger, and the gear-change for the three-speed Warner box was column-mounted. The FC-150 had a pickup bed over 6ft (1.8m) in length, and could carry a nominal three-quarter-ton payload.

In the following May a larger version was brought out, the FC-170. Although the cab was the same, this larger, heavier duty truck used a modified four-wheel drive Utility Wagon frame, with the Super Hurricane engine and transmission. The 63in (1,600mm) track and 103.5in (2,629mm) wheelbase remained the same, but the forward control configuration allowed for a pickup bed that was a huge 90in (2,286mm) long. Sales of the FC-170 actually ate into those of the FC-150, though neither model was a big seller in the US. The FC-170 was shown by Steele Griffiths at the Earl's Court

1963

'Jeep'®

FORWARD CONTROL TRUCKS

FC-150 TRUCK

If you want to be out front, you've got to be "up front," which is what Forward Control design was created for. The FC-150 is a short-wheelbase (81 in.), high-payload (1,727 lbs.) efficiency-engineered vehicle that puts the driver on top of any road situation. Easy handling—turns in an 18½ ft. radius —easy loading—bed height is 24½ in.—the FC-150 gives you the most cargo capacity on the least wheelbase of any pick-up in its weight class.
(Hurricane F-Head 4 cylinder)

FC-170 TRUCK

More muscle, more power, more payload—and still Forward Control, the FC-170 packs a big 3,510 lbs. payload in its 45 cu. ft. cargo box. On a wheelbase of 103⅜ in., the FC-170 turns in a 21 ft, 10 in. radius, and the driver can see the road ahead six ft. from the front bumper. Available as a pick-up truck, stake with single or dual rear wheels, or cab and chassis only, the FC-170 easily accommodates big loads, with balanced weight distribution.
(Super Hurricane 226 6 Cyl.)

FC-150 STAKE MODEL

FC-170 DUAL WHEEL STAKE MODEL

FC-150

FC-170

This brochure shows two versions each of the FC-150 and FC-170 with pickup and stake truck bodies and dual rear wheels. ('Doolies', as American truckers called them) See how much lower the FC-170's cargo bed sits, as much due to its Jeep truck frame. A major selling point for the FC was its visibility. The almost upright windscreen had an area of 2747 square inches, and the rear quarter lights gave a good rearward view.

Commercial Motor Show in October 1957, alongside a CJ-5, but it is doubtful whether it found many UK buyers.

The wider track of the FC-170 gave a more balanced appearance than the smaller model, and in 1958 the FC-150 received wider axles. Brooks Stevens put forward a number of different variants for the FC-series, including a minibus based on the FC-170, a utility for use in developing countries, and a commuter bus. Neither of these came to production: they were too early

for their time, coming along even before the VW Microbus went on sale in the US. The forward control concept, if not the FC-series itself, was to be more readily acceptable commercially in overseas markets.

Forward control variants

Like the FJ-3, the FJ-3A Fleetvan was two-wheel drive, but this box van was for public sale and was based on the FC150 chassis. With a Hurricane engine and the option of

FC-150 (1957–65)

Engine
Type	Willys Hurricane 4-cylinder, inlet over exhaust
Bore x stroke	3.25 x 4.125in
Capacity	134.2cc (2.2ltr)
Main bearings	3
Max. power	75bhp @ 4000rpm
Max. torque	114lb/ft @ 2000rpm

Chassis
Transmission	Warner 3-speed manual, synchromesh on 2nd & top
Turning circle	36ft
Transfer case	2-speed, part time four-wheel drive
Suspension	Semi-elliptic leaf springs front and rear
Brakes	4-wheel hydraulic, 11in drums front and rear

Dimensions
Wheelbase	81in
Track (front and rear)	48.5in
Overall length	147.5in
Overall width	71.375in
Overall height (top up)	77.375in
Curb weight	3,020lb

FC-170 (1957–65)

Engine
Type	Super Hurricane 6-cylinder in line, sidevalve
Bore x stroke	3.94 x 4.375in
Capacity	226cu in (3.67ltr)
Main bearings	4
Max. power	105bhp @ 3600rpm
Max. torque	190lb/ft @ 1400rpm

Chassis
Transmission	Warner 3-speed manual, synchromesh on 2nd & top
Turning circle	47.25ft
Transfer case	2-speed, part time four-wheel drive
Suspension	Semi-elliptic leaf springs front and rear
Brakes	4-wheel hydraulic, 11in drums front and rear

Dimensions
Wheelbase	103.5in
Track (front and rear)	63.5in
Overall length	180.5in
Overall width	76.5in
Overall height (top up)	79.375in
Curb weight	3,331lb

The tubular chassis of the M274, with 'Torsolastic' independent suspension. The centrally mounted, air-cooled engine drives through a Warner three-speed manual gearbox and a two-speed transfer case to all four wheels.

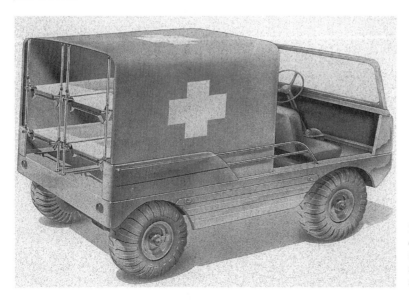

The M274, in its proposed ambulance guise. Other versions included a flat truck and a troop carrier with a canvas tilt.

The remarkable M274A1 Mechanical Mule, showing its four-wheel steering.

a three-speed manual transmission or a Borg-Warner automatic, it had a 1,000lb (454kg/just under ½ ton) payload and 170cu ft (4.8cu m) of space. The doors were almost 6ft (1.8m) in height and so gave good access to the walk-through cargo space, for quick and easy deliveries. Good visibility was claimed for the Fleetvan, as well as good manoeuvrability, thanks to a compact 12ft 10in (3.9m) overall length.

The US Military liked the FC concept and adopted their own versions, based on the FC-170. The crew cab M-677 gave seating room for at least four, plus a short pickup bed, whilst the M-679 was a steel-bodied ambulance. There were also the M676 and the M678, a carry-all and a pickup. Powered by 170cu in (2.7 litre) 85bhp three-cylinder turbocharged Cerlist diesel engines, they were used principally by the US Navy.

The Mechanical Mule

The M274 Mechanical Mule was an extraordinary military vehicle which took the utility concept to its extreme. In its prototype stage it was a basic four-wheel drive forward control platform, with a tubular chassis and a mid-mounted air-cooled engine. Besides the basic flat truck version, Willys featured in its promotional literature the choice of a flatbed carrier, a personnel carrier with a canvas tilt, and an ambulance. The additional superstructure was designed to be removable, so the base vehicles could be stacked one on the other for easy transport by sea or air. Two- or four-cylinder engines of capacities between 82ci (1.3 litres) and 195ci (3.2 litres) were proposed. Its payload was 1,500lb (680kg), nearly double that of the M38A1. Six vehicles were tested from 9 September to 11 November 1958; build quality was found to be lacking in certain respects, but once this had been put right, over 4,000 of the carrier version were supplied, mainly to the US Marines.

The simplest yet most versatile of the Mule variants was the M274A1. This had a twin air-cooled engine in the rear, and a flat bed. With permanent four-wheel drive and four-wheel steering, the tubular frame had no suspension; instead, the tyres were inflated to 15lb pressure. The driver sat at the extreme front, the pedals being carried in a cage out in front of the bed. The steering column could be swivelled forward and the vehicle driven in low range reverse with the driver following on foot.

BRITAIN DEMOBS ITS JEEPS

In 1956 the British armed forces sold off most of the remaining jeeps it had in regular service; the very last wartime jeep in use by a regular British regiment – postwar registration number 99 YH 99 – was sold off on 28 February 1959. The last known jeep in British military service, the transport of a British Army liaison mission officer in Korea, was sold off on 3 December 1966. The jeeps, and the Austin Champs, were replaced with Land Rovers.

THE LAND ROVER AND THE JEEP

The Land Rover was inspired by the jeep. Maurice Wilks, the head of Rover's technical department, was using an ex-WD jeep on his Anglesey farm in the 1940s. His brother Spencer, then Rover's managing director, asked him what he would do when the jeep wore out. As soon as Maurice replied that he'd buy another one, they realized what they should do – build their own! It would neatly solve Rover's current

most pressing problem of having to find an interim vehicle to keep production going, as the proposed M-type baby car had been scrapped. The Land Rover's simple body was made of aluminium because this was more readily available than steel in postwar Britain, and such a body would be easier to make and repair.

The first prototype Land Rover was built up by fitting a Rover car engine and gearbox into a Jeep chassis, mating it to the Spicer transfer box and axles; however, the production Series I was all Rover. Both Willys Motors and Rover gained much from export sales and overseas assembly, and by the end of the 1950s Jeeps and Land Rovers reached the same half-million production figure. Rover's biggest sphere of influence was the sterling area – Australia, New Zealand and the Commonwealth countries of Africa – which was exactly where Willys wanted to be.

In the spring of 1958 Rover's chairman, George Farmer, was approached by Willys Motors Inc. because they were seeking manufacturing facilities in England. Farmer and Maurice Wilks Rover's joint managing director, met Edgar Kaiser, and subsequently Farmer and his general manager, Mr Backhouse, visited Toledo. Both sides believed that 'considerable advantages' might be had by combining their expertise. Throughout the summer of 1958 teams from Rover and Willys therefore studied the possibilities of a merger – though it was as soon as early June that word had spread about the talks. To settle matters down, Rover issued a press release admitting that talks were going on between Rover and Willys, to 'see if there are mutual advantages in an association between the two companies in certain fields of production and distribution of four-wheel drive vehicles'.

Progress was not smooth: Willys were

A Jeep/Land Rover hybrid

During the negotiations between Rover and Willys, their engineers mated a CJ-5 body to a Land Rover chassis. It wasn't exactly a neat job. But why take Land Rover's chassis which was prone to rust and cracking, and fit on it a Jeep body that was equally susceptible to rot, when the Land Rover had a rust-free aluminium body and the Jeep's running gear was a combat-proven off-road performer?

Basically, the Jeep and the Land Rover were engineered to different principles. The Jeep was a battle wagon, and could travel at speed across country: its chassis was flexible, and its open-top, steel body flexed with it as it travelled over rough ground. The Land Rover, on the other hand, was designed from its outset as an agricultural vehicle: its aluminium body has no inherent strength, so its chassis is massively rigid. If a Land Rover body was mounted on the flexible Jeep chassis, it would shake to bits. The Jeep's body would not be adversely affected by being mounted on a rigid chassis, but it could not offer the Land Rover's full doors and better weather protection; also, it was high and ungainly, and the ease of repair of the Land Rover's body was lost. The vehicle was therefore less than the sum of its parts – in short, this hybrid had no vigour to recommend it.

The hybrid Jeep/Land Rover: an export CJ-5 body with a split windscreen, on a shortened Series II Land Rover chassis. Note how the front wheels are ahead of the centreline of the wheel arches. The fit of the body is governed by the location of the engine in the Jeep engine bay, and the Land Rover's front axle is further forward in the chassis compared to the Jeep. Because of the different profile of the Land Rover and Jeep floors, the Jeep body sits much higher.

The cut-down Land Rover chassis that would be put with the CJ-5 body. Chalk marks on the ground indicate the centre lines of the 81in (2,057mm) CJ-5 chassis. The Land Rover chassis is cut down to about 84in (2,134mm). The chassis is shortened from behind, and the rear spring hangers are relocated further forward.

The CJ-5 chassis that donated its body to the hybrid experiment, photographed in exactly the same spot as the shortened Land Rover chassis. The differences between it and the Land Rover are plain. The Jeep chassis is of channel section and is much slimmer, to allow it to flex as the vehicle travels over rough ground. Also clear by comparison is the location of each engine in relation to the front axle.

not happy that the transfer of manufacturing plant to Solihull could be carried out easily, and indeed the more they looked, the less they thought of the whole idea. Rover revealed to Willys that they were discussing a merger with Standard, and when Edgar Kaiser subsequently cancelled a meeting with George Farmer, this merely served to confirm Rover's suspicions that Toledo was having second thoughts. Whilst Willys said they were still interested, Rover felt that they could only continue if the Americans showed as much enthusiasm as they had at the start.

Farmer and Backhouse made a tour of the Willys plants in Brazil and Argentina in October, and whilst Edgar Kaiser indicated a willingness to continue with talks, Farmer decided to give Willys some time to think things over. The last real meeting between representatives of the two companies was with Willys's Steven A. Girard, who had been involved in the talks from the start. Stopping over from a trip to Europe in January of 1959, Girard promised to chase matters up. But the whole process would have taken too much money to have been viable, and as Willys's fortunes improved, the Rover talks were quietly forgotten.

JEEP IN AUSTRALIA

Had Kaiser been as open about its dealings with others as Rover had been regarding the Standard deal, Solihull might have pulled out sooner. Plans were begun as early as 1955 to set up an Australian operation: a sum of between six and eight million dollars was considered to be right for the project, the intention being to supply the Philippines and Indonesia. Willys Motors (Australia) was set up in Sydney in

1958; in the same year Kaiser also signed up the Australian firm of Shute-Upton Engineering in Brisbane, New South Wales, as the management unit, when they began assembly of Jeep vehicles. To comply with Australian law these were all right-hand drive, and a certain percentage of the components had to be locally made; 12v electrics were also required, making Jeeps compatible with Australian practice. The CJ-3B and CJ-6 were first to arrive, and the 6-226 truck, Station Wagon and CJ-5 followed in 1960. Australian-made hard tops with full doors were also available for the Universals, as was, later, an optional Ford Falcon six-cylinder engine.

Willys supplied an M38A1 to the Australian army for testing in late 1959. The test vehicle had a few miles on the clock, and after giving it a thorough work-out at the Army Design Establishment at Maribyrnong, Victoria, they decided they didn't like it at all. The Hurricane engine, the army report said, complicated mainte-nance in the field; also in this particular vehicle the chassis cracked, there were sev-eral oil leaks, and the windscreen shattered, apparently through stress. In summing up, the report said, 'The M38A1 at the time of original manufacture was probably in

---

US Postal Service Jeeps

'Through rain, sleet and snow, the mail must get through!' That famous slogan came from one of the most enduring of all US institutions, Wells Fargo, and it is as valid today for the US Postal Service as it was in the old stage-coach days. But for much of the post-war period America depended on the vehicle that really could get through anywhere: the Jeep.

The US Postal Service became motorized during the early years of the twentieth century. In 1931 they bought a fleet of 1,000 Ford AA trucks for large-scale deliveries, although the mailman still used a handcart or bag to deliver mail around the streets. After the end of World War II these old Fords were scrapped. However, many Americans then moved away from the town centres, into the newly built suburbs, which meant that the distances the mailman had to travel were much greater. At first the Post Office Department paid the mailmen to use their own cars, although at the same time it tried out a number of different vehicles for house-to-house deliveries. In 1952 the Jeep Panel Delivery was supplied to the US Post Office, and small three-wheeled vans known as Mailsters also went into service; powered by small, two-stroke industrial engines, these were not successful because they offered virtually no weather protection, and in the winter snows they were dangerous to drive.

Of all the vehicles tried by the US Postal Service, the DJ-3A Dispatcher of 1955 proved to be the best. Imagine the reaction of the mailmen, many of whom were ex-servicemen, when they were told they were to be given Jeeps! There was a smart new blue and white livery to replace the olive drab of the old vehicles, and the full box body gave them decent weather protection. If mailmen weren't going to get four-wheel drive, at least they were going to get Jeep durability by virtue of the Go-Devil engine and the Warner manual box. These DJ-3As were right-hand drive with slid-ing doors, so the mailman did not have to walk around the van to put the mail in the sidewalk mailboxes in America's sprawling new suburbs. Quite apart from the obvious safety factor, this was reckoned to save four hours a week in delivery time.

The mailman's Jeep was to become a familiar, friendly sight throughout the US for the next forty years. Then in 1958 about six DJ-3B prototypes, with tall bonnets and Hurricane engines, were made for the Postal Service. These did not go into production, however, and the Postal Service continued with its DJ-3As. The mailmen would have to wait until 1965 for something new.

advance of anything else then made. By today's standards it begins to fall short in comfort, handling and driveability.' The Australian army stuck to their Land Rovers and Champs.

JEEPS IN BRAZIL

During their negotiations with Willys, Rover were having difficulty in persuading the Brazilian government to renew their plant's manufacturing licence. After offering the plant to Willys, who declined it, Rover Brazil was wound up and the plant sold to Toyota. Jeep products, on the other hand, were doing well there. By 1960 Willys-Overland do Brasil had become 55 per cent Brazilian owned. Some 110,000 vehicles were scheduled for production, 95 per cent of the components being Brazilian-made, including those for the CJ-3B and the CJ-6-based 101.

BRITISH DIESEL POWER FOR JEEP

From 1957 diesel engine manufacturer Perkins had been engineering a conversion to fit their three-litre P4 engine in an MB. The P4 was too powerful for it however, and had to be detuned. During a downturn in fortunes in 1960, Perkins looked for alternative work, and discussed the possibilities of manufacturing Jeeps in or near their Peterborough factory.

This did not materialize, but Perkins continued an involvement with Toledo. As an option for the more cost-conscious US operator and for export markets, the new 4.192 diesel engine – '4' is for the number of cylinders, '192' the capacity in cubic inches (3.15 litres) – was adopted in early 1961. It was a narrow-bore version of the 4.236, which was to become one of the company's most successful power units. Although the actual horsepower was down a little, at 62bhp compared to 72 for the Hurricane, its 145lb/ft of torque was around 30 per cent higher.

The Perkins-engined CJ-5 on display at the 1961 Geneva Motor Show. Behind it are a CJ-3B and a Utility Wagon.

The first factory-approved, Perkins-powered Jeep, a CJ-5, was shown at the Amsterdam Motor Show in early 1961, on the stand of the Netherlands Jeep and Perkins distributor, Kemper van Twist of Dordrecht. Subsequently 4.192 engines were sent to Toledo for assembly in the CJ-5, the CJ-6 and the one-ton truck. Perkins also had some eighteen overseas manufacturing plants, including Argentina and Spain. The 4.192 was widely adopted in South American Universals, and it was fitted exclusively in earlier Spanish versions.

A CHALLENGING FUTURE

Jeep was not to have the home market for utility vehicles all to itself. In 1961 competition for the Universal and the truck came from International Harvester, with the introduction of the Scout. This was a two- or four-wheel-drive utility, with full doors in a full width body and a tough four-cylinder engine, and its sales over the next ten years were to equal or better the total of all Universal and FC Jeeps. International Harvester also made the four-wheel-drive 'Travellall' station wagon: whilst it was heavy, and based on a light truck chassis, the body was modern in appearance.

If Jeep's past was eventful, its makers had plenty to deal with in the years ahead.

5 The Kaiser-Jeep Corporation

The Jeep Utility Wagon was aimed at a different market to most other station wagons, but in spite of the toughness which was its main selling point, it was an ageing vehicle as the 1950s came to a close. The more modern International Harvester Travellall and the new Chevrolet Suburban also gave a hint of what Jeep was in for in the way of competition.

Jeep trucks' four-wheel-drive advantage was under threat, too. In the 1940s and 1950s Ford offered Marmon-Herrington four-wheel-drive conversions for its light trucks, Chevy a similar option by NAPCO, and Dodge had its own Power Wagon. Nevertheless, these were big, expensive to buy and heavy to drive, and the powertrain raised the ground clearance and made access to the cab less than ideal. Jeep trucks were much more versatile, with the benefit of a purpose-designed, selectable four-wheel-drive system. However, from 1957 Ford, and from 1960 the market leader Chevrolet, began building new, user-friendly four-wheel-drive trucks in-house. The truck market as a whole was expanding fast: by the late 1950s, close to 25 per cent of all light vehicle sales were trucks, and something was needed to keep Jeep in the game.

Brooks Stevens came up with some styling ideas to update the Utility Wagon for the old chassis, including a modern two-door body and a four-door design with a

The 6-230 Utility Wagon. Three chrome bars across the grille and the single chrome strip along the body side date it as a late vehicle.

CJ-5-style front end to carry over the Jeep icon, but these never got further than the prototype stage: the only way to go was with a wholly new vehicle. In 1959 the project was given to Achille 'Sammy' Sampietro, the chief engineer of Willys Motors Inc. since Barney Roos retired. The first thing to materialize in the comprehensive programme was a new engine, to take the place of the Super Lightning. The latter was the most powerful in the Jeep range – but by the late 1950s most other US auto engineers were discarding sidevalves. Jeep's new engine had to be powerful, with characteristics suitable for off-road and commercial applications; but it also had to be a six, thereby minimizing production costs because many of the machining operations from the Super Lightning could then be used.

THE TORNADO

Sampietro tackled the problem in a typically European way. He experimented at first by building pushrod hemi-heads for the Go-Devil/Hurricane and Lightning blocks.

The Tornado engine in the 6-230 Utility Wagon. A comfortable fit under the bonnet, it produced almost twice the horsepower, and twice the torque of the original Go-Devil engine.

He then developed a new, skinny, straight six block, with height, length and bore spacing identical to the old Super Lightning to ensure the new engine could be machined on the same transfer machines. The iron head had 'spheroidal', near-hemispherical, combustion chambers, and a single Morse chain drove a centrally mounted single overhead camshaft. Just one cam, operating via rockers, opened each cylinder's pair of inclined valves, and the four-bearing crankshaft was Tuftrided to cope with the power output.

The new engine, named the 6-230 'Tornado', had an identical stroke to the Super Lightning, but with a marginally wider bore, giving it a capacity of 230cu in (3.67 litres). It put out a useful 140bhp and an even more useful 210lb/ft of torque. From 3 May 1962 it was offered in two- or four-wheel drive as an option to the Hurricane in the Utility Wagon, the Utility Delivery and the truck.

THE J-SERIES

However, the Tornado engine was destined for a revolutionary new range of station wagons and trucks. Code-named the J-Series, there would be two principal lines: the J-100 station wagon and the J-200/300 trucks. Both had to have the toughness and off-road capabilities worthy of the Jeep name, but they also had to be nearly as stylish and as comfortable to drive as contemporary sedans: in short, this would be a package never before seen in one vehicle. For Brooks Stevens the styling job was at least straightforward. By now the fins-and-chrome era had peaked, and the trend was for more simple lines: a timeless, truly classic line was called for, and this fitted well with Jeep's enduring image. Nor did it need to be as big as a full-size station wagon,

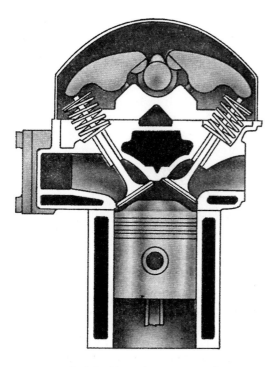

The top end of the Tornado engine, with its 'spheroidal' combustion chamber and single cam operating both valves.

although it did have to be at least big enough to offer the size and value demanded by the American public.

It was the running gear that needed the most serious attention, primarily because Jeep's reputation for off-road performance could not be compromised. Commercial and service users would be a prime target, but the new station wagon was also to be aimed at the family buyer who either lived in a part of the country that knew hard winters, or who wanted a dual-purpose car to take them into the backwoods for hunting and fishing at weekends. These people would put in most of their mileage on the highway, so there would be two-wheel drive or the option of selectable four-wheel drive. Power steering would be offered as well, to make the vehicle more acceptable to the

rapidly growing number of women drivers.

Underneath there was a new boxed-section ladder frame, with five cross-members for the 110in (2,794mm) wheelbase station wagon, and six for the 110in and 126in (3,200mm) trucks. There were four drive and suspension combinations: independent front suspension or solid front axles, with a choice of two- or four-wheel drive for each. Two-wheel-drive models would have independent front suspension as standard. Sampietro's solution for the suspension was as European-inspired as it was for the Tornado engine: it had longitudinal torsion bars, coupled to upper wishbones that mounted directly onto the chassis. A swing front axle, hung at its central pivot point on the cross-member by U-bolts, was used for both two- and four-wheel-drive models. The axle tubes, located by a leading control strut, acted as the lower suspension arms to give maximum ground clearance.

For the four-wheel drive, a front differential was built into the right-hand axle case, with which it swung integrally, and so was offset to line up with the front propeller shaft. The drive to the left-hand side was taken through a Spicer universal joint at the central point, and through a plain half-shaft inside the axle tube to the hubs. Universal-type steering knuckles allowed the front wheels to remain perpendicular as the vehicle's suspension coped with bumps and turns, and on the four-wheel-drive models, Rzeppa constant velocity joints transmitted the drive to the front wheels.

The independent suspension for two wheel-drive models would have a tube axle with a simple central fulcrum pin at its centre, also hung from the cross-member, and the same steering knuckles. The solid axle models were entirely conventional, with a live axle on the four-wheel-drive or a non-driven tube axle for the two-wheel-drive

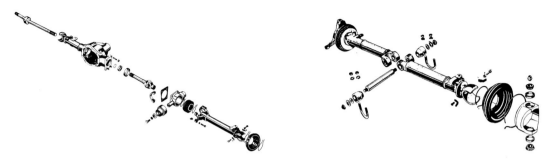

Exploded views of the two axles used in the J-Series independent front suspension. Left, the driven axle with the differential casing integral with the right-hand axle housing. Note the universal joint integral with the left-hand housing. Right is the non-driven axle, with a simple fulcrum pin, and the U-bolts used to hang it from the cross-member, in the centre. The steering knuckle, minus kingpin, is shown to the right of the drawing.

trucks, hung on longitudinal leaf springs.

On four-wheel-drive models the propeller shaft for the front axle was offset to the right-hand side of the transfer box, but the rear drive arrangement was a departure from the norm, with the propeller shaft coming off the centre of the transfer case; thus the differential on the rear axle was centrally placed. A three-speed manual transmission would be standard on the station wagons, with a dual-range transfer case for the four-wheel-drive models. Overdrive could be had too, and the trucks were to have the option of a four-speed manual gearbox. Warn free-wheel hubs

were also available for four-wheel-drive models. For the first time on a four-wheel-drive vehicle, an automatic transmission was available, from Borg-Warner, though only with a single range transfer case.

Some three years and $20 million after the development programme began, the Detroit Auto Show in October 1962 saw the introduction of the J-Series. No advanced notice was published in the auto press, despite their usual practice of previewing the new models. Named the Wagoneer, the station wagon fulfilled everything that Kaiser had envisaged. The two- or four-door body with its high ground clearance had the

The 1963 Wagoneer, a classic design that would become the second longest-running Jeep product in the US.

up-to-date but timeless look. At a shade over 15ft (4.5m), it was the same length as the new compact cars on the market, but still seated six. Thanks largely to the high. Boxy shape, the carrying capacity was massive. On the down side, the four-wheel-drive version's 44½ft (13.6m) turning circle was obviously not as good as a conventional sedan's – but then, one has to make allowances for contemporary technology!

The truck version, the Gladiator, came with either a 'Townside' pickup bed that lay flush with the cab sides, or the 'Thriftside' (Jeep's own name for that American favourite, the stepside). A stake truck and dual rear wheels were also available. Drive and suspension options were the same as the Wagoneer, although the top-weight model, at 8,600lb (3,900kg) GVW, could only be had with solid front axles, and had a drive-line brake and a four-speed gearbox as standard. A full line-up of utility accessories was offered for all models from the start, including a snow plough, a power take-off and a winch.

Despite their tough image, America's truck owners were enjoying more and more luxury items in their trucks. Jeep offered a Custom Cab option for the Gladiator, which included door arm-rests on both doors, a cigar lighter and twin sun visors. Midway between the Wagoneer and the Gladiator was the Panel Delivery: it used the Wagoneer's two-door body with the rear window area blanked off, and a pair of sideways-opening doors in place of the Wagoneer's tail-gate.

Willys called the four-wheel-drive system 'Drivepower four-wheel drive' in their advertising, and it could be selected 'on the fly' by moving a single lever on the floor. Testing the Wagoneer in early 1963, *Motor Trend* magazine's technical editor, Jim Wright, liked it: 'The Jeep Becomes a Gentleman' was the title of his road test of a manual transmission car – which, incidentally, had already been sold to a customer. Such was the demand that there was already a backlog of orders. The performance off-road, Wright found, could not be faulted, even on loose dirt. On the highway it was smooth, with a genuine 90mph (145kmph) available, and good reserves of power for overtaking. One thing Wright didn't like were the drum brakes, however: they faded too easily in hard work, and that, both on the highway and off road, was a serious fault.

J-300 TOWNSIDE

The Gladiator J-300 with a 'Townside' body. Although the peaked roofline over the windscreen would be altered many years later, the flared wheel arches would stay a feature of the truck for the whole of its life.

A NEW CORPORATE NAME HERALDS FOREIGN EXPANSION

In April 1963 Kaiser Industries' vice-president, Steven A. Girard, announced that Kaiser would drop the Willys name. The corporation was to be known as the Kaiser-Jeep Corporation, 'to properly identify the Toledo Company as one of the growing number of Kaiser family industries', and 'to more closely associate the company with its famous Jeep trademark as applied to its entire line of products throughout the world.'

One of the biggest of those world-wide

facilities was Industrias Kaiser Argentina at Cordoba. In under ten years, Cordoba had grown to a city of 60,000 people, with corporation housing and full social services including a hospital. In that time, IKA had made over a quarter of a million vehicles, a third of all Argentina's vehicle production, against competition from Fiat, Ford, Chrysler, General Motors and Mercedes-Benz. But Kaiser's financial stake was a minority one, since 60 per cent was now in Argentinean hands; the balance was shared with a number of component suppliers plus AMC, who joined up with Kaiser in Cordoba in 1961, and Renault. Eleven Jeep models and four models each from AMC and

The development of Jeep's four-wheel drive: The J-Series' silent transfer case

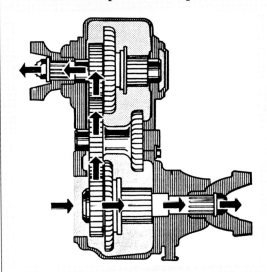

The 'silent transfer' case from the J-Series. When two-wheel drive is engaged, the drive is transmitted from the gearbox (arrowed from the bottom left), straight through. The centre layshaft is constantly in mesh. For four-wheel drive, the drive is taken through the layshaft to the front driveshaft and forward to the front axle.

No matter how well they are made, gears produce some sort of whine. Up until the advent of the J-Series, all four-wheel-drive Jeep vehicles had a transfer case with the propshafts offset to one side, and with the differentials similarly aligned. This meant that drive went through all the gears in the transfer case whether four-wheel drive was engaged or not, and the noise of the gears could be heard inside a closed car.

For utility vehicles and the Universals this noise wasn't too important, but the Wagoneer and Gladiator took four-wheel-drive motoring to new levels. The big station wagon was a fast, comfortable highway cruiser, and with two-wheel drive engaged, it was quiet. Sammy Sampietro achieved this by simply by-passing the gear train when two-wheel drive was engaged, as shown in the diagram of the 'Silent' transfer case. Only when four-wheel drive was engaged did the gear noise appear – and if it was needed, there were often other things to occupy the driver's mind than a gear whine from under the floor!

Renault were made in the complex. Total annual production in Argentina was heading for the 10,000 mark, and a $22 million expansion programme was in the pipeline.

Canadian operations were restarted in July 1959 when the old Willys plant in Windsor, Ontario was reopened. Windsor was almost a suburb of Detroit, albeit divided by a national border, and a natural home for Canadian operations. The M38A1 had ceased production at Toledo in 1957, but in 1967 the Windsor plant received an order for 800 military Jeeps for the Canadian armed forces; this was worth $C2,789,000. Even so, Windsor would only stay open for two more years; it closed in 1969.

APPROACHES TO UK MANUFACTURERS

Right-hand drive Wagoneers and Gladiators were offered from the start with a purpose in mind. Apart from Japan, Ireland and (then) Sweden, most Commonwealth countries drove on the left, and because of this Kaiser started negotiations with J. C. Bamford, the makers of JCB excavators, in early 1964 to import or licence-build Jeeps in the UK. However, after assessing the possibilities, JCB's boss, Joe Bamford, decided to stick with his core business, which was expanding well. Nevertheless, in the process of the talks, J. C. Bamford bought six left-hand-drive Wagoneers for use by their research department. Their engineers would often be driving between construction sites, and although Land Rovers were fine for off-road use, they were too crude for roadwork. Four-wheel drive in a large, comfortable estate car would seem to promise an ideal vehicle.

The magazine *Autocar* tested one of JCB's Wagoneers, a four-wheel-drive model fitted with a solid front axle and standard three-speed manual gearbox. They considered the car's highway performance to be good: it was on par with a Mk III Ford Zephyr 6 estate car, and it left the Land Rover and the Austin Gypsy in the dust. They also liked its equipment and load-carrying capacity – but like *Motor Trend*, they were less than impressed with the brakes. In concluding the road test, the writer said, 'We can think of many a farmer who would like such a spacious, cross-country work-horse one day, and a speedy and comfortable estate car the next. Both can be had for under £2,000.' Confirmation from the British press that Jeep had again 'done it first', this time seven years before the Range Rover.

After the withdrawal of JCB, Edgar Kaiser decided, in the summer of 1964, to make a second, informal approach to Rover. Rover's chairman George Farmer, and his general manager Mr Backhouse, visited Toledo – but these were boom years for Rover, and after considering how much work of their own they had, Rover's board declined Kaiser's offer.

MORE KAISER MILITARY VEHICLES

By the mid-1960s the Cold War was at its height, and US troops were being sent to Vietnam. The US government's defence spending was high, and in June 1964 Kaiser-Jeep's financial situation received a welcome boost from the US Army, with an order for 27,325 vehicles. Part of the order was for two-wheel-drive Gladiator trucks, and later on in the same year another contract for 3,975 standard 2.5-ton trucks, worth $16 million, was awarded; this second contract included 1,975 M-38A1 Jeeps. Production began in May 1965.

VIASA – Jeeps in Spain

The VIASA Jeep family, featuring four simple, rather austere, slab-sided forward-control models and a traditional Jeep. From the left, they are: the Duplex crew cab, the Toledo pickup, the Campeador motor caravan, the CJ and the Fourgon box van.

In keeping with Kaiser's business practice of licensing the building of Jeeps in overseas plants, VIASA (Vehiculos Industriales y Agricolas S. A.) in Zaragoza, Spain took over production of the Hotchkiss JH102 and HWL. These two-seaters were marketed as the Willys-VIASA CJ3 and CJ6 respectively, and powered by the Perkins 4.192 diesel. The short wheelbase CJ3 was eventually dropped, leaving the 101in (2,565mm) model, then known simply as the CJ. This long wheelbase chassis became the basis for VIASA's own series of forward-control Jeeps.

In 1968 VIASA merged with Materiel Movil y Construccions SA. Production was moved to Cogullada, and a version of the Commando was made alongside the CJ, whose chassis it shared. In the late 1970s VIASA was absorbed by EBRO. More modern prototypes – the CJ-35, based on the CJ-5, and the longer wheelbase CJ-65 – were made, but they did not enter production. Jeep production was ended in 1985 when EBRO was bought by Nissan of Japan, who introduced versions of their own vehicles.

This order derived from Kaiser's acquisition of Studebaker's Chippewa plant in the south-side Stude's home town of South Bend, Indiana. Studebaker had been building army trucks for decades, but the company was in chronic financial trouble. Its plants covered many acres of South Bend, and were costing the company far too much in overheads. But rather than concentrate on getting its haphazard automobile business into shape, Studebaker were diversifying, and this only added to their troubles. By the early 1960s the decision was taken to move auto production over to the Canadian plant, and the Chippewa plant was sold to Kaiser.

por fin un camión para uso múltiple!
aquí está el nuevo y robusto camión.

Jeep Frontal

para dos toneladas - motor a elección: naftero o diesel,
el único en su tipo en el mercado argentino.

Otra sólida realización JEEP para las más rudas y variadas necesidades del trabajo: el nuevo camión JEEP FRONTAL. En la misma robusta estructura, un motor adecuado a cada tipo de trabajo! Naftero: potente motor Tornado Special OHc 181 de 115 HP. y opcionalmente, Diesel: Con motor Diesel Borgward D-301 EL.Y en ambos: • 4 velocidades hacia adelante sincronizadas! • Extraordinario espacio para todo tipo de cargas! • Suspensión delantera independiente! • Robusto chassis de acero soldado! • Carrocería totalmente de acero, con amplia y cómoda cabina de visión panorámica! • Conducción frontal que asegura gran facilidad de maniobra! • Adaptabilidad para los más variados usos!
30 % al contado. 30 meses de plazo. 30.000 kilómetros de garantía.

ud. puede adaptarlo y carrozarlo a su conveniencia.

amplio furgón

chassis doble cabina

ómnibus para 17 personas sentadas

Y otros muchos modelos que Ud. podrá carrozar de acuerdo con su necesidad específica! Visite hoy mismo su concesionario JEEP y solicite una demostración.

IKA presenta también el

Jeep CARGUERO

con motor 4L-151 de 76-6 HP
para cantidades "industriales" de carga!

Apto para el trabajo en depósitos y almacenes, granjas, tambos, movimiento de bultos en playa de maniobras, acarreo de materiales. Capacidad de carga: 1 tonelada. Con suspensión a elásticos semielípticos con amortiguadores hidráulicos de acción directa y doble efecto. De reducido diámetro de giro (11,50). Muy maniobrable, resistente y seguro! Al igual que el Jeep Frontal, se lo puede carrozar según el uso a que se destine: "mulita" de carga, transporte de pasajeros, furgón, etc.

Producto de calidad de
INDUSTRIAS KAISER ARGENTINA
Vea TELENOCHE, lunes a viernes, por
Canal 13, a las 20 hs.

Argentina's Jeep Frontal was a forward-control commercial based on the Gladiator chassis. The range of bodies consisted of a box van, a truck, a crew cab and a minibus. Power was a choice between the Tornado engine or a Borgward diesel. Offered in two-wheel drive only, the Frontal used the J-Series torsion bar independent front suspension.

ENGINE DEALS WITH AMC

The 1966 model year saw the demise at home of the old Utility range; however, at the same time a new, extra-cost engine option for the Wagoneer and Gladiator was introduced, a 327ci V8 from the American Motors Corporation. Christened the 'Vigilante', the advertising blurb proclaimed it as having 'zesty zip' power – and this it certainly did, delivering 250bhp and 340lb/ft of torque. It came with a General Motors turbo Hydramatic unit, and a new two-speed transfer case. This resulted from a 1964 deal, whereby Kaiser Industries acquired a stake-holding in the American

---

Mahindra & Mahindra Ltd part 1

Mahindra & Mahindra Ltd of Mazagaon, Bombay, are India's tenth-largest privately owned company. Originally named Mahindra & Mohammed, the company was formed in 1945. However, Ghulam Mohammed parted company with J. C. and K. C. Mahindra in 1947, and the name Mahindra & Mahindra Limited was adopted. By the end of the twentieth century they were building some 40 per cent of India's light commercial and utility vehicles, most of them derived from original Jeep designs.

The first Jeeps to be assembled in India were CJ-2As, shipped in CKD form in 1947 from the Willys-Overland Export Corporation. Two years on, India's independence year, premises were leased from the British India Steam Navigation Company in Mazagaon. Mahindra & Mahindra Ltd continued to expand in many fields, including component manufacture in co-operation with Britain's Owen Organisation, but Jeep vehicles were to figure prominently throughout. In 1954 Kaiser began to phase in total indigenous vehicle manufacture, a process which saw a 70 per cent local content of Jeep vehicles by 1960.

In 1965, three years after a new plant at Kandivli was built, the FC forward-control range was bought from Kaiser. Two-wheel drive versions of the conventional utility vehicles came out in 1967. The average local content of all Mahindra vehicles was by then up to 97 per cent, and exports began to Sri Lanka, Singapore, Indonesia and the Philippines.

Motors Corporation and signed a contract with AMC and a consortium of Mexican business people to build a new engine plant in Mexico City. The plant would build AMC's all-new 232ci 6-cylinder OHV 'Torque Command' engine, for which a plant at their home town of Kinosha, Wisconsin had recently been built at a cost of $43 million.

MORE POWER FOR THE CJ

Also for 1966, Kaiser Industries sourced a more powerful engine option for the Universals: a V6, developed by the GM's Buick division for its Special model in the new BOP (Buick-Oldsmobile-Pontiac) compact series. The first engine for it and its Oldsmobile equivalent was a 215ci aluminium V8. However, although it was undoubtedly powerful, it was also expensive and troublesome to make, and so the prices of the Buick and Oldsmobile were higher; as a result these soon began to lose sales to the cheaper four-cylinder Pontiac Tempest. To bring prices down, Buick chose to make a cheaper engine, and using the alloy V8 as a starting point, produced an all-iron $90°$ V6 of 225ci (3.65 litres).

Jeep off-roaders had already discovered that the Buick V6 would fit into the CJ-5 with little modification: now Kaiser-Jeep was doing the job for them, and supplying a ready-made exhaust and service items, too! The V6 was wider and marginally longer than the Hurricane, and it only needed to be raised a little in the chassis to fit. Dubbed the 'Dauntless' by Kaiser-Jeep, its 155hp was double the power of the old Hurricane four-cylinder engine, and produced its torque in a flat, even curve for real pulling power. By 1965, GM had upgraded the Buick Special into a new, larger mid-sized car. The V6 was considered too small for it, and the tooling and the rights for the engine were bought up by Kaiser-Jeep.

The new CJ-5 was more comfortable and smarter, thanks to new bucket seats and

"a NEW truck for a NEW army"

Improved 4-WHEEL DRIVE and suspension

High-performance OVERHEAD CAM ENGINE

Exceptional CROSS COUNTRY MANEUVERABILITY

HEAVY-DUTY CONSTRUCTION THROUGHOUT

M 715 1¼ ton truck

ask the men who use them...

From the originators of "**Jeep** Reliability"

The M715 with its new overhead cam engine... keeps going when the going's tough.

KAISER Jeep CORPORATION developed and produced it... the Army is using it world wide...

Ask the men who use them. . . Not a wise suggestion after the event, considering the poor reputation of the Kaiser M-715 in service. Kaiser stole a march on the US Army's favourite one-ton truck, the M-37 Dodge, when this division of Chrysler failed to get its contract with the US Army renewed. The 1¼-ton Kaiser M-715 was based around the Gladiator. The J-Series cab and body was stripped of its roof, and a forward-raked windscreen and soft-top fitted. The engine was the 6-230 Tornado, but with the far greater weight of the vehicle – 5,200lb (2,359kg) – it struggled to perform, and its reliability suffered. Dodge were soon back in favour, the M-880 replacing the M-715 from 1976.

KAISER Jeep CORPORATION

TOLEDO, OHIO 43601

(Circle No. 84 on Inquiry Card for more data.)

THE LARGEST PRODUCER OF TACTICAL WHEELED VEHICLES SOUTH BEND MILITARY PLANT

optional hubcaps. One dubious step was the retention of vacuum windscreen wipers; also the suction pipe was mounted in an exposed position on the outside of the windscreen frame, and so was susceptible to damage. In a road test, *Motor Trend* magazine thought the location of the four-wheel-drive selector lever was too far to the right, obliging the driver to reach further over than was comfortable or safe, in that he had to take his eyes off the road, albeit momentarily. When the vehicle was stationary this did not matter, but four-wheel drive could be selected on the fly, and in practice this could be dangerous.

The Bantam BRC40 was the smallest of the three early production, quarter-ton 4x4s. This example has undergone a painstakingly thorough restoration.

The extreme conditions of the Western Desert and the needs of the Long Range Desert Group demanded some modifications to the jeep. The grille bars were removed and an extra header tank fitted for the radiator to provide extra cooling. Light machine guns provide the armament. This example is a replica of the actual vehicle used by Alistair Timpson MC and Thomas Mann of the G Foot Guards Patrol in 1942.

The GP-A was not the success its designers had hoped for, but today its rarity demands forgiveness for past inadequacy. After de-mob, this example is believed to have been used by a Scottish salmon farm as a general amphibious utility. It was restored in the late 1980s and later sold to a Land Rover specialist. The present owner bought it 'as seen', and gave the engine a much-needed overhaul. It has been driven in water, and performs well up to expectation.

A slat grille with headlights behind, and a right-angle front wing line identify this 1941 Ford GP, which has been fully restored.

This GPW was commissioned by the US Army in 1945 and 'inherited' by the RAF around 1947, where it remained until 1951 as a radio vehicle. Finished in authentic post-war RAF full gloss blue, it has been fitted with airfield disbursement equipment. It has been used in a film commemorating the Berlin Airlift, and to transport the crew of the RAF Memorial Flight between the Mess and the Lancaster aircraft at Biggin Hill Air Fair.

This 1952 M38 saw action in Vietnam with the US Special Forces. After military service it was bought by Colorado State Fire Department, who painted it red and used it as spotter vehicle for forest patrol. Now restored to Korean War livery, it carries serial numbers from that era.

A 1948 Jeepster VJ-2, fully restored to original specification, which has been used by Chrysler Jeep UK as VIP transport at the Goodwood Revival historic race meeting.

This M38A1 was built in Holland by Nekaf for the Dutch Army. It is finished in US Army colours and used in Vietnam War military displays. Dutch M38A1s are often restored in this manner, as they are easier to come by than Toledo-built examples.

Probably unique in the UK, this FC-170 stake truck has been fully restored, including an engine and gearbox overhaul.

A 1956 Jeep four-wheel-drive pickup, with a Hurricane engine. This truck was totally rebuilt by its owner over a period of three years.

The Mechanical Mule is one of the most versatile lightweight four-wheeled vehicles ever made. It can carry more than its own weight in either cargo or passengers. It can be driven by someone walking behind it, and with permanent four-wheel drive and four-wheel steering, can go virtually anywhere. Most of those that survive command high prices; they are bought as working vehicles, such is their usefulness.

A 1963 Utility Wagon with a Tornado OHC six. This wagon was driven overland from Baja, California, to Peru by a previous owner, who decided to do the journey on a whim.

Perhaps the only example in the UK in standard condition, this 1971 CJ-5 was built in Brazil by Ford, hence the blue oval on the front wing. It was restored from literally a pile of junk, with many of the body parts completely fabricated from sheet metal. Power is from a Willys six-cylinder F-head Super Hurricane engine.

This Kaiser M-715 was brought over by the film company who made Full Metal Jacket.

A 1978 Cherokee Chief, imported from California in 1997. Powered by a 360ci V8, it is almost rust free. The colour has been changed: originally it was bright orange, a colour favoured by hunters, who knew that the bright shade would prevent them from becoming an accidental target in the woods.

Postal DJ-5s are rare in the UK, but the fact that this one is in original condition is even more unusual, as many have been cut down into open-top models. It is a DJ-5C, with the AMC 232ci in-line six accommodated by the bulbous grille. The distinctive mirrors are a safety feature, as Postal Jeeps are right-hand drive.

An official import 1977 J-20 truck with 132in (3,353mm) wheelbase and optional pickup-bed top.

Fully restored, this basic 1978 CJ-6 is a rare vehicle in itself, let alone in right-hand drive form.

This 1979 Silver Anniversary CJ-5 has fewer than 40,000 miles (64,360km) on the clock, and has never been off-road.

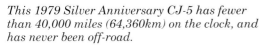

The Laredo was the top-line model during AMC's tenure of the Jeep. This is a US model CJ-7 in left-hand drive, with a 304ci V8, automatic gearbox, a Warn winch and extra-big tyres. More than a quarter of a century on from when it was made, it still can show the opposition what off-roading is all about.

Many Jeeps are modified in one way or another. This 1982 CJ-7 has a 350ci Chevrolet V8. It was imported by Howes Jeeps, new, as a left-hand drive model, and converted to right-hand drive using the correct steering box and pedal box.

Rare enough in the UK as it is, this CJ-8 is actually an ex-US Postal Service vehicle, with purpose-built right-hand drive. Its 258ci in-line six is coupled to a Torqueflite auto gearbox, which – even more unusual for a US model – has a floor-mounted selector.

Perhaps the rarest J-series, this CJ-10 is understood to be the only long wheelbase example in the UK. It was destined for Australia, but was unloaded at Liverpool docks by mistake. In virtually original condition, it was stored in dry premises until bought and registered by its first owner in the late 1990s.

A left-hand drive, basic two-door XJ Cherokee with a 2.5-litre, four-cylinder engine.

The Wagoneer and its variants lasted an amazing twenty-eight years. This is a 1987 model, with a 360ci V8, Selec-Trac four-wheel drive, and air-conditioning and power steering as standard. This is the final form of the Wagoneer, which was axed by Chrysler in 1991.

The Comanche was a natural development of the XJ Cherokee and Wagoneer, as American Motors had nothing in the light truck market. This example is two-wheel drive, with a 2.5-litre four-cylinder engine and an American-made top for its pickup bed. Despite only having drive on the rear axle, it can still perform well off-road.

This J-10 of 1987 is one of the last made, and features air-conditioning and a tail-lift. It is relatively unusual in having the longer 132in (3,353mm) wheelbase instead of the standard 120in (3,048mm).

Probably one of only three or four Sahara Special Edition Wranglers in the UK; the sand colour is very unusual.

Another rare, special edition YJ so far as the UK is concerned, the Islander was also available in red or white.

A personal-import, 1991 Cherokee Limited. Apart from a different interior, the trim is finished in gold, as are the wheels, and the 'Limited' badges are castings rather than decals.

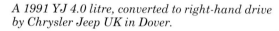

A 1991 YJ 4.0 litre, converted to right-hand drive by Chrysler Jeep UK in Dover.

Mahindra utility vehicles were imported into the UK in the mid-1980s. This is one of a batch of CJ340DP 'Bushranger' models from a cancelled order for the Australian Army.

Military Jeeps for 'approved users'

Military Jeep variants were made available to friendly or neutral countries, such as Switzerland and Israel: the US government described these as 'Approved Users'. Made in the old Willys assembly plant in Oakland, California, which Jim Mooney had re-opened in the 1940s, there were three models. The M606 was a military CJ-3B: it featured 12v electrics, full blackout lighting and a pintle towing hook, and could ford up to 20in (50cm). The M606A2 was the CJ-5 equipped similarly to the M606 and sold under Kaiser's model number instead of the US Army's. The M606A3 was an A2 with fully suppressed 24v electrics to run the standard radio equipment; a kit was also available from Kaiser-Jeep to fit the radio kit to the M606

Israel was a user of the M606A1, as portrayed by this replica.

and M606A2. The long wheelbase M170 was sold as a military ambulance, and what is more, with full engine waterproofing, which was not available on either the M606 or the M606A2.

The M151 MUTT

Jeeps had served the US Army well, but they were being overtaken by the demands of modern warfare. As early as 1951 the Army Ordnance Corps requested the Ford Motor Company to design a new, all-purpose quarter-ton vehicle, and on 1 July 1952 gave Ford a contract to build six prototypes. Ford set up the Ordnance Vehicle Project, and by 30 June 1954 came up with the XM151 'MUTT', or 'Military Utility Tactical Truck'. Its unitized construction made it lighter, at 2,320lb (1,052kg), than the Willys MB. It had all-round independent suspension and a 141ci (2.29ltr) four-cylinder engine.

The M151A1 MUTT.

After tests in 1960, the first production version of the M151A began the following year at Ford's Livonia plant. The M38A1 was phased out, and gradually replaced by the new quarter-tonner. In a neat twist, Willys Inc. were awarded two contracts to build extra numbers of the new vehicle in the Toledo plant: one in May 1962, and the second in the following December.

A major overhaul in 1966 for the Wagoneer: the new grille fronts AMC engines, either a 232ci six or a 327 'Vigilante' V8.

THE DJ-5

At the other end of the scale, the two-wheel-drive DJ-5 Dispatcher 100 arrived in late 1965. It was advertised as the lowest-priced delivery truck in the US market, and it was aimed at the same customers as the DJ-3A, which it replaced. Just like the DJ-3A, its biggest single user was the US Postal Service; theirs were Hurricane-powered models, but the DJ-5's private and commercial users could have the Dauntless V6. A long wheelbase DJ-6 version was produced, but it did not prove popular in the US.

WAGONEER UPGRADES

For 1967 Kaiser-Jeep added luxury to the J-Series with the introduction of the Super Wagoneer. There were bucket front seats, it was carpeted throughout, including the rear load bay, and it had an electrically operated tail-gate window. A fake wood-finish trim to the doors was echoed by 'antique gold' and black colour flashes on the sides. A horizontal grille enhanced the new, more up-to-date appearance, as did mag-style wheel trims and a padded vinyl roof capped with a chrome roofrack. Also supplied as standard were seatbelts, a padded sun visor and dashboard top, two-speed wipers and self-adjusting brakes.

Kaiser's publicity handout said of the Super Wagoneer that it '. . .constituted a unique and dramatic approach to the station wagon market. . . designed for the prestige buyer who is rapidly becoming aware of the safety and other advantages of four-wheel drive. While being the ultimate in detailed elegance, the new vehicle still has all the traditional "Jeep" versatility and ability to go on or off road.' Here was the concept taken further than ever: the best in American style luxury, added to the

Willys CJ-5 & CJ-6 with Dauntless engine (1965–72), CJ-5A, CJ-6A Tuxedo Park (1964–67)

Engine
Type	Buick 90° ohv V6
Bore x stroke	3.25 x 4.125in
Capacity	225.2cc (3.66ltr)
Main bearings	4
Max. power	160bhp @ 4200rpm
Max. torque	235lb/ft @ 2400rpm

Chassis
Transmission	Warner 3-speed manual, synchromesh on 2nd & top
Turning circle	CJ-5, 36ft, CJ-6, 39ft
Transfer case	2-speed, part time four-wheel drive
Suspension	Semi-elliptic leaf springs front and rear
Brakes	4-wheel hydraulic, 9in drums front and rear

Dimensions
Wheelbase	CJ-5, 81in, CJ-6, 101in
Track (front and rear)	48.5in
Overall length	CJ-5, 135.5in, CJ-6, 155.5in
Overall width	71.75in (including spare wheel)
Overall height (top up)	69.5in
Curb weight	2,413lb

The CJ-5 V6. The only clue to this Jeep having the big engine is the small square badge on the scuttle, below the 'Jeep' name.

best of off-road performance in one package. Jeep was definitely moving up-market.

The AMC V8 stayed in the J-Series, but the Tornado went – it was still just a six when the V8 had come of age. Its major drawback was that it suffered from a high oil consumption, which from a customer's point of view was unacceptable: when the oil level got too low, as it might after prolonged freeway driving, the engine was likely to suffer damage. Rather than rework the Tornado, it was simpler and cheaper to buy in the new AMC 232cu in in-line six for the base models and trucks; this lighter, reliable, seven main bearing unit put out around the same horsepower, as well as living up to its own epithet of 'Hi-Torque'. Dropped also was the independent front suspension and the two-wheel-drive option. In operation it was too fragile for its task, and it was very difficult to keep dirt out of the moving parts of the driveline. Now all Wagoneers would be four-wheel drive with solid axles – and so would the eight-model-strong J-Series trucks, which were re-named J-2000, J-3000 and J-4000. The square grille on the standard Wagoneer was replaced by a full-width one for 1967, but the trucks had to wait until 1970 for the facelift.

THE LEISURE MARKET EXPLORED: THE TUXEDO PARK

The Jeep had always been a working vehicle – even the DJ-3A Gala, for all its fancy colour scheme, was designed for commercial use in the leisure industry. The 1960s were a time of ever-increasing prosperity, and the number of two-car families had doubled over the previous ten years. The Ford Mustang had unleashed the potential of the youth market, and British sports cars were enjoying tremendous success in the US.

Jeep's market for the CJ-5 was largely in rural America, in the wide open spaces of states like California, Texas and New Mexico, and most of them were bought as second cars. Sales of the V6 were far greater than for the Hurricane, and quite a few after-market accessory manufacturers sold wide wheels and roll bars for Jeeps. Kaiser-Jeep decided to have a look at this market for themselves, and from 1961 introduced the Tuxedo Park option. This was a cosmetic job, with chrome bumpers and smarter seats, and over the next few years the extra equipment was gradually added to; finally in 1964 the CJ-5A and the long wheelbase CJ-6A Tuxedo Park were introduced as separate models for the 1965 model year. The following season a special edition 'Prairie Gold' CJ-5 was brought out, featuring chrome trim and a smarter interior. However, this was not a big success; Jeep buyers wanted functional extras, not just dress-up items.

THE NEW JEEPSTER

The market for a specialist utility vehicle had already been opened by the International Harvester Scout, and now Kaiser's real thrust at the leisure market was with the revival of an old name, 'Jeepster', introduced in late 1966. 'Fall in love with the fun makers', said the Jeepster brochure: and here was a car designed to take you to out-of-the-way places where you could take part in other outdoor sports such as surfing, skiing, fishing or hunting, in any place that a conventional two-wheel-drive vehicle would have difficulty getting to; and yet still be a perfectly good everyday road car.

The 101in (2,565mm) CJ-6 chassis and

Jeepster Commando (1966–72)

Engine
Hurricane
Type	4-cylinder, inlet over exhaust
Bore x stroke	3.25 x 4.125in
Capacity	134.2cu in (2.2ltr)
Main bearings	3
Max. power	75bhp @ 4000rpm
Max. torque	114lb/ft @ 2000rpm

Dauntless V6
Type	Buick 90°ohv V6
Bore x stroke	3.25 x 4.125in
Capacity	225.2cu in (3.66ltr)
Main bearings	4
Max. power	160bhp @ 4200rpm
Max. torque	235lb/ft @ 2400rpm

Chassis
Transmission	Warner 3-speed manual, synchromesh on 2nd & top, with GM Turbo Hydra-Matic optional with Dauntless V6
Transfer case	2-speed, part-time four-wheel drive
Suspension	Semi-elliptic leaf springs front and rear
Brakes	4-wheel hydraulic, 10in drums front and rear

Dimensions
Wheelbase	101in
Track (front and rear)	50in
Overall length	175.3in
Overall width	65.2in
Overall height (top up)	64.1in
Curb weight	3,000lb

its engine options, the Hurricane and the Dauntless V6, were to be the base for the Jeepster. Unlike the original Jeepster, the chassis would have four-wheel drive, with power steering and the GM Hydramatic auto gearbox as an option on the V6. Variable rate, single-leaf springs gave a better ride on the highway than the CJ-6's multi-leaf ones. Furthermore there was a choice of body styles: the Jeepster convertible with wind-up windows and an optional power top (the first offered on a 4x4); the Commando Roadster; the Commando hardtop; and a pickup.

When it was first announced, the new Jeepster caused something of a stir. Older drivers recalled the original, and some even mistook the new car for a restored old model. Dual-purpose vehicles are always a compromise, and whilst the Jeepster had off-road performance close to its CJ cousins, crosswinds affected it at highway speeds. Access to the rear seats was difficult, especially for a girl in a tight mini skirt, and the soft-top models had no space for a suitcase, let alone a surfboard or scuba gear. Not having power steering

Every inch a Jeep to look at, the Jeepster Commando Truck had a decent-sized pickup bed and full doors with wind-up windows. The grille is much wider than the CJ-5, incorporating indicators. Although a purposeful-looking truck, it was expensive compared to the Ford Bronco and the International Harvester Scout.

made parking difficult, too.

Nevertheless, the special CJ-5 models and the Jeepster were clear manifestations of Kaiser's train of thought, and in 1969 a concept car, the XJ001, was announced. Based on a CJ-5 chassis, it was an open top, door-less, two-seat 4x4 sport featuring a full width, glassfibre body. According to the press release it was an experimental vehicle, built – like so many of the auto industry's dream cars of the post-war decades – to test the market's reaction. Lack of money prevented the idea being taken forward, because to build such a plastic body would need tooling expertise not found within Kaiser's group.

The Jeepster Commando Station Wagon tackles some tough country. The roofrack adds to the already useful amount of space in the back.

The Renegade I

The CJ-5A venture had taught Kaiser-Jeep a thing or two about what Jeep buyers really wanted, and in 1969 they introduced the 462 package. This offered a full roll bar, skid plate, swing-away rear tyre mount and additional instruments; it was available for both V6 and Hurricane models. The 1970 model year saw all the 462 goodies offered on the new Renegade I model, distinguished by a bonnet stripe with the legend 'Renegade I'. In short, as the leisure market grew, Kaiser-Jeep were beginning to offer true Jeep enthusiasts some really worthwhile factory options.

DEVELOPMENTS IN SOUTH AMERICA

The old Station Wagon and truck were given a new lease of life when Brooks Stevens designed new front end sheet metal and a four-door body. It appeared as the Jeep Rural in Brazil, and the Estanciera in Argentina. In Brazil the Rural was joined by the Scaci, a revived version of the Jeepster that shared the Rural's underpinnings and new front end style. Despite a warm, critical welcome, the Scaci was not to be a production model.

By the end of the decade Kaiser-Jeep had established thirty overseas manufacturing plants, with Jeep vehicles sold in 150 countries; but Edgar Kaiser knew that he did not have the resources to introduce new passenger cars in the South American markets. Brazil's unstable government made for a temperamental market, a far cry from the conditions in Argentina. In 1967 Ford, expanding rapidly all around the world, bought out Willys do Brazil, including Renault's fourteen percent share. They continued to make the CJ-5, the CJ-6 and the utility range, eventually replacing the Super

Jeep / Renault's utility vehicle range from 1968. They are, lined up on the left from the top down, the CJ-6 and CJ-5, both with 161ci F-head Super Hurricane engines, and the Renault 4 Furgoneta. Centre is the Gladiator-based Jeep T-80 with Tornado engine and four-speed ZF gearbox, optional four-wheel drive and torsion bar IFS. Right is the Estanciera, the Argentinean version of Brooks Stevens' redesigned Station Wagon. The Estanciera also had the Tornado engine, and standard four-wheel drive.

Hurricane six that was the standard power-plant with their own 2.3 litre OHC engine.

Kaiser sold out its Argentinean interest to Renault in late 1968. The new company, Ika-Renault, continued to make a range of Jeep vehicles alongside its own models. The Jeep range included the CJ-5 and 6, the Estanciera, and a version of the J-Series truck, the T-80.

AMC ENGINES FOR THE J-SERIES

The Vigilante V8 was a short-lived addition to the J-series: AMC were to drop this ageing engine entirely, and the new Typhoon V8 would not be ready for outside customers. Kaiser-Jeep looked again to Buick. In 1964 Buick had extended the iron V6 to make a 300cu in iron V8 for the new mid-sized cars: for 1968 this engine was bored and stroked to 350cu in, (5.69 litres), and found a home

Wagoneer and Gladiator (1963–72)	
Engines	
Tornado	
Type	Six cylinder in-line, single overhead cam
Bore x stroke	3.35 x 4.38in
Capacity	230cu in (3.8ltr)
Main bearings	4
Max. power	140bhp @ 4000rpm
Max. torque	210lb/ft @ 1750rpm
Vigilante V8	
Type	American Motors Corporation 90°ohv V8
Bore x stroke	4.00 x 3.25in
Capacity	327cu in (5.3ltr)
Main bearings	5
Max. power	250bhp @ 4000rpm
Max. torque	340lb/ft @ 2500rpm
Hi-Torque Six	
Type	American Motors Corporation ohv in-line six
Bore x stroke	3.75 x 3.50in/3.75 x 3.9in
Capacity	232cu in (3.8ltr)/258cu in (4.2ltr)
Main bearings	6
Max. power	100bhp @ 3600rpm/110bhp @ 3500rpm
Max. torque	185lb/ft @ 1800rpm/195lb/ft @ 2000rpm

Dauntless V8

Type	Buick 90°ohv V8
Bore x stroke	3.8 x 4.85in
Capacity	350cu in (5.7ltr)
Main bearings	5
Max. power	230bhp @ 4400rpm
Max. torque	350lb/ft @ 2400rpm

Chassis

Wagoneer

Transmission	Warner 3-speed manual, synchromesh on 2nd & top, with Borg Warner 3-speed Automatic optional with Tornado engine, GM Turbo Hydra-Matic optional with Buick and AMC engines. Overdrive optional with manual transmission
Transfer case	2-speed, part-time four-wheel drive (single range with automatic)
Suspension- front	IFS with torsion bars or solid axles with leaf springs
Suspension-rear	Semi-elliptic leaf springs
Brakes	4-wheel hydraulic, 11in drums front and rear

Gladiator

Transmission	Warner 3-speed manual, synchromesh on 2nd & top. 4-speed optional, manual standard with J-400. Borg Warner 3-speed Automatic optional with Tornado engine, GM Turbo Hydra-Matic optional with Buick and AMC engines
Transfer case	2-speed, part-time four-wheel drive
Suspension- front	IFS with torsion bars or solid axles with leaf springs (solid axles standard with heavy duty models)
Suspension-rear	Semi-elliptic leaf springs
Brakes	4-wheel hydraulic, 11in drums front and rear, optional power assistance

Dimensions

Wagoneer

Wheelbase	110in
Track (front and rear)	57in
Overall length	183.7in
Overall width	75.6in
Overall height (top up)	64.2in
Curb weight	3,700lb

Gladiator

Wheelbase	120in or 132in
Track (front and rear)	63.5in (63.75 J-3800)
Overall length	183.8/205.64in
Overall width	75.93in
Overall height (top up)	71in
Curb weight	3,555lb–4,018lb

in the Wagoneer in the same year. It was named in Kaiser-Jeep's line-up as the 'Dauntless V8', to echo its V6 stable-mate's name. Thanks to its V6 origins, it mated nicely to the existing manual and automatic transmissions. The AMC in-line six continued as the base engine option; however, this would not be the last we would hear of AMC V8s, or the American Motors Corporation.

6 American Motors: Jeep Becomes a Leisure Vehicle

The American Motors Corporation, the fourth largest auto maker in the US, was fighting its way back into profit. Roy D. Chapin Snr had formed the Hudson Motor Company back in 1909; now, in 1967, his son, Roy Jnr, was appointed AMC's joint chief executive officer, and William V. Luneburg the chairman when Roy Abernethy resigned. AMC lost $12.5 million in 1966 because Abernethy made some serious mistakes in realigning the model line, thereby losing AMC's traditional customers. In the early 1960s, huge investments had been made in two new engine plants in Kenosha: from 1964 these were making the Torque-Command six-cylinder series, and from 1966 the Typhoon V8. Factories in South and Central America were doing steady business, and so was the Canadian plant in Brampton, Ontario. But the slump in sales at home failed to recoup the investment money in either the engines or the tooling for the mid-sixties models that had sold so poorly.

The American Motors Corporation

The US auto industry post-war was dominated by the expansion of the Big Three. With huge financial resources at their disposal, they could undertake massive research projects, develop powerful new engines and follow a policy of annual model changes. In a bid to survive, Studebaker and Packard merged, and lasted in the auto business until 1964. But much more successful was American Motors, a merger between Nash-Kelvinator and Hudson.

Hudson's story goes back to 1909, when Roy D. Chapin introduced a car financed by Hudson's department store in Detroit. The range throughout the 1920s and 1930s was conventional, but the Terraplane straight-eight of the early 1930s gained a reputation as a sharp performer. The Canadian-made chassis became the basis of two British models, the Railton and the Brough Superior.

Hudson's post-war cars were of unit construction with all-round coil spring suspension, but they were powered by old-style sidevalve engines, which belied their ageing design with consistent championship wins on the NASCAR and AAA stock-car racing circuits. The race wins did not translate into sales success, however, for the company struggled to fund new models, and had to buy in the new Packard V8 engine. The introduction of a smaller car, the Jetliner, swallowed all their development money, but was a flop.

Charles Nash had worked for William Crapo Durant at the Durant-Dort Carriage Company. When Durant formed the fledgling General Motors Corporation, Nash took over the management of its Buick division; this was in 1910. In 1916, after losing a power struggle with Durant, Nash left GM. He bought Thomas B. Jeffery's business in Kenosha, Wisconsin, and turned it into his own motor company. Nash was an excellent manager of both production techniques and financial matters, and the company prospered. In 1936 a merger with domestic appliance manufacturers

---

On 1 May 1954 the American Motors Corporation was born. Hudson president A. E. Barit, left, shakes hands with Nash's George W. Mason (centre) and George Romney.

Kelvinator resulted in the formation of the Nash-Kelvinator Corporation.

Post-war Nash cars had a conventional straight-six engine, but an 'aerodynamic' body that helped fuel economy. Nash was the first American maker to build small cars after the war; in 1953 a tie-up with BMC saw the production in Longbridge of the little two-seat Metropolitan, and at this time the Rambler would be America's only successful home-built compact.

In 1954 Nash-Kelvinator and Hudson merged to form the American Motors Corporation, with Nash's George W. Mason as chairman and president. But before the end of the year Mason was dead, and his place was taken by the outspoken George Romney, who had joined the company in 1948. Hudson's Detroit factory closed, and production was transferred to Nash in Kenosha. Hudsons became badge-engineered Nashes, although by 1957 both names had been killed off. Subsequently all AMC's cars carried the Rambler name, derived from the old Jeffery model.

George Romney was to engineer the most successful post-war period in AMC's history. He introduced well made, economical models that eschewed style changes and that appealed to America's older, more conservative buyers. Then in 1962 Romney left to become Governor of Michigan; his place as president of AMC was taken by Roy Abernethy.

Chapin cut the prices of the smaller models, introduced the sporty AMX and Javelin, and persuaded AMC to become involved in a factory racing programme. The 'Rambler' brand name was gradually dropped, and henceforth all cars from AMC's Kenosha factory carried AMC badges. The Kelvinator domestic appliance division was sold off to gain some cash. Roy Chapin's plan looked like succeeding; the best news of all was that 1968 saw the first profits for many years.

At Kaiser Industries, another son of an entrepreneurial father was at the helm. Edgar Kaiser took a long, hard look at his operations world-wide, for the non-automotive side of the business was in need of some financial input. But where was the cash to come from? Kaiser-Jeep had potential for the future, but Kaiser could not afford to invest in new vehicles. They did not want to lose control of a possible source of income, but it was the most suitable asset for realizing capital. Since the mid-1960s Kaiser had owned a share-holding in AMC, and it was to them that Edgar turned. From as early as 1966 rumours had spread about a merger between AMC and Kaiser, but when Roy Chapin had studied the idea of buying into Kaiser-Jeep, the advice that he had received from his investigator, Gerald C. Meyers, had been to 'leave well alone'; Meyers considered it would do no good for American Motors as a whole.

Chapin thought differently. He had been involved in overseas sales, and had negotiated the deals with Kaiser in Argentina and Mexico. He knew the value of Kaiser's overseas markets, and the potential of the Jeep. Although Chapin faced a lot of flak from both shareholders and the auto press, American Motors bought into Kaiser-Jeep on 12 December 1969 for a cash-and-shares package that amounted to around $70 mil-

lion. The deal would give Kaiser a return on their holdings, but to AMC the benefits of the deal were more specific: they would get an entry into the light truck field; they would acquire a military vehicle building operation; and best of all, they would take a quantum leap into the four-wheel-drive market with the most famous name in the world.

AMC wasted no time in reshaping the new acquisition. By March 1970 Jeep was split into two divisions: the Government Contracts Division, and the Jeep Corporation. The Government Contracts Division would build military vehicles and DJ-5 Postal Service vehicles in Kaiser's Chippewa plant in South Bend, Indiana; in 1971 this division was set up as a wholly independent subsidiary, and renamed AM General.

The other division, the Jeep Corporation, took a big step into the off-road leisure market, which was growing fast.

IMPROVED CJ MODELS

The Jeep Corporation continued to build civilian Jeeps at Toledo, Ohio. The 'Universal' name was dropped, after twenty-seven years. The CJ-5 and CJ-6 were still marketed as working vehicles in the US, but the off-road leisure market was the big direction in which AMC would take Jeep.

Initially the Kaiser-Jeep specifications were carried over, but new models were released for the 1972 model year, and it was soon clear that AMC Jeeps would be a significantly different breed from Kaiser models; the top-to-bottom changes showed just how much work was done in that short time. There were new engines: the AMC 232ci and 258ci straight sixes and the 304ci V8 replaced both the V6 and the antiquated Hurricane. The wheelbase of the

US Postal Service Jeeps

The US Postal Service had used DJ-3A Dispatchers since 1955. From 1965 these were replaced by the more modern DJ-5, with a Hurricane engine. There was also a new livery, white with red and blue stripes to replace the blue and white. The extra-large sliding doors were carried over from the DJ-3A, as was right-hand drive.

A bought-in Chevrolet four-cylinder engine with a GM Power-glide two-speed auto 'box replaced the Hurricane and the three-speed Warner manual in 1968, but when AMC bought Kaiser-Jeep,

The DJ-5 built for the US Postal Service was right-hand drive. Safety was the main concern in fitting some odd-looking mirrors on the door and (US) offside front wing. Traffic coming from the rear could easily be seen, and when turning into a main road, the oncoming traffic there was better viewed.

AM General was formed, and Postal Jeeps would become more remote from the mainstream civilian models. The Chevy engine was dropped, and the 232ci in-line six was squeezed into the new DJ-5B. To get the auto 'box in under the body without radically altering the scuttle and the frame, the engine was moved forward in the chassis, and a bulbous grille pressing added to the front to clear the radiator. The wheelbase remained at 81in (2,057mm), unlike the revised CJ-5, which was stretched by 3in (76mm).

The six-cylinder DJ-5 – numerous transmission changes pushed the variant number up to F – lasted until 1978, when some VAG 2-litre four-cylinder engines were installed in the DJ-5G, mated to a Chrysler Torqueflite auto box. This was followed by the DJ-5L, with the GM 151ci 'Iron Duke' four, and the last of the postal DJs had AMC's new four from the XJ Cherokee.

In 1982 the Postal Service began replacing its Jeeps with the Grumman LLV, and from 1997 the much larger Ford Aerostar box van. By the end of century it was estimated that 27,000 DJ-5s would still be in service – but after they are decommissioned, the Postal Jeep will be no more.

There were a few variants to the mainstream DJ-5s to meet different needs, and there were some experiments with alternative motive power. In the mid-1980s, right-hand-drive CJ-8 Scrambler panel vans went into service on longer rural rounds. Electric power was experimented with on the DJ-5E in 1976, but the batteries doubled the weight of the vehicle, and the trials were not followed through. Harking back to the old Panel Delivery, an FJ-9 version of the Cherokee was tried in 1975.

Two unique DJ-5s were modified by Perkins engines of Peterborough who, in response to the fuel crisis of 1974, installed specially designed 2.5-litre four-cylinder diesel engines in them. One was shipped to the US, the second remained in the UK where modifications could be made to the engines, and tested, before new components were shipped out to the States for the Postal Service to fit to the other. However, the low-revving nature of the engines was not compatible with the automatic gearbox, making the vehicles slow. Perhaps too, the noise of a diesel engine in the early morning generated complaints. The Perkins diesel DJ-5 never went further than this experiment, although the UK model was kept at Perkins and used as a factory runabout.

AMC's 1972 line-up of Jeep models was promoted by the slogan: 'With the guts to come on stronger than ever'. Although the leisure market was a priority, the workhorse image was still put forward strongly, as with this 'Highway Patrol' shot. The cleaner lines of the reworked body are clear, with the battery cover and snorkel cut-out no longer in evidence. The hard top and doors were optional extras.

CJ-5 and 6 were each lengthened by 3in (76mm) to accommodate the new engines. A new range of Dana 30 open-ended axles was introduced, giving a wider track and a much welcomed, tighter turning circle – 32.9ft (10m) instead of 36ft (11m) on the CJ-5 – and cutting down on the steering shimmy encountered with the old Model 27 axles. The new, stiffer, stronger frame was boxed along its entire length, and the body was retooled. It was stretched between the scuttle and the front wheel arch to take up the extra length. The bonnet lost its snorkel cut-out. The battery was moved under the bonnet, so the cowl lost its battery cover, and the fuel filler was moved to below the right-hand tail-light.

Four-speed manual transmissions were supplied with the six-cylinder motors, whilst the V8 came with an all-synchromesh three-speed. There was a Trac-Loc limited slip differential option, bigger brakes and high capacity heaters. The much-criticized, dash-mounted handbrake was replaced with a foot-operated emergency brake. Also the Renegade's swing-away spare tyre mount was available on all models. Pedals were now hung from the dash, instead of coming out of the floor: no more wet feet when hitting a water splash!

The Renegade II

The Renegade I had been well received, and now a new, special edition 'Renegade II' CJ-5 spearheaded Jeep's advance toward the leisure market. Its 304ci V8 produced 210bhp – treble that of the old Hurricane, and half as much again as the Dauntless V6. Power brakes and power steering were optional. The standard roll bar, additional instruments and fuel-tank skid plate were all carried over. It was also good value: at $299 the package added 10 per cent to the CJ-5's base price. A second special edition, the 'Super Jeep', was also offered, being a 'dress-up' package on the six-cylinder models. The Renegade II was a big hit, and for 1973 it was made a full production model.

AMC CJ-5 (1972–83), CJ-6 (1967–72) and CJ-6A export model (1972–81)

Engines

In-Line Six

Type	American Motors Corporation ohv in-line 6
Bore x stroke	3.75 x 3.50in/3.75 x 3.90in
Capacity	232cu in (3.8ltr)/258cu in (4.2ltr)
Main bearings	7
Max. power	100bhp @ 3600rpm/110bhp @ 3500
Max. torque	185lb/ft @ 1800rpm195lb/ft @ 2000rpm

V8

Type	American Motors Corporation ohv 90° V8
Bore x stroke	3.75 x 3.44in
Capacity	304cu in (4.9ltr)
Main bearings	5
Max. power	150bhp @ 4200rpm
Max. torque	245lb/ft @ 2500rpm

Chassis

Transmission	Warner 3-speed manual, synchromesh on 2nd & top, optional 4-speed manual with 6-cylinder engine
Turning circle	CJ-5, 32.9ft, CJ-6, 37.6ft
Transfer case	2-speed, part time four-wheel drive
Suspension	Semi-elliptic leaf springs front and rear
Brakes	4-wheel hydraulic, 10in drums front and rear, power assist available with V8 engine
	10.98in front discs, 11in rear drums from 1976

Dimensions

Wheelbase	CJ-5, 84in, CJ-6, 104in
Track	51.5in front, 50.5in rear
Overall length	CJ-5, 138.9in, CJ-6, 158.9in (including side-mounted spare wheel)
Overall width	71.75in (including side-mounted spare wheel)
Overall height (top up)	68.3in
Curb weight	CJ-5, 3,750lb, CJ-6 3,900lb

RATIONALIZATION

Exit the Jeepster

With the CJs uprated to meet the demands of the leisure sector, the poor-selling Jeepster was to be killed off. The run-out model, the 1971 Hurst Limited Edition Commando, featured some smart extras, including Hurst's dual-gate change, plus rally stripes and wide tyres. Hurst were manufacturers of special gear-change equipment, much favoured by drag racers. However, only about one hundred of these Dauntless V-6-powered special models were sold – a very poor take-up.

A brief revamp for the Commando . . .

The Commando name was carried over to the rest of the range for 1972, but now also featured AMC engines. The in-line sixes and the 304ci V8, with optional auto boxes, replaced the Hurricane and Dauntless. To accommodate the longer engines and the new 104in (2,642mm) CJ-6 frame, the front end was redesigned with a full-width style. The less practical convertible option was dropped, whilst the more useful station wagon remained, gaining bucket seats as standard. However, in comparison to the competition – the Blazer, Bronco and Scout – sales of the Commando were poor. The best year had been 1968 when almost 14,000 were sold, though this was less than half of the Scout's estimated annual average. Nevertheless, although AMC could never hope to match Ford's potential volume or the meteoric rise of the Chevy Blazer, they could not afford to abandon completely such a blossoming market. They had to reassess

the whole line-up, so after only a year in production, the expensive, less-than-ideal Commando was dropped entirely.

. . . and a realignment of the J-Series

Not surprisingly, for the 1972 model year the Buick Dauntless V8 was replaced in the Wagoneer by a choice of AMC's 304ci or the 360ci V8s, whilst the 258 six replaced the 232 as the base. The engine options were carried over to the truck line, which was rationalized into the 120in (3,048mm) wheelbase J-2000 or the 132in (3,353mm) J-4000. For 1972 the Gladiator name was dropped, and the vehicles became known simply as Jeep trucks. All used either Warner manual transmissions or GM Hydramatic automatic gearboxes. The Borg-Warner transfer case stayed – but the big news for 1973 was the introduction of Quadra-Trac. Offered at first on the V8 engine and automatic transmission combination only, Quadra-Trac's centre dif-

The new Commando, with the revised front end. It accommodated a more powerful engine, but the vehicle lost the essential 'Jeep' look.

The 1972 Wagoneer featured a new grille, but more importantly, a stronger frame, and the new generation AMC V8 joined its six-cylinder stable-mates.

ferential enabled permanent four-wheel drive to be offered for the first time. Trucks would still be referred to as the J-Series, but the Wagoneer would have a revised code to suit its size and status: SJ, for Senior Jeep.

By 1974, American Motors' across-the-board realignment of the J- and SJ-Series shaped up to meet the competition. There was a new, stronger frame. The running gear was updated, with new Dana open-end

axles cutting the Wagoneer's turning circle down to 38.4ft (11.7m). Those drum brakes were to be consigned to the skip, and discs were at last offered as an extra-cost option.

The Custom Wagoneer was new. Building on the idea begun by the 1967 Super Wagoneer, the Custom offered more luxury and equipment in a four-wheel-drive vehicle than had ever been seen. Power steering and automatic transmission were standard, with alloy wheels an

Jeep trucks were given a make-over, too. This is the J-4000, the long wheelbase heavyweight.

option, and the 360ci V8 became the base engine for all Wagoneers. Everything the American buyer expected on a luxury car was to be had, and the Wagoneer, never a cheap car, now became a top line model with a premium price.

The Chevrolet Blazer had raised the stakes for Kaiser-Jeep when it was introduced in 1969, but now AMC pulled an ace out of the hole: the Cherokee. This was a budget-priced two-door SJ, with prices starting at $3,986, compared to $6,246 for the Custom Wagoneer – though it must be said that, whilst the Custom had just about everything included in the price, the Cherokee's options list was pretty long, and included such items as an electric clock and air-conditioning. The base model Cherokee was powered by the 258ci six, with 360ci and 401ci V8s as options. Quadra-Trac was available for six-cylinder and V8 engines in both the J-Series passenger models and trucks.

For 1975, disc brakes were standardized across the whole J and SJ range, and a new, stiffer chassis frame was introduced in 1976. By this time fuel-emission controls were being toughened up by the US government, and electronic ignition helped to clean up all AMC engines.

The Cherokee Chief made its bow in 1976, with wider wheel arches to accommodate the bigger tyres and wheels demanded by off-roaders. The Cherokee was an excellent seller, and a four-door model was introduced in 1978. In common with the rest of the non-Quadra-Trac J-Series it offered a new, two-speed Dana transfer box. The J-Series trucks, renumbered as J-10 and J-20, kept the 258ci six as their base engine.

Jeep's four-wheel-drive systems: Quadra-Trac

Quadra-Trac™ . . . Jeep automatic 4-wheel drive

Quadra-Trac™, a unique 4-wheel drive system developed by Jeep Corporation for Jeep vehicles, automatically supplies exactly the right amount of power at all times to both front and rear axles. The result is optimum traction and control in all driving situations.

Continuous power is transmitted through a limited slip third differential to the axles in direct proportion to their needs.

With Quadra-Trac the vehicle is constantly in 4-wheel drive. No floor shift lever is required to convert to 2-wheel drive as is the case with conventional 4-wheel drive systems.

A smooth power flow is achieved through a silent chain drive, instead of gears, in the transfer case. With the third differential, axles are not locked together allowing all wheels to rotate independently at different speeds.

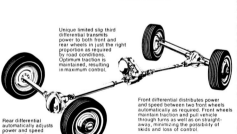

Unique limited slip third differential transmits power to both front and rear wheels in just the right proportion as required by road conditions. Optimum traction is maintained, resulting in maximum control.

Front differential distributes power and speed between two front wheels automatically as required. Front wheels maintain traction and pull vehicle through turns as well as on straight-away, minimizing the possibility of skids and loss of control.

Rear differential automatically adjusts power and speed between two rear wheels as required. Rear wheels maintain proper traction and push while on straightaway or in turns.

As we have seen, the main problem with running a four-wheel drive on hard roads is finding a way of allowing the front wheels to rotate independently of the rear wheels yet still provide power. For this, some kind of centre differential is vital, but it took the Americans until 1973 to develop something good enough to market. After four years' work, Borg-Warner in Detroit produced the Quadra-Trac system for Jeep. Engineer Jack Engle, dubbed 'Mr Quadra-Trac', developed a centre differential using cone clutches. It could also supply different torque to each axle dependent on demand. However, although this new system was effective, it was expensive to produce and noisy in operation.

The driveline of the 1974 Wagoneer, with the optional Borg-Warner Quadra-Trac permanent four-wheel-drive system. Note the offset differential on the new rear axle.

AMC SJ Wagoneer (1972–91), Cherokee (1974–83), J-Series Truck (1972–1987)

Engines
In-Line Six
Type	AMC ohv in-line 6
Bore x stroke	3.75 x 3.50in/3.75 x 3.90in
Capacity	232cu in (3.8ltr)/258cu in (4.2ltr)
Main bearings	7
Max. power	100bhp @ 3600rpm/110bhp @ 3500rpm
Max. torque	185lb/ft @ 1800rpm195lb/ft @ 2000rpm

V8
Type	AMC ohv 90° V8
Bore x stroke	4.08 x 3.44in
Capacity	304cu in (4.9ltr) (Cherokee)/360cu in (5.9ltr) (Wagoneer)
Main bearings	5
Max. power	175bhp @ 4000rpm
Max. torque	285lb/ft @ 2400rpm

Chassis
Wagoneer
Transmission	Warner 3-speed manual, synchromesh on 2nd & top, optional 4-speed manual or GM Turbo Hydra-Matic
Transfer case	2-speed, part-time four-wheel drive (single range with automatic), Quadra-Trac permanent four-wheel drive available from 1974
Suspension-	Semi-elliptic leaf springs front and rear
Brakes	4-wheel hydraulic, 11in drums front and rear, 12in discs on front from 1974

J-Series Truck
Transmission	Warner 3-speed manual, synchromesh on 2nd & top, optional 4-speed manual or GM Turbo Hydra-Matic
Transfer case	2-speed, part-time four-wheel drive (single range with automatic), Quadra-Trac permanent four-wheel drive available from 1974
Suspension-	Semi-elliptic leaf springs front and rear
Brakes	4-wheel hydraulic, 11in drums front and rear, 12in discs on front from 1974

Dimensions
Wagoneer
Wheelbase	108.7in
Track (and)	59.4in front, 57.8in rear
Overall length	183.7in
Overall width	75.6in
Overall height (top up)	66.7in
GVW	3,555lb–4,018lb

J-Series Truck
Wheelbase	120in or 132in
Track (front and rear)	63.5in (63.9 J-4500-4800)
Overall length	205.8in
Overall width	78.93in
Overall height	69.5in

Jeepster Commando (1972–73)

Engine

In-Line Six

Type	American Motors Corporation ohv in-line 6
Bore x stroke	3.75 x 3.50in/3.75 x 3.90in
Capacity	232cu in (3.8ltr)/258cu in (4.2ltr)
Main bearings	7
Max. power	100bhp @ 3600rpm/110bhp @ 3500rpm
Max. torque	185lb/ft @ 1800rpm195lb/ft @ 2000rpm

V8

Type	American Motors Corporation ohv 90°V8
Bore x stroke	3.75 x 3.44in
Capacity	304cu in (4.9ltr)
Main bearings	5
Max. power	150bhp @ 4200rpm
Max. torque	245lb/ft @ 2500rpm

Chassis

Transmission	Warner 3-speed manual, synchromesh on 2nd & top, with optional GM Turbo Hydra-Matic
Transfer case	2-speed, part-time four-wheel drive
Suspension	Semi-elliptic leaf springs front and rear
Brakes	4-wheel hydraulic, 10in drums front and rear

Dimensions

Wheelbase	104in
Track	51.5in front, 50.5in rear
Overall length	178.3in
Overall width	65.2in
Overall height (top up)	64.1in
Curb weight	3,000lb

AMC IN TROUBLE AGAIN

By 1975 AMC had built their 400,000th Jeep, but whilst these niche-market vehicles continued to sell well, sales of the passenger cars began to suffer. Roy Chapin had made mistakes of his own in choosing new model lines, and in particular the second model Javelin and the big Matador flopped in the marketplace. The new Pacer was a unique model for AMC, sharing its bodyshell with no other. General Motors were going to supply a Wankel rotary engine for it, but the fuel consumption, the dirty emissions and the plain unreliability of this engine caused GM to scrap it, and the Pacer came out with AMC six-cylinder engines. In its first year, 1975, it sold well, but in successive years this initial success tailed off, as a recession bit hard into the pockets of those AMC customers in the lower price bracket. The new full-sized Matador failed to make any effect in the markets dominated by the Big Three. The 1970s' compacts, the Hornet and the Gremlin, were successful models, but their

After a gap of some twenty-five years, the Automobile Association took another look at Jeeps. This CJ-6 was supplied in 1974 for assessment, and used in the Hampshire area. The 'Relay' motif on the hard top indicates that its towing capability was an important reason for its trial. It was popular with the crew, but the AA decided once more to stick to British vehicles. Certainly the big AMC six would not have returned the fuel economy of a four-cylinder Land Rover! (Note, incidentally, the absence of a fuel filler on the nearside; AMC moved it to the rear, below the tail light.)

sales, plus those of Jeep, were not enough to make up the difference. AMC began losing millions.

CHANGES DOWN UNDER

Complaints had been seen in the Australian motoring press that Jeep's local agents, Shute-Upton Engineering, had not made enough attempts to sell the product line. If this were true, it was the company's downfall, and they went broke in 1973, leaving Jeep with no source of manufacture. From the late 1960s, Ford Falcon in-line six cylinder engines had been fitted to CJs, and money was outstanding to Ford of Australia. In lieu, Ford took Jeep transmission units and axles and fitted them to a number of Falcon pickups ('utes'), selling them exclusively in Queensland. Jeep would not return to Australia for another seven years.

JEEP IN THE UK

AMC was looking beyond its markets in the USA, Canada and Latin America, across the Atlantic to Europe, and the next sequel in its history was that the American Motors Corporation (Great Britain) Ltd was set up in Hudson's old premises by the Chiswick flyover in West London, and a depot established at Swindon, Wiltshire. The UK was to be a base from which AMC would launch its passenger car lines and Jeep vehicles in the European Common Market, of which Britain was the latest member.

Selected models from the CJ and SJ range were offered, including CJ-5, CJ-6, the Cherokee and the J-Series truck. Obviously the working abilities of Jeep vehicles were stressed in the promotional literature, but so was the fact that they were a pleasure to drive. Furthermore, although only a three-speed manual gearbox was available, it was an all-synchro unit, and this, too, was emphasized; at this time Land Rover appeared to have the advantage with a four-speed manual, but it had synchromesh on third and top gears only. At least two thousand CJ-5s and CJ-6s were to be imported during 1974, which would, it was hoped, rise to five thousand by 1977, with the declared ambition to take 25 per cent of the 4x4 market from Rover. These figures never materialized, however, despite the prices of CJ models being competitive with Land Rover: a CJ-5 with the standard soft top, 232ci six and three-speed manual gearbox was £1,572, as compared

to a 2.2-litre, petrol 88in (2,235mm) Land Rover with canvas tilt at £1,308.

The first CJs and Senior Jeeps imported were left-hand drive, but were converted to right-hand drive by TKM of Andover. They used a Wooller-Hodec chain-drive system mounted behind the dash. The upper steering column was shortened, and the left-hand-drive steering box left in place. Contemporary road testers complained that the conversion was crude: master cylinders were left in their original place, and the pedal operation was transferred by extension rods similar to a driving-school car's dual controls. The foot-operated parking brake was more difficult to operate, too.

The transfer box, spare wheel and battery had been built on the opposite side to the driver in the US left-hand-drive models so as to balance the weight distribution, and could not be changed over for the right-hand-drive versions. Over the course of a year or so, some of the right-hand drive CJs developed a distinct right-hand list as the springs began to sag under the extra weight of having the driver on the opposite side. The problem was rectified by adding an extra leaf to the offside springs, though this was at the customers' expense. However, some factions in the British motoring press, rooting for the Land Rover against the import, grabbed this opportunity to put the Jeep down by making the problem larger than it truly was.

A further disadvantage was that although service agencies had been set up for all AMC products throughout the UK, they were not as numerous as Rover dealers; more over the right-hand-drive conversions on the whole did nothing to help Jeep's cause. Also buyers had to compare the more powerful Jeep against the Land Rover's better weather protection. Although later CJs were purpose-built with right-hand drive, the venture was a failure.

Not only did Jeep sales amount to no more than fifty a year, AMC's passenger cars were a victim of the hike in oil prices. By the end of 1974, AMC cut its losses and closed the UK operation.

THE CJ-6

The CJ-6 was withdrawn from the US market in 1976. Out of all the CJs made in twenty-one years, only one in ten were CJ-6s: perhaps its utility image did nothing to help sales, even though a full selection of accessories such as snow ploughs and winches were offered across the Jeep range. Its longer wheelbase improved weight distribution, giving better traction; thus in a straight line it was more stable at speed and in high speed braking. Moreover, when driving hard off-road, understeer could be corrected by the throttle at higher speeds with less risk of turning over than with the CJ-5. However, the message did not convince enough Jeep aficionados, and there were plenty of conventional four-wheel-drive trucks available in the US to make the CJ-6 obsolescent. By this time the CJ-6's real forte as a basic workhorse was valued more in overseas markets. Small numbers were made of the CJ-6A export model until 1977, but the CJ-6 continued in overseas production until 1980.

The 1976 CJ-5 Renegade, with standard soft top and soft doors.

THE CJ-7

After six years of owning Jeep, AMC brought out a new CJ series, the CJ-7. It replaced the CJ-6, although the CJ-5 continued alongside the new baby. The CJ-7 had a longer wheelbase – at 93.5in (2,374mm) it was not quite as long as the CJ-6 – but the extra length was mainly in front, to make room for the optional Hydramatic auto box and the new Quadra-Trac permanent four-wheel-drive system. With its longer wheelbase, the CJ-7 would inherit some of the CJ-6's extra stability at speed.

The standard engine for the CJ-7 was the 232ci six, with the 258ci six or the 304 V8 as options, and the choice of three- or four-speed manual transmission alongside the auto. Although tuning specialists offered Quadra-Trac and automatic gearbox conversions in CJ-5s (and a 401ci V8!), AMC would not do so, claiming that the extra length of the whole transmission assembly resulted in too acute a driveshaft angle to the rear axle. Disc brakes were offered for both the CJ-7 and the CJ-5, as an optional extra. The US Army had experimented with them on an M38A1 in 1959, but had rejected the idea because the pad wear was too great. Now they were available for the first time on production CJs.

There was more leg-room in the passenger compartment, and more luggage space behind the back seat. And with the polycarbonate hardtop version, the CJ-7 had a real luxury: solid doors, with wind-up windows on the hardtop models. The longer chassis was boxed along its entire length, as was the 1977 CJ-5, and was much stiffer as a result. Now the doors could be relied upon not to bang against the enlarged shuts. They could also be locked, giving added security.

AMC GO BACK TO THE UK

AMC returned to the UK in 1978, this time trying a different tack. They would sell only Jeep vehicles, and use a British distributor. Against competition from Lohnro and the Lex Group, the franchise for the new company, Jeep UK Ltd, was given to TKM of Andover, Hampshire, with Chris Tennant as managing director. The CJ-6, CJ-7, Cherokee, Cherokee Chiefs and trucks were listed for importation. The Cherokees would have the 360ci V8, whilst the truck and the CJs would have the 258ci six. There was the Golden Eagle option for the CJ-7, and Golden Eagle and Honcho options for the truck. Initially, the CJ-5 was not to be brought in, as Jeep Division of

The 1976 CJ-7 Renegade, with soft top removed. Note the bigger door openings on comparison with the CJ-5. The roll bar was a standard fitting. A tilting steering column, plus air conditioning for the hard top models, would follow in 1997.

Jeep Corporation CJ-7 (1976–86)

Engines

In-Line Six

Type	AMC ohv in-line 6
Bore x stroke	3.75 x 3.90in
Capacity	258cu in (4.2ltr)
Main bearings	7
Max. power	110bhp @ 3500rpm
Max. torque	195lb/ft @ 2000rpm

V8

Type	AMC ohv 90° V8
Bore x stroke	3.75 x 3.44in
Capacity	304cu in (4.9ltr)
Main bearings	5
Max. power	150bhp @ 4200rpm
Max. torque	245lb/ft @ 2500rpm

4-Cylinder (from 1980)

Type	GMC ohv in-line 4
Bore x stroke	4 x 3in
Capacity	151cu in (2.45ltr)
Main bearings	5
Max. power	82bhp @ 4000rpm
Max. torque	125lb/ft @ 2600rpm

Chassis

Transmission	Warner 3-speed manual, synchromesh on 2nd & top, optional 4-speed manual with 6-cylinder engine
Turning circle	CJ-5, 32.9ft, CJ-6, 37.6ft
Transfer case	2-speed, part time four-wheel drive, Quadra-Trac permanent four-wheel drive available from 1974
Suspension	Semi-elliptic leaf springs front and rear
Brakes	4-wheel hydraulic, 10.98in front discs, 11in rear drums

Dimensions

Wheelbase	93.5in
Track	51.5in
Overall length	147.75in
Overall width	68.5in (including side-mounted spare wheel)
Overall height (top up)	67.5in
Curb weight	2,650lb

AMC wanted to offer an automatic gearbox, which was not available for it. All CJ-7s would feature Quadra-Trac, at least to begin with.

The whole range was imported in right-hand drive form, using components originally sourced from Australian and Postal Service models. The SJs were significantly cheaper than the Range Rover, and this time there was a far better sales

The 1976 Cherokee, with two doors. The following year a four-door Cherokee would join the line-up.

record. The Rangie was in short supply, which encouraged buyers to look at the Jeeps. If they bought the Cherokee, they found the fuel consumption to be comparable, but the acceleration to be far better: 0–60mph (0–100kmph) in 12.3 seconds. Turnover for Jeep UK Ltd exceeded £6 million in the first ten months, through fifty-two dealers. A further fifteen dealers

Chris Tennant, managing director of Jeep UK and TKM Motor Services with a CJ-7 Renegade and a Cherokee Chief. Both vehicles are Toledo-built with right-hand drive. Note the Lucas indicators and sidelights on the front wings of the CJ-7. The flared wheel arches of the Cherokee Chief were a JS customer-led modification to allow the fitting of serious off-road tyres.

were to be signed on by the end of 1979, and Jeep's share of the UK four-wheel-drive market would climb to a high of 18 per cent.

A NEW SMALL ENGINE

AMC still did not have a four-cylinder engine for its passenger cars, and it was losing out to Ford's Pinto and Maverick, and GM's Vega. There was not the money to develop a new four-cylinder engine of their own. Instead, in May of 1975 negotiations began with Volkswagen-Audi to manufacture the 122ci (1984cc) OHC VAG engine in a $40 million plant in Richmond, Indiana. This engine had been used in VW light trucks and the Audi 100 saloon. In the meantime German-built VAG engines were brought over and installed as an option in the Concord and the Gremlin.

CHANGES AT THE TOP

In May 1977, William Luneburg reached retirement age and left American Motors. In October, Roy Chapin moved from CEO to chairman, and his post was taken by Gerald C. Meyers, the man who had recommended that Jeep should be left well alone. Meyers must have been glad his advice had been disregarded. The changes made by AMC throughout the entire Jeep range were right: for instance, at the end of 1971 US sales of CJs had dropped to 12,000 units for the year; two years on, and the figure was up to over 31,000. Jeep as a brand won 40 per cent of the American off-road market in 1976, peaking at over 43,000, and in 1979, sales of the new CJ-7, even alongside the CJ-5, would reach a record at over 55,000. The 1977 model year saw even more detail and engineering improvements across the Jeep range.

The J-20 truck with a 132in (3,353mm) wheelbase and after-market top for the pickup bed. Eight-stud wheels were fitted to the heavier capacity version. This is an official UK right-hand-drive import.

It would have been celebrations all round at American Motors had the sales of the passenger cars matched those of Jeep – but they didn't, and despite Jeep Division's success, it was a small enterprise in comparison to the passenger car division, its profits nowhere near enough to counter the loss made by the rest of the Corporation. 1978's losses of close on $84m threatened the development of an exciting new Jeep model, but help was already at hand from across the Atlantic.

This picture is taken from the 1977 British brochure; it shows two versions of the CJ-7, the Golden Eagle (right) and a 'working' model in the newly rebuilt St Katherine's Dock, by Tower Bridge. The Golden Eagle package offered a roll bar, sports wheels, a Levi's hood, ABS wing extensions, extra instruments and a spare tyre lock. Colours available were thrush brown, gold, white and black. Both vehicles are purpose-built in right-hand drive, and include UK specification Lucas indicators.

7   French Partners and a New Concept

At the end of the 1970s, France's Régie Nationale des Usines Renault – state-owned since 1945 – was the third biggest car producer in Europe. In terms of cars and trucks produced, it was number eight in the world, turning out close on two million vehicles for home and export markets. This was in sharp contrast to AMC, who only managed a little over half a million. Despite a roller-coaster ride in the chaotic economic climate of the 1970s, Renault averaged a good profit.

Now Renault was looking across the North Atlantic. The USA was becoming more receptive to European-sized cars, but it was Japan that was taking an ever-increasing share of the two million units – fast approaching 20 per cent of the market – that the US imported in 1977. Renault had tried selling in the US before, but with disastrous results: in the late 1950s the Dauphine had virtually destroyed Renault's reputation by rusting away to nothing in just a couple of years. Renault's 1977 try looked more promising, and sales of the little 5, marketed as 'Le Car', doubled on the previous year to over 13,000.

At this juncture Renault looked to harness AMC's dealer network, to establish themselves as a big name in the US. There had been connections between AMC, Kaiser and Renault in Argentina, and in 1968 Renault bought the Cordoba opera-tion. In March 1978 Renault signed a 'Letter of Intent' with the American Motors Corporation for AMC dealers to sell

Renault cars in the US and Canada.

Roy Chapin retired in October 1978, and Gerald Meyers took on the post of CEO and, for a brief time, that of chairman. The subsequent appointment of Paul Tippet from the Singer Sewing machine company as the new chairman raised a few questions, but Meyers then surprised the auto

Gerald C. Meyers, appointed CEO of American Motors in 1978.

123

A 1983 CJ-7 Renegade in UK specification right-hand drive, with new-style front indicators and side lights. This model could be had with a choice of the 258ci six or the 151ci four.

world by announcing that AMC would join a world-wide group of car makers, and that he had entered serious negotiations with Renault with this in mind. In January 1979 the dealership agreement was signed with Renault, and now AMC could offer the new 18 and Le Car in the sub-compact market. The agreement would extend to sales of Renault cars in Canada and South America, too. A new Renault, the X42, was being designed for a world market. It would fit between Le Car and the 18, and AMC would build it for US sale. Renault had anticipated that some contribution to plant costs might have to be made, as AMC would not be able to afford the expense on its own of funding the tooling for the new car, but the way in which it was done surprised all. There had been no mention of any merger between AMC or Renault, but in October 1979 it was announced that Renault would purchase some 22 per cent of AMC stock.

Thanks largely to Jeep and their non-automotive subsidiaries, AMC was profitable in 1978. The following year, 1979, started well because America bought enough of the new Concord and Spirit, but sales collapsed in the last quarter. The Shah of Iran was deposed in January 1979, and after only a few months of the new regime of the Ayatollah Khomeni the price of crude oil rose considerably. The US economy went into recession, inflation rose to over 15 per cent, and the price of a gallon of gas doubled. Those big cars were left on the dealers' lots, and everyone wanted small cars. AMC had them, but with big sixes or V8s they weren't the most fuel-efficient. AMC's loss for 1980 was an incredible $155,672,000: America's fourth-largest auto makers were in desperate straits. Even Jeep suffered. 1980 was the third lowest production year in the history of the brand, after 1954 and 1971, and the worst for profitability. Total production more

than halved, from over 134,000 vehicles to 62,000.

RENAULT TAKE A BIGGER SLICE

These losses forced Gerald Meyers into a move he hadn't intended: the sale of further AMC stock to Renault. $122.5 million would give the French a 46.4 per cent stake in AMC. Jeep had the potential to return to profitability, but its revenue was too small to wipe out AMC's massive debt. The only alternative was oblivion. When AMC's top executives showed their Renault counterparts round the whole of the business, they naturally wanted to demonstrate how great the Jeep was; to this end, a visit was organized to a Jeep Jamboree. For Jeep enthusiasts this is the trip of a lifetime, where they can really get out into the

The year 1979 was a double silver anniversary, when American Motors celebrated twenty-five years of its founding, and twenty-five years of the CJ-5. This is the special edition Renegade built for the occasion.

mountains and backwoods and enjoy their Jeeps. AMC's executives played up the importance of this market, but the spectacle was quite unappreciated by some of the Frenchmen. Certainly Renault's marketing people were quick to realize the opportunities, but some of the engineers found it hard to come to terms with what Jeep and the whole off-road business was all about. Old Hotchkisses were sold off to farmers and small traders, but using such a vehicle for leisure was what hippies might do; it just wasn't *chic*.

ECONOMY ENGINES

A new four-cylinder. . .

The VAG engine was abandoned. It wasn't powerful enough for either the passenger cars or the CJs, and it would cost more to make than the existing six-cylinder – and there wasn't the time or the money to cut *this* engine down to a four-pot. Instead, AMC went to General Motors for the four-cylinder OHV Pontiac 'Iron Duke' from the 1975 Astre. This 151ci, 82bhp engine would give the best fuel consumption and emissions figures yet for any AMC Jeep.

Both CJ-5 and CJ-7 models were available in the UK market, but this CJ-5, like the Honcho, is left-hand drive, nor does it have European specification lights. Wind-up windows were available for the soft-top CJ-7 for 1980. Weight reductions were made, with light alloy gearboxes and lighter Dana 300 transfer cases and a lighter auto gearbox.

...And diesel power once more

There was very little interest in diesel power in the American market, but for the rest of the world, Jeep had to offer an oil-burner in the CJs to compete with Land Rover and Toyota. The light diesel engines made in the US were unsuitable because they were low-revving commercial units, so Jeep had to look further afield. Perkins was one of the early companies investigated, but the new engines under development proved unreliable. Eventually General Motors was found to have what was wanted; they were already supplying four-cylinder petrol engines to AMC, and they had a financial holding in the Japanese Isuzu company – so the 2.4-litre, four-cylinder

Isuzu diesel was chosen.

Renault undertook a reciprocal arrangement to sell CJs in over 9,000 dealers in France and also in Belgium; moreover in a country with very high petrol prices, they naturally wanted to offer a diesel engine. But Renault would not accept a Japanese engine in France, and put forward an argument for either their own 2.1 litre four-cylinder or a 2.5 litre Fiat. The choice fell, not surprisingly, on the Renault. It was shipped to Toledo for installation in the CJ-5, tipped over to the right by five degrees to clear the bonnet, and mated to a five-speed manual gearbox and two-speed transfer case. For the French market there would be a base model, plus Renegade and Laredo options, and later the Texan version of the

The legend on the bonnet of this CJ-7 says it all. Although there was little or no interest in diesel vehicles in the US – the Americans preferred the four-cylinder petrol engine as an economy option – the Jeep Corporation needed a diesel engine for the export market. With the exception of France, that need was met by a 2.4-litre four-cylinder Isuzu.

CJ-7. The GM four-cylinder petrol engine was available as an option to the diesel. Thus in March 1981, Hotchkiss notwithstanding, and in far happier circumstances, the first shipment of American-made Jeeps since 1944 set off for France!

SJ- AND J-SERIES DECLINE

In the shadow of increasing fuel prices and demand for smaller cars, the Wagoneer soldiered on. A new Quadra-Trac system gave the old campaigner unprecedented performance off road and on. Part-time four-wheel drive was offered for the Cherokee and Wagoneer, and in 1980 a 258ci in-line six returned in the top-line model. This was a new, much lighter, fuel-efficient version, with aluminium replacing iron for components such as the water pump. J-Series trucks began losing sales, despite a new, smoother roof-line for 1981, and the re-introduction of the stepside body and an optional five-speed manual gearbox. SJ sales were dropping too, although the decline of the luxury end was halted by the introduction of the super-luxury Wagoneer

The 1980 Cherokee Laredo, with chrome wheels, roof rails and graphics. In the Senior Jeep series, Cherokee Limited and Wagoneer models were also offered in the UK. A new, lightweight four-speed manual gearbox was standard for the Cherokee for 1980, as was the option of Quadra-Trac with a dual-range transfer case.

Six-cylinder J-10 Jeep trucks were sold as part of the UK range, including this 1980 120in (3,048mm)-wheelbase Honcho. This is an idyllic rural English setting, although unlike the models actually sold here, the example shown is left-hand drive. The J-10 shared the Cherokee's weight-saving four-speed manual gearbox and Dana 300 transfer case. The larger J-20 would offer a 'creeper' first gear for really heavy loads. As well as being tough, the trucks would also offer luxury features like power windows, power door locks, a radio/cassette player and carpets.

Limited, and in 1981 the even better specification Brougham.

THE CJ-8 SCRAMBLER

Compact leisure trucks with enough space for a motorcycle or surfboards in the back, were a boom market. Japanese-made models, either sold under their own names or badged by one of the Big Three, were selling well: Renault did not make a strong half-ton

pickup, AMC did not have those all-too-useful Japanese connections, and there was nothing in the existing Jeep range that would compete. The CJ-6 had gone from the domestic market by 1976. The smallest that AMC could offer was the CJ-7, but it didn't have a decent pickup bed that could take a useful load for the tradesman, or a couple of motorcycles for the leisure user. The answer was simple: stretch the CJ-7. The result was the CJ-8 Scrambler, which hit the showrooms in the spring of 1981. The wheelbase

CJ-8 Pickup offers a generous cargo bed for work or recreational gear.

CJ-8 Utility is designed to carry 9 passengers.

The CJ-8 Scrambler in (top) pickup version, with a standard soft half top and optional hard top and steel doors; and (bottom) the nine-seat Utility with a full soft top and fabric doors – six passengers could be sat sideways in the rear of the Utility, with three abreast on the front seat. There were dress-up versions too: the SR and SL Sport at first, but for 1985, the trim options were aligned with the CJ-7. There was the Renegade or the more expensive Laredo models; in the latter, in addition to the Renegade's standard roll bar, wheel arch extensions, spare wheel lock and special paint and decals, the Laredo had chrome bumpers, grille and wheels, and distinctive striping and lettering.

was some 10in (254mm) longer than the CJ-7 at 103.5in (2,629mm), but another 10in of pickup bed gave the Scrambler an overall length of 117.3in (2,979mm). All Scramblers were offered with the new lightweight 258ci six, the 151ci GM four-pot, or the 2.4-litre Isuzu diesel. The 304ci V8 was no longer available, either for Jeep or AMC passenger cars.

Jeep Corporation CJ-8 Scrambler (1981–86)

Engines
6-Cylinder
Type	ohv in-line 6
Bore x stroke	3.75 x 3.90in
Capacity	258cc (4.2ltr)
Main bearings	7
Max. power	110bhp @ 3500rpm
Max. torque	195lb/ft @ 2000rpm

4-Cylinder
Type	GMC ohv in-line 4
Bore x stroke	4 x 3in
Capacity	151cu in (2.45ltr)
Main bearings	5
Max. power	82bhp @ 4000rpm
Max. torque	125lb/ft @ 2600rpm

Chassis
Transmission	Warner 4-speed manual, all synchromesh, optional Chrysler Torqueflite 3-speed automatic
Turning circle	37.6ft
Transfer case	2-speed, part time four-wheel drive
Suspension	Semi-elliptic leaf springs front and rear
Brakes	4-wheel hydraulic, 10.98in front discs, 11in rear drums

Dimensions
Wheelbase	103.5in
Track	51.5in
Overall length	177.3in
Overall width	68.6in
Overall height (top up)	67.5in
Curb weight	2,759lb

CRISIS POINT FOR AMC'S PASSENGER CARS

American Motors' new home-designed models – the Concord, the Spirit and the four-wheel-drive Eagle – were all based on the Hornet platform. Power was from the General Motors' four-cylinder engine or the 258ci six. These models were not selling, well however. The sub-compact sector was met as planned by two Renault models, Le Car and the 18, but AMC's models were hardly state-of-the-art, and nobody was queuing to buy them; nor would America spend hard-earned money on cars from a company with such a doubtful future – they would for most of the Jeep lines, and to a lesser extent for Renault, but for AMC's passenger cars, it was a different story. Sales of these would drop even more, spelling serious trouble for Kenosha.

MORE CHANGES AT THE TOP

The loss of confidence in AMC's own passenger cars meant a change at the top. Renault were now calling the shots at American Motors. Gerald Meyers was moved out of the CEO post in January 1982, to be replaced by a Renault man, Jose Dedeurwaerder; Paul Tippet became the new chairman. AM General had developed the largest successor to the Jeep ever seen: the HUMVEE, or Hummer. Now, as cash was desperately needed, AM General was sold off to LTV for $170 million.

NEW RENAULT MODELS

Renault's new compact sedan, the X42, was introduced globally in late 1982. Known in Europe as the 9, the US version was named the Alliance, and it went into production in Kenosha at the same time. Welcomed unanimously by the dealers, it made a good start, *Motor Trend* magazine voting it car of the year; however, two effects worked against it. Reliability and durability problems soon appeared, and the price of gasoline fell: as a result of the latter, America once again began buying bigger-engined cars, and sales of the Alliance collapsed. Even the arrival of the 1.7-litre Encore hatchback (known as the 11 in Europe), failed to effect a change. However, there was something of an unexpected reversal of fortunes in 1984, when AMC made their first real profit since 1978, whereas Renault's losses as a company were $1.7 billion. Ironically the Concord and Spirit were dropped for 1984; only the Eagle remained.

A RETURN TO AUSTRALIA

In 1980 American Motors looked once more at the Australian market. Mitsubishi,

Nissan, Daihatsu and Toyota had pushed Land Rover out of the running as the major supplier of cross-country vehicles, due as much to reliability as the availability of more comfortable models. This time Jeep Corporation would run the business themselves, setting up Jeep Australia Pty Ltd. A local company, LWC Industries, would assemble knock-down kits of the CJ-7, and also the Cherokee; the latter would be the only passenger model Senior Jeep ever assembled on foreign soil. The Australians share with Americans a love of the pickup truck, but they have their own name: the 'ute' – and two Jeep 'utes' joined the line-up. They were the hybrid J-10 truck in short and standard wheelbase versions; and the CJ-8, sold in Australia as the Overlander. The CJ-10 was a hybrid that manifested itself in two forms: a short wheelbase model, built on a CJ-7 frame; and a much larger model on a J-Series truck frame. The smaller was primarily a military vehicle, used as an aircraft tug in the USA, but also bought by some buyers in Australia. The larger was an 'export only' model, sent to both Venezuela and Australia. The large Australian models, powered by 258ci sixes, were bought for use as light trucks in the mining industry.

It was difficult to judge how truly successful Jeep vehicles might have been in Australia, for they were the victims of a change in the exchange rate. During the early 1980s the value of the US dollar against the Australian dollar almost doubled, increasing the value of the imported components – and thus the price of Jeeps – to an unrealistic high. Renault, now in control at American Motors, pulled the plug on the Australian operation in 1984. The sudden withdrawal was described by one Australian motoring writer as 'the most successful retreat since the ANZACs at Gallipoli'. It was even more regrettable in

Jeep's four-wheel-drive systems: Quadra-Trac and the new generation

Whilst part-time four-wheel drive had been an essential part of Jeep's equipment since its beginnings, its use was for off-road conditions. But permanent four-wheel drive could be a great asset to safety in bad weather on the highway. For this, a centre differential was vital, to avoid drive-line wind-up and excess axle and tyre wear. Borg-Warner's Quadra-Trac centre differential had its drawbacks. It was virtually hand-built, and in consequence expensive. It was also noisy, and it could only handle engines of up to 285bhp.

Harry Ferguson Research in Coventry had been working on the problem of developing a really versatile centre differential since the late 1950s, coming up with their own mechanical system, the Monolock, around the early 1960s. A version was fitted to the Jensen FF, but proved troublesome in use. But it was the Ferguson company's invention of a viscous control unit (VC) in 1968 that made permanent four-wheel drive a practical proposition for road cars. This was patented under two names: A. P. R. Rolt (Tony Rolt, one of the founders of the company); and Derek Gardner, the engineer who put in a great deal of work in its development. In 1986, Rolt was awarded the Institute of the Motor Industry's Castrol gold medal for the development of the viscous coupling.

New Process Gear was a joint venture between Chrysler and General Motors. The company took out a licence for Ferguson's (by this time FF Developments) VC in 1978, and built a wholly new Quadra-Trac system for Jeep. The viscous coupling consists of two sets of concentric vanes running in an enclosed chamber. One set is attached to the input shaft, the other to the output, but they are interspersed with each other. The secret of the coupling is a remarkable oil that, unlike other oils, actually gets thicker as it gets hotter.

This oil allows the VC to detect changes in traction and wheel speed, to almost instantaneously supply power at different propshaft speeds, and provide the right amount of power to the wheel that demands it, whatever the speed or the going. The viscous coupling was also cheaper to build, and silent in operation. The VC-equipped Quadra-Trac system, designated as Model NP 219, was available for the 1980 model year on Wagoneers, Cherokees and trucks. Operated by a single control, 4WD high lock, 4WD high, neutral and 4WD low could be selected.

NP 208 TRANSFER CASE

This New Process Gear case was standard on the Senior Jeeps from 1980. It was a basic system, although refined and in a lightweight alloy casing, and available with manual or automatic transmissions. The drive could be set to 2WD, 4WD high, neutral and 4WD low via a single lever.

DANA 300

The Dana 300 transfer case would be standard on all CJs, giving 2WD high, 4WD high, neutral and 4WD low. The new NP 219 Quadra-Trac would be available as an option for CJ-7 from 1980.

COMMAND-TRAC

Command-Trac, standard on the XJ Cherokee and YJ Wrangler, was a simple system, with a direct drive to both axles. It is a part-time system, very much in the mould of the original Spicer transfer case used in the old flat-fender Jeeps, although more finely engineered. Just like the original transfer case, Command-Trac was only for off-road or on snowy highway conditions, to prevent drive-line wind-up.

SELEC-TRAC

Selec-Trac has a centre differential, but unlike Quadra-Trac it is, as its name suggests, a selectable part-time system: two-wheel drive, disconnecting the front axle to minimize tyre wear and improve fuel consumption, or four-wheel drive. Selec-Trac can be used in four-wheel-drive mode on a dry highway for extra traction at higher speeds or in wet weather. The drive options can be easily selected with a single lever. As well as being an option for the new XJ Cherokee, Selec-Trac became available for the revised SJ from 1983.

that those AMC executives running the Australian business felt that Renault should have stood loyal to their commitment for the long term: they had their own dealer network that could have saved overheads, and more significantly, there was a revolutionary new model on the way that might have brought success quite quickly.

THE ALL-NEW CHEROKEE

On the drawing board by the end of the 1970s was a revolutionary replacement for the Senior Jeep; it would be the first completely new design since the J-Series in 1963. Originally it was to be a big, conventional body-on-frame model in the mould of the SJ. However, the 1979 fuel crisis, so far as the new car's development programme was concerned, came at the right time. Now the need for a light, compact vehicle totally altered the concept of the XJ. The four-wheel-drive Eagle was of unitary construction, with strong, welded-on frame rails. The experience gained with it undoubtedly gave AMC the confidence to go ahead with what they described as a 'Uniframe' construction for the XJ. With a rigid body, the suspension system would have to handle the tortures of off-road work on its own. One particular Renault engineer, François Castaign, would be on the team designing the suspension system. The XJ would be in sharp contrast to his previous job: chief engineer of Renault's highly successful Formula One team.

The XJ would have live axles front and rear, and this would give far greater articulation off-road than IFS, and would not strain driveshaft joints when the suspension was at full articulation. A wholly new four-link 'Quadra-Link' front suspension was also designed which would not only give that full articulation, but would guar-antee a more comfortable ride on the highway, too. The pinion of the front differential was placed above the axle centre-line instead of below it, as convention would expect, as this reduced the angle of the front driveshaft in a such a short vehicle. Coil springs would take up too much luggage space in the rear of the compact XJ, so leaf-spring rear suspension was used for the rear axle.

XJ's light weight would allow a smaller, fuel-efficient engine, and this would be AMC's first ever four-cylinder engine. A conventional 2.5-litre, five main bearing, overhead valve, in-line engine, it would also replace the 'Iron Duke' in the Eagle. It shared internal components such as connecting rods, rockers and pushrods with the 258ci six, but it was a new block, more square than the 258. The bore was 3.88in compared to the 258's 3.75in, and the 3.19in stroke was shorter than the six's 3.9in. Even with full pollution control and catalytic converter, this engine, with electronic ignition, turned out 105bhp at 5,000rpm and a tidy 132lb/ft. of torque at 2,800rpm. Most significant for the XJ was the choice of two four-wheel-drive systems: standard was the part-time Command-Trac, with vacuum-operated, shift-on-the-fly facility; or there was the extra cost Selec-Trac.

A bigger engine option was needed, but rather than use the improved 258ci in-line six, AMC turned once again to General Motors, and bought in the new 60° engine of 173ci (2.82 litre). Producing 115bhp and 145lb/ft torque, it had been designed for GM's new mid-sized, front-wheel-drive models. Coupled to it and the four-cylinder base engine there was the choice of five-speed manual or three-speed automatic transmissions.

Just like Brooks Stevens some thirty-odd years before, Jeep's stylists had to come up with a timeless design that not only embod-

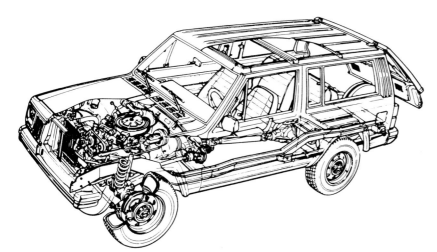

The XJ Cherokee in cut-away. The frame rails of the Uniframe construction can be clearly seen, as well as the layout of the driveline, the coil springs for the front axle and the leaf springs at the rear.

ied a Jeep look, but bridged the gap between a conventional sedan and a credible off-roader. The best place to start was at the front, with a vertical slat grille that identified the XJ as a Jeep product. The trend in the late seventies and early eighties was for sharp-edged lines: these would give that rugged look, but follow contemporary passenger-car styling. The XJ would offer a choice of two or four doors at the start, giving it a head start on its intended rival, the Chevy Blazer, which was just a two-door design. Besides, the Blazer and the Ford Bronco had the appearance of being a pickup with a passenger body stuck on, which in reality was what they were, but the XJ had an integrated design making it as much a passenger car as it was an off-roader.

It was as compact as the designers intended. Although its wheelbase was 1in (25mm) longer than the Chevy Blazer, it was 5in (127mm) shorter overall, and a full 21in (533mm) shorter than the SJ. At 2,886lb (1,309kg) it was the lightest of the three, as compared to the Chevy's 3,150lb (1,429kg) and the SJ Wagoneer's huge 4,025lb (1,826kg).

There were to be two main model lines,

and Jeep stuck with tradition when they named the new babies: the base model would be the Cherokee, with trim options called Pioneer and Cherokee Chief, and it would be available with two or four doors. Up-market models would be the Wagoneer, available in four-door only. For this top-liner there would be the Brougham version, and the Limited, with fake wood side panels.

The Toledo plant was geared up to make the XJ. Renault had an interest in Cybotech, a company that manufactured robot assembly machines, and these robots were installed on the XJ production lines. The XJ was launched in late 1983, for the 1984 model year. The $250 million the XJ had cost was money well spent. Almost immediately it took market share from its rivals from GM and Ford, and the public's welcome was echoed by three major off-road magazines, who named it '4x4 of the Year'. Following the XJ's announcement, AMC's marketing group vice-president, Joseph Cappy, said: 'Market studies indicate that by 1985 more than half the sales of four-wheel-drive vehicles will be in the compact segment, as compared to only 2 per cent in 1978'. Cappy's estimate was

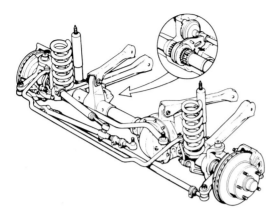

The Quadra-Link front suspension from the XJ. Two parallel leading links are mounted at the extreme ends of the axle. The two inner ones are angled in to provide firm lateral location without using an anti-roll bar, which would limit axle articulation off-road. The insert shows the 'axle disconnect' facility for easier servicing.

conservative: the share actually grew to 70 per cent.

THE GRAND WAGONEER

For 1983, understandably, the SJ Cherokee bit the dust. The top line SJ model stayed, re-named Grand Wagoneer. Surprisingly, this 'Grand Daddy in four-wheel drive' seemed to take on a new lease of life, with an almost 50 per cent increase in sales. Its buyers were the more affluent, older Americans who did not have to worry about the price of gasoline, and simply preferred the size of car they had enjoyed for decades.

FAREWELL TO THE CJ-5

There were safety questions raised over the CJ-5. It was prone to roll over in novice hands, and was unstable in braking from high speeds. Even so, after twenty-nine years of production, the CJ-5 had done as

The 1986 XJ Wagoneer, identified by its stacked headlights. Only around one in ten XJs were top-line Wagoneers.

Jeep Corporation XJ Cherokee, Wagoneer and Comanche (Wagoneer 1984–87, Cherokee 1984–90)

Engines
4-Cylinder

Type	ohv in-line 4
Bore x stroke	3.88 x 3.19in
Capacity	150.45cu in (2.5ltr)
Main bearings	5
Max. power	105bhp @ 5000rpm
Max. torque	132lb/ft @ 2800rpm

V6

Type	GMC ohv V6
Bore x stroke	3.50 x 2.99in
Capacity	151cu in (2.8ltr)
Main bearings	4
Max. power	115bhp @ 5000rpm
Max. torque	145lb/ft @ 2400rpm

Renault 4-Cylinder Turbo Diesel

Type	ohv in-line 4
Bore x stroke	3.49 x 3.51in
Capacity	126cu in (2.1ltr)
Main bearings	5
Max. power	82bhp @ 32500rpm
Max. torque	132lb/ft @ 3000rpm

Chassis

Transmission	4-speed manual, all synchromesh, optional Chrysler Torqueflite 3-speed automatic (not available with diesel engine)
Turning circle	36.1ft
Transfer case	Command-Trac or optional Selec-Trac 2-speed, part time highway compatible four-wheel drive
Suspension (front)	Quadra-Link four-leading links with two coil springs, solid axle
Suspension (rear)	Solid axle with semi-elliptic leaf springs
Brakes	4-wheel hydraulic, 10.98in front discs, 10in rear drums

Dimensions

Wheelbase	101.4in
Track	58in
Overall length	165.3in
Overall width	70.5in
Overall height	64.1in

Jeep in British Fire Brigades

In a time when many British Fire Brigades were investing in 6x4 Range Rover crash tenders, two brigades, Staffordshire and East Sussex, chose Jeeps instead. In the 1970s East Sussex Fire Brigade were using Ford Transits, but these didn't have enough power to haul all the equipment needed and keep up a decent speed. They investigated the Range Rover conversions, but these were getting a reputation for being a little unstable. For power and carrying capacity the only alternative would be an American vehicle.

The first J-20 rescue tender bought by East Sussex Fire Brigade.

AMC were exporting Jeep vehicles to Iran. When the Shah was toppled in 1979, a shipment, including J-Series models, was left lying off the Iranian coast for some months, with its cargo slowly rusting on the deck. The ship was eventually diverted to the UK via Saudi Arabia, and the cargo sold off. A Jeep J-20 chassis with a 350cu in V8, Torqueflite transmission and Quadra-Trac became available to East Sussex Fire Brigade. The chassis was stretched and a floating rear axle added. Specialist builder Pilcher Green of Burgess Hill, West Sussex fitted it with a crash tender body. The Fire Brigade's own engineering section added all the specialist equipment needed for rescue work both in road traffic accidents and the kind of emergencies encountered in the open countryside, farms and the adjacent Ashdown Forest.

East Sussex ordered two more J-20s in 1983, and a fourth the following year. This time the body was supplied by Angloco of West Yorkshire, on a chassis lengthened by West Midlands American Vehicles. The powertrain was a little different too, with a two-speed transfer box, but no Quadra-Trac.

All four of the 4.5 tonne trucks served well, although the last vehicle to be delivered was written off in an accident. The remaining three were retired from mainline duties in the early 1990s, when they were transferred to training purposes and replaced by GMC 4x4 V8 diesel units. Oxford Airport also used a J-20 fire truck. The original J-20 and the surviving Sussex models are all now in preservation. The last, which is pictured, went to a private owner in August 1998.

much for civilian sales as the old MB had to introduce the jeep to the world. Over 600,000 had been built, not far short of the total wartime production. Now, as 1983 drew to a close, it was no more.

XJ IMPROVEMENTS

The Renault 2.1 diesel, in turbocharged form, was offered in Cherokee and Wagoneer for 1985. AMC predicted a fuel consumption of 31mpg (11ltr/100km) in city driving. Although it was offered in the American market (California excepted),

Comanche (1985–92)

Engines
Type   As per Cherokee and Wagoneer

Chassis
Transmission   4-speed manual, all synchromesh, optional Chrysler Torqueflite 3-speed automatic
Turning circle   36.1ft
Transfer case   Command-Trac part-time or optional Selec-Trac 2-speed, part time highway compatible four-wheel drive
Suspension (front)   Quadra-Link four-leading links with two coil springs, solid axle
Suspension (rear)   Solid axle with semi-elliptic leaf springs
Brakes   4-wheel hydraulic, 10.98in front discs, 10in rear drums

Dimensions
Wheelbase   119.9in
Track   57in
Overall length   195.5in
Overall width   71.7in
Overall height   64.7in
Curb weight   3,200lb

the principal aim for this engine was Europe, as Renault were to offer the XJ through their own dealerships. 'The Jeep from Renault' said the stickers in the back windows of all XJs sold in France. A two-wheel drive version of Cherokee, the Sportwagon, was introduced from March 1985. It used a simple tube axle, hung on the Quadra-Link front suspension, and was a cheap-to-make answer to the two-wheel-drive Chevy Blazer. The Cherokee boosted Jeep's sales by 90,000 for 1984, their best ever year, with a daily average output from Toledo of 824 vehicles.

UK DISTRIBUTION

Howes Motors of Eaton Bray, Berkshire, and other dealers took over Jeep distribution on an independent basis from Jeep UK Ltd, but it looked as if things would change again. As well as selling Jeeps in France and Belgium, Renault planned to sell them in the UK through their own dealers, and announced their intention to do so by August 1982 – but in the spring of the following year, they backed out. By September 1984, Jeep Concessionaires of Stockport were to be the new Jeep agents for the UK. However, UK Jeep buyers would only have the Renegade at this time: officially the XJ would not be available for the UK, and nor would the SJ Grand Wagoneer.

THE COMANCHE

For the 1986 model year an XJ-based pick-up, the Comanche, was introduced. This was the first new generation of Jeep pick-ups since the J-series in 1963, and was soon to replace the CJ-8. Where the Scrambler

The Comanche pickup, introduced in 1986, was offered with a choice of trim levels to cater for the leisure and commercial markets: the base 'Custom' was for the business user, and the more up-market 'X' and 'XLS' was for the sport user, and offered exterior decor packages.

merely held a presence for Jeep in the light truck market, the Comanche, with its longer 119.6in (3,038mm) wheelbase made a significant contribution of its own. It was unique not only as a unit construction truck, but in its weight range too: it was slightly bigger than the Japanese models, though not as heavy as its home-built rivals. In two years, some 100 pre-production vehicles were tested to destruction over 500,000 miles (804,500km), to ensure that the Uniframe construction was strong enough for the job. This was vital, as the pickup bed was fixed to the floorpan alone, and not integral with the cab.

At 119.7in (3,040mm) the wheelbase was some 18in (46mm) longer than the XJ passenger car. A two-wheel-drive version was also made, as some 75 per cent of the light

truck market was for two-wheel-drive vehicles, and there were Command-Trac or Select-Trac four-wheel-drive options. The engine options were the same – the 2.5-litre four, the 2.8-litre V6 or the 2.1-litre Renault turbo diesel – as were the four-speed manual, and the optional five-speed manual, plus three-speed auto transmissions for the petrol models.

THE WRANGLER

In late 1985, AMC's vice-president of sales and marketing, Joe Cappy, set the automotive world on its heels by announcing that the Jeep was to be killed off. The market, he said, was moving towards lighter, more modern station-wagon type vehicles like

The YJ Wrangler, introduced in the spring of 1986, after Joe Cappy stunned the off-road world by announcing the death of the Jeep.

the XJ. Reaction to this news by Jeep fans was one of dismay and outrage, but Cappy was in fact executing a clever publicity programme. The motoring world's attention was now fixed on one of the true great classics, for it is true that you only really appreciate something when it's gone. In reality, Cappy's great coup was that he had only killed off the CJ-7.

All ready for production at a brand-new Canadian factory in Brampton, Ontario, was the third generation of the traditional Jeep, the new YJ Wrangler: it was announced in March 1986. The principles of construction were the same as the CJ's, being body-on-frame, but that frame was totally different. It was a much more rigid perimeter type, using much of the mechanical components from the XJ, but with leaf springs on the front end instead of the XJ's Quadra-Link coil set-up.

Power was from the new AMC 2.5-litre four, or the revamped 258ci in-line six. Command-Trac was standard, coupled to a five-speed manual gearbox or a Torqueflite three-speed auto. Plastic wing extensions covered the much wider, 58in (1,473mm) track of the XJ axles. A basic CJ-7 rear tub was used, though new sheet metal in broadly traditional style was on the front; also the top half of the grille was angled back slightly – and the rectangular headlights that were set into it had the purists choking on their camp fire-brewed coffee.

Jeep Corporation YJ Wrangler (1986–96)

Engines

In-Line Six

Type	ohv in-line 6-cylinder
Bore x stroke	3.75 x 3.90in
Capacity	258cu in (4.2ltr)
Main bearings	7
Max. power	112bhp @ 3200rpm
Max. torque	210lb/ft @ 2000rpm

In-Line Four

Type	ohv in-line 4-cylinder
Bore x stroke	3.88 x 3.19in
Capacity	150.45cu in (2.5ltr)
Main bearings	5
Max. power	117bhp @ 5000rpm
Max. torque	135lb/ft @ 3500rpm

Chassis

Transmission	4-speed manual, all synchromesh, optional 5-speed manual or 3-speed Torqueflite automatic
Turning circle	33.6ft
Transfer case	Command-Trac 2-speed, part time 4WD
Suspension	Semi-elliptic leaf springs front and rear
Brakes	4-wheel hydraulic, 11.02 front discs, 9.84in rear drums

Dimensions

Wheelbase	93.5in
Track	58in
Overall length	152in
Overall width	66in
Overall height (top up)	68.1in
Curb weight	3,100lb

Unlike the 'old hands' who knew the inherent dangers of off-road driving and used their Jeeps sensibly and much more often off-road, the new breed of Jeep owners used them as daily drivers on the street. And when these 'greenhorns' took their CJs into rough country, or cornered them too hard on the highway, they were lost when trouble occurred. Although its height to the top of the windscreen was about the same as an early CJ-5 (on standard wheels and tyres), the Wrangler had a much wider track and a lower centre of gravity, and was safer as a result. A full roll cage was standard; it added the safety dimension, and it contributed to the overall stiffness of the vehicle. By making the Wrangler inherently safer, AMC engineered their way neatly and responsibly out of any potential law suits.

Whilst the chassis improvements helped soften the road ride in comparison with the CJs, it was still a Jeep in its off-road performance: there were no compromises on that

The Cherokee Sportwagon was the base model in the XJ series. This version is the two-wheel-drive Pioneer.

score. AMC had taken the traditional Jeep features and re-configured them with modern technology. If you hated a firm ride on the highway and hated the wind noise at over 30mph (50kmph), tough. If you accepted these as the price you paid for unequalled performance off-road, you were a true Jeep enthusiast and you weren't disappointed with the Wrangler. The lower profile, necessary for highway safety, reduced the ground clearance somewhat. For the serious, experienced off-roader, it was nothing that a 2in (50mm) suspension lift wouldn't cure. . . but weren't you going to do that anyway?

TALKING UP THE ODDS

'This is our year: 1987!' said AMC's Joe Cappy, now promoted to chief executive officer. Jose Dedeurwaerder was made president, and Pierre Semerena the new chairman. At the end of 1986 Cappy was speaking optimistically about the launch of a new Renault model, the Medallion (known in Europe as the 21), claiming that the new car would more than hold its own in the face of Japanese and other European competition.

On the surface, Cappy had something to shout about, particularly as there was another new Renault passenger car in the pipeline: the X58, and its coupe version, the X59. Styled by Giorgio Guigiaro, it was a booted version of the big V6 25, named the Premier, for which both Régie Renault and Kenosha had great hopes. With it, AMC would have all the sub-compact range covered. Like the YJ, it would be built at Brampton, and would meet Ford's highly successful Taurus (a version of the Scorpio) and Chevrolet's Corsica (equivalent to the Opel Omega/Vauxhall Carlton) head on.

The 1986 J-10, in 132in (3,353mm) wheelbase form. The roofline has been altered, removing the peak above the windscreen to give a little less wind resistance.

The YJ Wrangler had met with a terrific reception.

The XJ Cherokee was not only the most successful Jeep to date: it would be one of the best-selling passenger cars AMC had produced in its entire history. The ZJ, the XJ's replacement, had been approved as early as 1983, and was scheduled for introduction for the 1990 model year.

But in truth Cappy's optimism was unfounded. Although Jeep sales continued to blossom, it was the same old story that had dogged Jeep's owners since the early fifties. The four-wheel-drive legend was thriving, despite having a host that was dying on its feet. History would therefore repeat itself: Jeep would be an irresistible lure to another rescuer.

8   Chrysler and 'the Jewel in the Deal'

Lee Iacocca had done what the experts had thought impossible, and dragged the Chrysler Corporation back from the brink of oblivion. The new, compact K-car got a terrific reception in the American market, and its MPV derivative had revolutionized suburbia's view of the station wagon. Now Chrysler were looking for more production space, for both its M-bodied mid-sized cars, and for the replacement for the Plymouth Horizon and Dodge Omni sub-compacts that were a left-over from Chrysler Europe. The proposed Peugeot designs for such a car had been abandoned by Peugeot in the face of falling sales of European models in the US, and Chrysler intended to design its own.

By contrast, American Motors were selling fewer Renaults and Eagles. Renault had suffered some appalling losses, although they were on a gradual upward trend: compared to 1984's loss of £1,271 million, that for 1986 was cut to £456 million, and they anticipated a return to profit in 1987. But they were disillusioned with America. None of the Renault models had received a sustained welcome, and the Régie wanted out, despite the best opportunity so far to achieve some success. There was already a link between Chrysler and AMC: Chrysler were supplying Torqueflite automatic transmissions for the Wagoneer, and New Process Gear, who made Jeep's transfer cases and viscous couplings under licence from FF Developments, was a part-owned Chrysler subsidiary. On 30 June

1986 Chrysler signed a deal with AMC to make the M-cars at Kenosha, and also discussed the idea of making the Omni and Horizon replacement there, too.

But it wasn't just production space that Chrysler were looking for. They had never made sport utility vehicles (SUVs), and now within their grasp was Jeep. Whilst AMC as a corporation were haemorrhaging money – over $91 million were lost in 1986 – Jeep was still profitable. Now the balance between sales of AMC's regular passenger cars and Jeeps had shifted dramatically, and basically passenger car sales had crashed. Jeep, once a small proportion of the corporation's turnover, had grown to represent three-quarters of AMC's total vehicle production, doubling in ten years to just under a quarter of a million units. CJ-7 sales had grown about 10 per cent in the 1980s. And the XJ, with sales going into six figures in their first full year of production, became not only the best-selling Jeep in the brand's history, but arguably the most successful car the American Motors Corporation had ever produced. America's car-buying public might have lost faith in AMC passenger cars, but they never lost faith in Jeep.

Lee Iacocca authorized Project *Titan* where Chrysler Corporation would enter into negotiation with American Motors. After some preliminaries towards the end of 1986, Chrysler announced in March 1987 that it would buy AMC. It took until 5 August to finalize everything, which

The Chrysler Corporation

'Ford for cheapness, General Motors for value, and Chrysler for engineering': so ran the old slogan the US auto-buying public and whilst market forces have closed up the differences between the three over the years, Chrysler still prides itself on its engineering abilities.

At forty-five years old Walter P. Chrysler was already a millionaire when he walked out of the presidency of the Buick division of General Motors in 1920, after a row with William Durant. The son of a Kansas farmer, Chrysler had taken an apprenticeship in the railroad business in Chicago, working his way up to a management position with the Pittsburgh American Locomotive Company before moving to Buick.

On leaving General Motors, Walter Chrysler concentrated his vast experience on the nuts and bolts of cars –he had been tinkering with them since he was a boy – and in business management: he was responsible for re-organizing a number of makes, including Chalmers and, significantly for our story, Willys. But things really happened when he bought the ailing Maxwell company, which he transformed: in 1924 his success was manifested in the first car to carry his name. It was an all-new, six-cylinder model, low-slung by comparison with its contemporaries on its smaller-than-average diameter wheels and balloon tyres, and with 60mph (100kmph) performance. With this car Chrysler had shown himself to be not so much a revolutionary manufacturer, as an evolutionary one. It remained conventional in its overall layout, but it had hydraulic brakes and shock absorbers, and a high-compression engine with full pressure lubrication, which helped its reliability and made it much more of a pleasure to own and to drive. It was a huge success in the mid-priced sector of the market. Then on 6 June 1925 the Chrysler Corporation was formed, and the simple format was set for all successive models: engineer them well, and make them look good!

By 1929 Chrysler was the third biggest manufacturer in the US, and for a brief while the magnificent Art Deco Chrysler Building in New York was the world's tallest, before it was surpassed by the Empire State Building. Even the Wall Street crash of 1929 did no permanent harm to Plymouth and De Soto, the two budget makes created by Chrysler, or to Dodge, which had been acquired in 1928.

From that beginning, high quality engineering, and a policy of taking a lead in automobile styling, have been the hallmarks of Chrysler's success. There were notable exceptions: the Airflow of the mid-1930s was too advanced for the buying public's taste, and the early 1950s cars were considered too dowdy. But when the formula was applied right, it was a successful one. For instance, Virgil Exner's 'Forward Look' of the late 1950s was seen on some of the most flamboyant cars of the age, bringing the 'fins-and-chrome' vogue to its zenith. Even Harley Earl, who had first put fins on a Cadillac in 1949, had to sharpen up all the 1959 General Motors range, for fear of losing vital market share.

Chrysler were the first manufacturers in the world, in 1949, to offer disc brakes on a production car, and what was to become the most powerful engine seen in a mass-produced American car, the fabulous 'Hemi' V-8 was introduced across the range in 1951. This engine, in the early Chrysler 300 series 'Letter Cars', was to dominate NASCAR stock-car racing for several years, and became a favourite of hot-rodders across the US.

Ford's revival pushed Chrysler back down to third place in the 1950s, ahead of American Motors and Studebaker, but in the 1970s the corporation began to lose its way. It did not update its management to keep up with its competitors, and, deep in debt, it faced oblivion. Ironically their saviour would come from a major rival, the Ford Motor Company: his name was Lee Iacocca.

Lee Iacocca

Lee Iacocca will probably always be known as the 'Father of the Mustang': this is one of the most successful Ford cars ever made, and the one that made Iacocca famous across America. He worked for thirty-two years with Ford, and it was during this time that he learned about the automobile business. Lido Anthony Iacocca was born in 1924 in Allentown, Pennsylvania, the son of an enterprising Italian immigrant, Nicola Iacocca, and his young wife, Antoinette. A bout of rheumatic fever contracted in his early teens kept him out of military service in World War II, and instead he studied engineering at Lehigh University in Bethlehem, Pennsylvania. Here he developed his ambition to work for Ford.

When he graduated, young Lido was offered a choice: go to Ford as one of the fifty graduates they took on annually, or go to Princeton University to study for a Master's degree whilst Ford held a place open for him. Iacocca chose to go to Princeton. But by the time he had finished his Master's, the recruiting officer at Ford had been drafted into the forces and nobody at Ford knew anything about the promise made. However, Iacocca told his story to the new man at Ford, and was accepted as the fifty-first recruit for 1946.

Starting in the engineering department, he soon moved over to sales, and made rapid progress until 1960, when at the recommendation of Robert MacNamara he was promoted to general manager of Ford Division; in 1974 he finally achieved his ambition of becoming president of the Ford Motor Company. But in his best-selling autobiography (*Lee Iacocca with William Novak* Sidgewick & Jackson, 1989) he talked about Henry Ford II's dismissal of Semon 'Bunkie' Knudsen, and claimed that 'Henry was a king who could tolerate no equals'. Unfortunately for him, this attitude also applied to his own rise within Ford; Henry feared that his dynasty would lose control of the company. Iacocca lost out in a protracted battle waged by Henry to remove him, officially resigning in October 1978. In a brusque statement reminiscent of the manner in which old Henry had dismissed Charles Sorensen in 1944, the younger Ford simply said, 'Well, sometimes you just don't like somebody.'

Chrysler's president, John Riccardo, head-hunted Iacocca almost immediately, as the only one he considered capable of reorganizing his chaotic, demoralized and almost moribund corporation. Iacocca raised loans from a bewildering number of banks, getting them covered by hard-won government guarantees. The recovery was based around a completely restructured management system, and the new, compact, front-wheel-drive 'K-car' platform, which the still-talented engineering department had developed. With this and its innovative Dodge Minivan and Plymouth Voyager MPV derivatives, Chrysler worked its way back, both into the black and into the hearts of the American automobile buying public. With his appearances in Chrysler TV commercials, the whole episode made Lee Iacocca a household name once more.

(Profile taken from *Iacocca*, by kind permission of the Macmillan Press)

included the purchase of Renault's share, but in announcing the take-over, Chrysler described Jeep as 'the jewel in the deal'. The burden of AMC's debts, a colossal $885 million, plus its pension liabilities, were well compensated for by the acquisition of the Kenosha, Brampton and Toledo plants. There was also the export market that Jeep would bring with it, for Jeep represented about 75 per cent of total US vehicle exports.

RATIONALIZATION

Chrysler's board began to wield a big scalpel. All AMC was incorporated into the new Jeep/Eagle division, under the

The Grand Wagoneer. This 1987 example has Selec-Trac, and standard air-conditioning. The final edition was very little different to this example.

direction of former AMC chief executive officer Joseph Cappy. This included the run-out Renaults, the Eagle four-wheel drive and all the Jeep models. Despite an original pledge to keep Renault models in production for five years, they would not last too long. Neither would the Eagle, and production of the four-wheel-drive car ceased at the end of 1987.

The Jeep range in its entirety was not safe, either. Chrysler Corporation's medium-sized Dodge trucks – the D150, D200 and D300, with carrying capacities between a half ton and a full ton – included the four-wheel-drive Power Wagons. The D-Series was the oldest in Chrysler's

Wood-effect trim extends to the tail-gate of the Grand Wagoneer.

line-up – they had been around since 1972, earning themselves the nickname of 'Grandpa'. However, they were youngsters compared to the J-Series, which because of its age and the advancement of production techniques, was a very expensive truck to make. There was a new range of Dodge trucks lined up for the near future, and rather than perpetuate two elderly lines, the end of 1989 saw the axing of the J-Series Jeep trucks. It wasn't only the J-Series that disappeared in 1989: in that year the Kenosha plant, which echoed to the ghosts of Thomas Jeffery and his Rambler automobiles of 1909, was demolished by Chrysler.

The writing was on the wall for the Grand Wagoneer, too. Its sales had remained surprisingly buoyant for such an old vehicle, although through the late 1980s they began to tail off. But during the first two years of Chrysler's tenure the figures dropped dramatically, and it was decided that it was time to say good-bye to this old friend; production finished at the end of 1991.

The GM V6, not loved by many in the XJ, also had to go. AMC already had a replacement engine under way, and Chrysler followed through with its introduction in 1987. It was a complete overhaul of the old faithful AMC in-line six that could trace a line from 1964. This time the capacity was 4 litres (242ci), and the engine was identified to the buyer in its metric capacity instead of the old-established American practice of using cubic inches. Sharing many internal components with AMC's 150ci four, it turned out a class-beating 173bhp and 200lb/ft of torque, pushing the XJ from rest to 60mph (96.6kmph) in under ten seconds. A new four-speed automatic box, produced jointly by Borg-Warner and Aisin of Japan, became an option to the five-speed manual gearbox. The Renault

Add-on graphics identify this 1998 YJ Wrangler, with 258ci straight six and five-speed manual gearbox. This is a privately imported example.

turbo diesel was also dropped from the XJ in 1988.

Despite some objections by the old die-hards at its introduction, the XJ Series was a runaway success. On 22 March 1990 the one-millionth Jeep XJ rolled off the tracks at Toledo. As well as being a huge success in the US, its compact shape and competitive price had contributed to its becoming

An early special edition YJ was the Sahara. This 1988 model was finished in one colour – sand – and was trimmed in special light-coloured fabric seats. The running gear included 225 section tyres and Up-Country suspension with heavy-duty shock absorbers.

Chrysler's best-selling export to Europe. With the end of the Grand Wagoneer in 1991, the XJ simply carried the Cherokee name. The YJ was also a terrific success: 1988's figures of over 52,000 vehicles were the best ever annual sales for any traditional Jeep, and they would get better.

THE GRAND CHEROKEE

With the end of the SJ, there was a sector of the market that Jeep had created, but in which they were no longer playing: the luxury four-wheel drive. This was ruled now by up-market Fords and Chevys, and the imported Range Rover and Mitsubishi Shogun. The ZJ project had been started in 1983 by AMC as the XJ's replacement, and the Concept 1 vehicle was exhibited in 1984. However, as the SJ's sales had been steady, Chrysler had put the ZJ on 'hold' whilst they worked on their own product lines. But in 1990 it was decided it was time to move back into the luxury sector, and to add another tier above the XJ. With the ZJ, Jeep Division's declared intent was

Chrysler moved to attract a younger buyer to the YJ with the Islander special edition. Power for this model was from the 258ci six, and three paint colours – red, white or blue – were offered. Extra equipment included in the package was a heated rear window and a rear wash/wipe for the hard top, cruise control, and a radio/cassette player.

The YJ's dash was much more car-like than its CJ predecessors. It caused some concern amongst CJ fans, but it appealed to new SUV buyers, and that is what mattered to Jeep's marketing people.

to create a 'benchmark' vehicle in true Jeep tradition, for the up-market sector. The ZJ would be the Chrysler's first Jeep model, and the second new platform to be created by the Platform Team, brought over from American Motors.

Using modern management practice, the Platform Team brought together the design engineers, the manufacturing engineers and the component suppliers to co-ordinate every aspect of the ZJ's design from the outset. The design team's objectives were simple, but considering the pedigree behind them, and the competition they had to face, they were also demanding. These declared objectives were as follows: to make ZJ the highest quality Jeep vehicle ever; to create a fresh, new appearance whilst retaining Jeep identity; to improve the interior package without creating an unsuitably large exterior; to maintain Jeep performance superiority and four-wheel-drive system leadership; to improve on-road ride and handling without

The ZJ Grand Cherokee 4.0-litre Limited, in right-hand-drive form. Standard fitments were air-conditioning, a computerized vehicle information centre, leather seats, heated in the front, 16in alloy wheels, and a roof console with map-reading lamps and a compass. Roof rails and a sun roof were optional extras.

compromising off-road capability and performance; and to provide the premium safety and convenience features expected by up-market buyers.

The name 'Platform Team' suggests that once more, the ZJ was to be a unit construction vehicle. It was, but much had been learned from the XJ, and the new shell was some 20 per cent stiffer than the older vehicle. A 190bhp version of the 4-litre (242ci) Power Tech 6, delivering 225lb/ft of torque, would be the base engine for the ZJ. But this vehicle was a flagship, and the shell was re-engineered to take Chrysler's 5.2-litre (318ci) V8 as an option. The V8, a design harking back to the 273ci engine of the 1964 Plymouth Valiant, put out 220 horsepower, but most significantly its

285lb/ft of torque matched the AMC 360ci V8 in the much heavier Grand Wagoneer. The choice of a five-speed manual gearbox or a four-speed auto came with the six, whilst the auto was the only transmission available for the V8. A choice of four-wheel-drive systems were offered: Command-Trac part-time as the base, and Selec-Trac permanent as an extra-cost option. Quadra-Trac was offered as standard on the V8 models, and optional on the six-cylinder cars.

Once more, the need to balance highway comfort and off-road ability was paramount. Chrysler chose to stay with solid axles, because they gave the right amount of articulation and ground clearance, and solved the problem of trying to keep dirt

Chrysler Jeep Division XJ Cherokee (1987–date)

Engines

In-Line Six

Type	ohv in-line 6
Bore x stroke	98.4mm x 86.7mm
Capacity	3960cc
Main bearings	7
Max. power	176bhp @ 4400rpm
Max. torque	222lb/ft @ 3000rpm

In-Line Four

Type	ohv in-line 4-cylinder
Bore x stroke	98.5mm x 81mm
Capacity	2464cc
Main bearings	5
Max. power	117bhp @ 5000rpm
Max. torque	135lb/ft @ 3500rpm

VM Diesel

Type	ohv in-line 4 cylinder turbocharged diesel
Bore x stroke	92.0mm x 94.0mm
Capacity	2499cc
Main bearings	5
Max. power	114bhp @ 3900rpm
Max. torque	221lb/ft @ 2000rpm

Chassis

Transmission	5-speed manual synchromesh with 2.5ltr petrol and diesel, standard 4-speed automatic with 4.0ltr engine
Turning circle	10.9 metres
Transfer case	Standard Command-Trac 2-speed, part time four-wheel drive, optional Selec-Trac highway compatible four-wheel drive
Suspension (front)	Quadra-Link four-leading links with two coil springs, solid axle
Suspension (rear)	Solid axle with semi-elliptic leaf springs
Brakes	4-wheel hydraulic, power assisted vented front discs, rear drums

Dimensions

Wheelbase	2,576mm
Track	1,473mm
Overall length	4,240mm
Overall width	1,790mm
Overall height (top up)	1,700mm
Curb weight	1,640kg

The Grand Cherokee 5.9 Limited LX, made in only left-hand drive.

out of complex drive and steering joints. To give a better ride, the Quadra-link coil spring system was fitted to the rear suspension as well as the front.

Air bags were a new safety feature by this time, but AMC had not included them in the initial design. Chrysler fitted them, but had to overcome a tricky problem, namely: how would the air-bag sensor know whether a Jeep had collided with another car on the highway, or come to an abrupt stop when it hit a hidden tree stump when driving off-road? Certainly it gave Chrysler's engineers a problem, and they sacrificed some fifty or so test vehicles before they got it right.

Delaying the ZJ enabled Chrysler to design and build a completely new assembly plant. Up on Jefferson Avenue, Detroit, Chrysler had an old plant that in 1907 had been home to Chalmers. It was flattened,

and for a price of $1 billion, the 1.75 million square foot Jefferson North assembly plant was erected and equipped.

Some time was taken thinking what to call the ZJ, until Lee Iacocca took the decision to name it the Grand Cherokee. In a beautifully set up, spectacular stunt, it was launched at the 1992 Detroit Auto Show. Chrysler's president, Bob Lutz, drove a brand new, specially prepared ZJ off the tracks at the Jefferson North plant, and took it thought the streets of Detroit to the COBO Center, the home of the show. Not stopping for anyone to open the doors for him, Lutz drove straight through glass walls of the Center. He then got out of the car and said to the crowd of astonished motoring journalists: 'That was one helluva ride, but that's to be expected, because Grand Cherokee is one helluva vehicle!'

Chrysler Jeep Division ZJ Grand Cherokee (1993–99)

Engines

In-Line Six

Type	ohv in-line 6
Bore x stroke	98.4mm x 86.7mm
Capacity	3960cc
Main bearings	7
Max. power	174bhp @ 4600rpm
Max. torque	222lb/ft @ 2400rpm

V8

Type	ohv 90° V8
Bore x stroke	3.875in x 3.375in
Capacity	318cu in (5.2ltr)
Main bearings	5
Max. power	225bhp @ 4000rpm
Max. torque	285lb/ft @ 3600rpm

Diesel

Type	ohv in-line 4-cylinder turbocharged diesel
Bore x stroke	92.0mm x 94.0mm
Capacity	2499cc
Main bearings	5
Max. power	114bhp @ 3900rpm
Max. torque	221lb/ft @ 2000rpm

Chassis

Transmission	5-speed manual synchromesh with 2.5ltr petrol and diesel, 4-speed automatic with 4.0ltr engine
Turning circle	11.4 metres
Transfer case	Standard Command-Trac 2-speed, part time four-wheel drive, optional Quadra-Trac permanent four-wheel drive
Suspension	Quadra-Coil four-leading links with two coil springs, solid axles front and rear
Brakes	4-wheel hydraulic, power assisted 279.6mm vented front discs, 285mm solid discs rear, ABS

Dimensions

Wheelbase	2,690mm
Track	1,492mm
Overall length	4,500mm
Overall width	2,081mm
Overall height	1,752mm
Curb weight	1,640kg (4.0ltr model)

MODEL CONSOLIDATION

Chrysler continued to improve the Jeep range, next consolidating its powertrains. With the scrapping of the Grand Wagoneer, the YJ was the only Jeep vehicle using the 258ci six, and it was considered time to phase it out; the 4-litre Power-Tech 6 from the XJ was therefore grafted into the 1991 Wrangler Renegade. This was a simple job, as the YJ already used a lot of the running gear from the XJ.

Sales of the Comanche pickup had dropped by one third since the introduction of Chrysler's mid-sized Dodge Dakota truck. The Comanche's success, such as it was, had been in the leisure truck field, rather than as a working vehicle – it even had some race wins, and took the SCCA Racetruck Challenge manufacturers' championship. 1992 was the last production year of the ground-breaking Comanche, and from that point on, all of Chrysler's truck production would be under the Dodge banner. With the introduction of the Grand Cherokee, the old XJ was realigned in the market to appeal to a younger buyer. Still with a two-door option in the home market, there was a base model, the Sport, and a new name, the Country.

The YJ Wrangler was improved: it was given full-height steel doors and an automatic transmission option for the four-cylinder models for 1994. Sales continued to climb, because this, the most advanced of all the 'traditional' Jeeps, took into its design all the technology of the modern industry, yet still held to a tradition that could be traced back to the MB.

Both press and public loved the Grand Cherokee. It was *Motor Trend*'s 'Truck of Year' (the Americans see it as a truck, even though the British may think it odd to class a luxury car like the ZJ as such!); *Four Wheeler* magazine named it 'Four Wheeler

of the Year'; and it was *4-Wheel & Off Road* magazine's '4x4 of the Year'. The Grand Cherokee had particular appeal to women buyers, the biggest growth sector in the sport-utility market, probably because its strength and its high driving position gave them a feeling of security. For its first year, the public bought nearly a quarter of a million Grand Cherokees, exceeding the sales of its little brother by 100,000. But the XJ's sales rose too, by 7,000. This was satisfaction indeed, that Jeep was back with two top models which could outperform anything in the market.

OVERSEAS EXPORTS

The US auto industry had been downsizing its cars since the mid-1970s, and now a number of Chrysler's models were right for markets that had been the domain of European and Japanese makers. The K-car – in production as the Plymouth Reliant – the Chrysler LeBaron and the Dodge Aries were runaway successes, and the MPV variants – the Dodge Minivan and the Plymouth Voyager – were top sellers. Chrysler remained the number three auto maker in the USA, behind General Motors and Ford, but the whole industry was now on a global scale; even the sheer size of the US market would not allow Chrysler to overtake its rivals on its own. The damage done in the 1970s could not be made good.

Just as it was for Willys-Overland and Kaiser, the key to greater expansion for Chrysler was export; right-hand-drive models of the XJ and ZJ had therefore been designed in from the start. Willys-Overland had effectively set up Mitsubishi's – Jeep's main rival – four-wheel-drive manufacturing capabilities when it had licensed the production of CJ-3B variants: it must therefore have been particularly gratifying

The ECCO

The little ECCO concept car. With its aluminium and plastic unitary body, independent suspension and two-stroke engine it was the most advanced Jeep made.

Brooks Stevens was constantly trying new ideas for Jeep vehicles. Many of them were variations of existing lines, to explore market sectors, for the Jeep division of Kaiser Industries had little money to develop all-new cars. Chrysler have always loved their concept cars, and under Lee Iacocca and latterly Bob Lutz they have had a habit of putting them into production if the public's reaction is right. The Plymouth Prowler, a retro-style hot rod, is one example of this, but the most spectacular success has been the Dodge Viper. (Incidentally this is marketed in Europe as the Chrysler Viper; Renault have owned the European rights to the Dodge brand since buying Chrysler Europe's truck manufacturing facilities in 1980.) The practice continues with Jeep in the 1990s, although up until the millennium no Jeep concept vehicle has gone into production.

The ECCO of 1993 was perhaps the most advanced off-road vehicle to be produced by Jeep. Nothing is carried over from previous models, apart from its styling cues and a continuation of the philosophy of 'no compromise' in off-road performance. The engine was an all-aluminium, 1.5-litre, lean-burn three-cylinder two-stroke, producing 85bhp and 120lb/ft of torque. This was the smallest engine ever to power a Jeep, and it did not need to be bigger: the featherweight ECCO was made entirely of aluminium and plastic, making it wholly recyclable. All-independent suspension was also a complete departure, showing that Jeep was not going to stick with tradition for its own sake.

to Chrysler-Jeep that the first American right-hand-drive vehicle ever exported to Japan was a Jeep – in fact, a Cherokee.

Ford and General Motors had built up European and Australasian manufacturing businesses from the very early days; Ford, for instance, had an assembly plant in Trafford Park, Manchester, before the Great War, and GM moved into Europe in the 1920s with the acquisition of Vauxhall and Opel. Chrysler had not sold vehicles in the UK since the end of the 1930s, when they had an assembly plant by the River Thames, less than a mile from Kew Gardens, Surrey. The operations at Kew ceased after World War II.

Chrysler's first post-war venture into Europe was, in the end, a failure. Chrysler International was started in Geneva in 1957, and acquired a share-holding in the French company Simca. From 1964 Chrysler began buying into the troubled Rootes group in England. By 1970 Rootes, who were to lose £10.7 million that year, became Chrysler United Kingdom Limited, a wholly owned subsidiary.

But Chrysler was in a mess at home, and the UK operations were in deep trouble too. New models – the Coventry-designed Alpine, the French 160/180 and 2-litre and the Horizon – were of European design, but against General Motors, Ford, the big European makers and the ever-encroaching Japanese, they failed to turn the European operations around. The whole venture was sold to Peugeot in 1978.

By the late 1980s Chrysler was growing in stature once more, and was looking to expand into the European markets; but they needed a European manufacturing base to make it a viable proposition. The hugely successful MPV, marketed in Europe as the Chrysler Voyager, began assembly in Graz, Austria, in 1991, in co-operation with Steyr-Daimler-Puch. With 2.5-litre, four-cylinder engines it would find a place in the upper end of the market.

The British market was soon in Chrysler's sights. The Motor Division of the huge retailing and industrial conglomerate, Inchcape, negotiated for a five-year concession for Chrysler Jeep vehicles in

Chrysler Jeep UK's conversion of the YJ Wrangler to right-hand drive included fitting a new handbrake linkage instead of the foot parking brake, and a new centre console. The transfer box lever still remained in its original position, to the left of the gear lever.

October 1992. A team of just six, including the managing director of Chrysler Jeep Imports UK Ltd, Richard Mackay, was set up with premises in Paulton Close, Dover, Kent; within a year the staff had grown to twenty-two. But getting the operation off the ground was not an easy task. Car dealers remembered the old Chrysler days – the disastrous 180, the Alpine and the left-over Avenger – and at first they didn't want to know; but when Mackay's team tempted them with the bait that the first vehicles to be imported would be Jeeps, they started to listen.

First to go on sale was the XJ Cherokee, and there were three models: the 2.5 litre and 4.0 litre Limited, and the 184bhp 4.0

Chrysler Jeep UK's managing director, Richard Mackay.

A 1993 XJ Cherokee Limited, officially imported, with chrome trim from the US model fitted to the grille. These earlier imports had US specification trim, too.

European lighting regulations demanded that the tail-lights of imported YJ Wranglers be moved inboard slightly. This was done by fitting these adapters.

Litre Limited SE. This was followed in May by the special edition 4.0 litre Stealth. Total vehicle sales for 1993 were a respectable 3,914. The Grand Cherokee, fitted with disc brakes all round and the 4-litre in-line six, came into the UK in 1994. A turbo-diesel XJ Cherokee, with a 2.5 litre 116bhp 206lb/ft four-cylinder VM unit, came along in the May of 1995.

Mackay's team were sure there was a market for the YJ Wrangler, and that it was big enough for investment into a right-hand-drive version. They told Chrysler so, but failed to convince them. Concessionaire

---

The Cherokee in British Police work

Chrysler Jeep UK saw the XJ Cherokee as a good alternative to the Range Rover as a police vehicle, and in 1993 a special XJ police model was shown at the Police Equipment Exhibition in Devizes, Wiltshire. Taking note of the claims of better performance and a cheaper purchase price, Essex Constabulary bought a number for use as armed response vehicles (ARVs). Another reason for choosing the Cherokee was because of the county's exceptionally rural character, the off-road capability being considered highly important if police wanted to get anywhere in a hurry. The four-litre engine gave sparkling performance, and Essex patrolmen found this extra power, and the four-wheel drive, of great advantage when towing. But like all police vehicles they were fitted out with a substantial amount of equipment, and the Kevlar reinforcement in the doors added noticeably to the Jeep's weight. This affected the braking capabilities, and the Cherokee suffered when driven hard in pursuit by comparison to saloon cars.

The diesel Cherokee found favour as a rural beat vehicle in Essex. For routine police work, its dual-purpose nature did not compromise any aspect of its duty, and the fuel economy of the oil engine was appreciated. Sadly, all Cherokee models were withdrawn in 1999, having reached the end of their normal service life. As the ARV Cherokees were very rarely called off-road, they will be replaced by saloon cars.

The 1994 Cherokee Stealth. Named for the US Air Force Stealth aircraft, it shares the black paint, but with a high gloss clear coat. The car features special black alloy wheels, a black finish big-bore exhaust, a lower body styling kit and a rear roof spoiler.

status does give a little more freedom than being part of the parent company, so Chrysler Jeep UK imported left-hand-drive Wranglers and converted them to right-hand drive in their own workshops. The 3,000-odd right-hand-drive models sold convinced Detroit that there was a market for the Wrangler, and left-hand-drive models were imported. With the top-line Wrangler Sahara, in left-hand-drive form, the line-up of UK specification Jeep vehicles was complete. But no right-hand-drive YJ was ever built at the factory because there was something else in the pipeline.

The Cherokee Stealth's leather and carbon-fibre fascia, with a six-disc CD player and special leather steering wheel. The trim is also black leather.

9 DaimlerChrysler and the Future

THE TJ WRANGLER

The YJ Wrangler had set new standards in both on- and off-road ability, with its rigid frame and more flexible leaf-spring suspension. But the off-road market had grown considerably, and whilst Wrangler still had a 50 per cent US share, its competitors had upped the stakes. Refinement, comfort, handling and highway performance had found a place of equal value to the buyers of off-road vehicles, for many of them would never take their 4x4s anywhere near rough country. For many people, vehicles like these were a fashion statement. Jeep could build a boulevard cruiser, but with such a pedigree there could be no compromise. The YJ's replacement, under development by 1993, had to be the ultimate off-road vehicle and every bit an American icon. Jeep owners who actively went off-road demanded the best, and they would get it.

The end of the alphabet had been reached with ZJ, so the numbering system turned back to the old SJ Wagoneer, and the next letter picked was 'T': the new Jeep would be the TJ. As regards design, the YJ Wrangler's tub and rigid ladder-type perimeter chassis was carried over. The wheelbase was identical to the YJ at 93.4in (2,373mm), as was the 58in (1,473mm) track. The Dana solid axles were used again, but this time the Grand Cherokee's Quadra-Coil all-coil suspension would give the TJ a degree of axle articulation never before experienced on a traditional style, production Jeep. The recirculating ball steering box gave the TJ a very comfortable 33.6ft (10.25m) turning circle. Also, the TJ would be the first ever 'traditional' Jeep with right-hand drive designed in from the start. There would be no more conversions: now new markets, including Australia, South Africa and Japan could be targeted.

The TJ Wrangler Sport, the base UK model, with the 2.5-litre, fuel-injected, four-cylinder engine and steel wheels. Transmission is a five-speed manual with Command-Trac part-time four-wheel drive. Colours available are flame red, lapis blue, bright jade, deep amethyst, moss green and black. On-the-road list price for 1999 was amazingly low £14,225.

The engines were to be carried over in principle from the YJ, although the 4-litre in-line six was given a major re-work, with new pistons, a lighter, stronger block and a re-profiled camshaft. Power was 181bhp, with a very useful 222lb/ft of torque. The base 2.5-litre four-cylinder motor was to be used again. This was no weakling, with 120bhp and torque figure of 140lb/ft. Both engines shared a bore size of 3.9in (100mm) – barely larger, incidentally, than the 3.75in (95mm) of the Go-Devil and the Hurricane – but at 3.4in (86mm), the six's stroke was longer than the 3.2in (81mm) of the 2.5-litre four.

A choice of a five-speed manual transmission or a three-speed automatic gearbox was coupled to the Jeep's most important attribute, the four-wheel-drive system. This was Command-Trac, the part-time set-up which featured a dual-range transfer case, with shift-on-the-fly. Operated by a single lever, there was the usual choice of two-wheel-drive high, four-wheel-drive high or four-wheel-drive low.

In 1995 the YJ Wrangler stopped production and the new TJ was announced for the 1996 model year. Following the Jeep tradition of continuance of names, it too was called the Wrangler. Its appearance was all Jeep, and the return to round headlights emphasized this. The interior was all new, featuring dual air bags and a new-style dashboard. The carpets were made to be easily removable so that the floor could be hosed down after off-road work, returning the Jeep to a comfortable commuter vehicle.

UPGRADES FOR THE XJ AND ZJ

In late 1995 the XJ Cherokee received the new 4.0-litre six from the TJ Wrangler, and for the UK market there was the 4.0-litre Sport. Then in 1996 the ZJ Grand Cherokee

Top of the Wrangler range in the UK is the 4.0-litre Sahara. An automatic transmission is available, but the 'Grizzly' alloys are standard, as is a removable hard top with glass windows and a rear wash-wipe. Two extra speakers are fitted on the roll bar for the CD-compatible radio/cassette. The 1999 price for a Sahara auto is less than £19,000.

underwent a top-to-toe revamp. There was a new interior and instruments, and a revised powertrain and steering. The Quadra-Trac four-wheel-drive system was improved to give variable ratio power delivery from 100 per cent:0 per cent rear/front on dry, hard roads, up to a fifty-fifty split, giving whatever is required automatically, in a split second. The re-worked 4-litre six with new pistons, a stiffer block and a new cam for more response and refinement, took its place alongside the 5.2-litre V8.

Once destined for replacement by the ZJ, the XJ went from strength to strength. It was revamped for the 1997 model year,

Chrysler Jeep Division TJ Wrangler (1996–date)

Engine
6-Cylinder
Type	ohv in-line 6
Bore x stroke	98.4mm x 86.7mm
Capacity	3960cc
Main bearings	7
Max. power	176bhp @ 4400rpm
Max. torque	222lb/ft @ 3000rpm

4-Cylinder
Type	ohv in-line 4-cylinder
Bore x stroke	98.5mm x 81mm
Capacity	2464cc
Main bearings	5
Max. power	117bhp @ 5000rpm
Max. torque	135lb/ft @ 3500rpm

Chassis
Transmission	5-speed manual synchromesh, standard, 3-speed automatic optional
Turning circle	10.25 metres
Transfer case	Standard Command-Trac 2-speed, part time four-wheel drive
Suspension (front)	Quadra-Link four leading links with two coil springs, solid axle
Suspension (rear)	Quadra-Link four leading links with two coil springs, solid axle
Brakes	4-wheel hydraulic, power assisted vented discs front, drums rear

Dimensions
Wheelbase	2,373mm
Track	1,473mm
Overall length	3,883mm
Overall width	1,740mm
Overall height (top up)	1,782mm
Curb weight	1,610kg

The revised XJ Cherokee has a much softer look around the grille and indicators. The tail-gate has lost its sharp corner over the rear lights, and the grille now has Jeep's trade-mark seven slats. This is the 4.0-litre Limited model with standard alloy wheels. Also standard are air-conditioning, cruise control and front fog lights. Leather facings are an extra-cost option for the power-adjustable seats. This model, with cloth seats, retailed in 1999 for £23,225.

with a new interior and a softer look: the sharp corners of the rear door, over the tail-lights, were removed, and the lights re-shaped; and the new grille incorporated re-styled indicators, and gained the trade-mark seven slats. The new Cherokee helped make 1997 a record year for Chrysler and Jeep sales in the UK, and a total of 17,519 vehicles of all types (including Voyager and Neon) were moved. This made the UK the third-largest Chrysler Jeep market in the world, whilst Chrysler Jeep UK was Europe's top distributor.

JEEP – STILL A GLOBAL VEHICLE

The XJ's continuing global appeal is reflected in the fact that one in three Toledo-built Cherokees are exported. As with the UK, Jeep is almost always the first Chrysler vehicle to be offered in each new market – by 1998 Jeep vehicles were being sold in 100 countries. There were subsidiary companies assembling or distributing Chrysler and Jeep vehicles in Canada, Belgium, Mexico, Singapore, Venezuela and, significantly, Brazil and Argentina. There were also joint ventures to build the vehicles: the Eurostar assembly plant in Graz, Austria; the Arab American Vehicles Company in Cairo, Egypt; the Thai Chrysler Automotive in Bangkok, Thailand; and the Beijing Jeep Corporation in China. Affiliated companies assembled Jeeps in Djakarta, Indonesia; Kuala Lumpur, Malaysia; and Changun, China.

Chrysler in Europe

Walter P. Chrysler began exporting his cars almost as soon as he had got the first one into production. His empire spread overseas first to Belgium, with an assembly shop in Antwerp in 1926, then the following year it was England, with premises on the banks of the Thames at Kew. Complete cars from Chrysler's Canadian factory were unloaded from ships onto barges in the London docks and floated down to the river frontage. Canadian cars were sent because, being Empire made, they were not subject to the McKenna duties levied on imported cars.

By 1930, cars were assembled from KD kits, and the British content was gradually increased to 65 per cent to make them what Whitehall deemed to be British made. Versions of Chrysler, De Soto and Plymouth cars were all sold under the Chrysler badge with locally inspired model names such as Kew, Wimbledon and Hurlingham. Dodge trucks, originally assembled at Park Royal, joined the passenger cars at Kew in 1932.

In World War II the plant was turned over to truck assembly and aircraft component manufacture, and was damaged by enemy bombing. However, peacetime passenger car production did not restart, and the Dodge truck manufacturing business was eventually sold to the Rootes Group. Today the site is a retail park; it is also home to the Public Records Office.

Chrysler returned to Europe in 1957 when an office in Geneva was opened. Connections were also made with the Italian styling house of Ghia, who produced some striking concept cars. Subsequently, Chrysler bought the French company Simca, who had not long taken over Ford's French operations. In 1963 Chrysler approached Rootes Group, who had endured a disastrous two years, and a financial holding was acquired the following year. By 1967 Chrysler had control, and in 1970 Rootes became Chrysler United Kingdom Ltd. The French and UK concerns were merged to become Chrysler Europe.

Unfortunately, Chrysler as a whole were in severe difficulties, and the whole European operation was sold to Peugeot in 1980. Following its rescue by Lee Iacocca, Chrysler turned its export sights to Europe once more. Its factory in Graz, Austria, the result of a 1991 venture with Steyr-Daimler-Puch, began building Voyager MPVs, and both left- and right-hand-drive Grand Cherokees.

Jeep and Orvis: two American outdoor legends

In addition to the Limited and Laredo models, the Orvis special edition Grand Cherokee was launched at the 1998 UK Motor Show at Birmingham's National Exhibition Centre. Orvis as a company are relative newcomers to the UK, but in the USA the name has a long history. Charles F. Orvis opened a fishing shop in Vermont in 1856, and his hand-made fly rods soon became known as America's finest. That tradition continues, and the company now sell carbon-fibre fly rods, shotguns, sports accessories and clothes, and a range of high quality fashion leisure clothing for men and women.

The Orvis name was adopted for the top Grand Cherokee model, to link two names associated with America's love of the great outdoors. But the Orvis name was not put on a Jeep with utility trim: far from it. Orvis was a top-line luxury model. A full leather interior with burr walnut trim is the most prominent feature of the Orvis, and this superbly appointed vehicle also has a sun roof, full climate control, a six-disc, ten-speaker auto-change CD player, a digital compass, eight-way power-adjusted seats and twin air bags.

The UK Jeep range: outstanding value

Jeep vehicles have always sold on their performance, but one reason that they have sold exceptionally well in the UK in recent times is the price. The ZJ Grand Cherokee

The ZJ Grand Cherokee Orvis, outside one of the Orvis company's UK shops. The Orvis models were available in a choice of three Pearlcoat colours: bright platinum, deep slate or forest green.

Chrysler Jeep Division WJ Grand Cherokee (1999–date)

Engines
6-Cylinder

Type	ohv in-line 6
Bore x stroke	98.4mm x 86.7mm
Capacity	3956cc
Main bearings	7
Max. power	188bhp @ 5000rpm
Max. torque	218lb/ft @ 3050rpm

V8

Type	SOHC 90° V8
Bore x stroke	93.0mm x 86.5mm
Capacity	4701cc
Main bearings	5
Max. power	217bhp @ 4700rpm
Max. torque	288lb/ft @ 3200rpm

Chassis

Transmission	4-speed automatic, alternate second gear ratio on V8 model
Turning circle	11.1m
Transfer case	Quadra-Trac II permanent four-wheel drive
Suspension (front)	Solid axle, Quadra-Link leading arms, coil springs
Suspension (rear)	Solid axle, lower trailing arms, triangular upper arm, coil springs
Brakes	Vented discs front, solid discs rear, ABS

Dimensions

Wheelbase	2,690mm
Track	1,511mm
Overall length	4,605mm
Overall width	2,239mm
Overall height	1,773mm
Curb weight	1,975kg

Orvis, for all its luxury, is no exception. Against the top Range Rover, the difference between the 1998 price of each model is staggering; for instance, the 4.6 litre V8 Range Rover Autobiography was listed at £60,330, whereas the ZJ Orvis, with the 4-litre six, was £33,520. Even the V8 Grand Cherokee Limited (the Orvis package was not available in the UK with the V8) was, at £31,000, some £4,000 cheaper than the V6 Toyota Land Cruiser, and a huge £9,000 cheaper than the standard Range Rover. One might argue which is better off-road. The Range Rover, like the Jeep, has an enviable reputation, but the difference is hardly ever tested by most buyers. They would not go too far off-road anyhow – and if they did, Jeep's capabilities would be far in excess of what most of them would need.

The Orvis special edition package became available on the XJ Cherokee as from February 1999. The Cherokee gathered a loyal following amongst UK buyers: these people were happy with the compact size of the XJ, and when they wanted to trade up they did not want to buy the bigger ZJ, but were happy with a luxury XJ.

DAIMLERCHRYSLER

The cost of developing new vehicles had grown to astronomic proportions. Legislation was imposing ever-more stringent safety regulations for vehicles, and designing, testing and producing new cars demanded a tremendous outlay to meet these; so, too, did the ever-tightening emissions legislation. On a much grander scale the position that faced Chrysler was the same as the one that faced Willys-Overland in 1952: namely, in order to stay in the game, Chrysler needed to pool its resources with another organization, not only to fund the costs of designing future vehicles, but so it could take advantage of that organization's existing export markets to increase global sales. Chrysler found such a partner, and the announcement caught the world by surprise, for there was no real inkling of the merger.

'Daimler-Benz and Chrysler combine to form the leading global automotive company,' said the press release of 7 May 1998. The new company was christened DaimlerChrysler, with the German com-

pany holding 57 per cent of the shares and Chrysler holding the remaining 43 per cent. From the start it was headed by Jurgen E. Schrempp, chairman of Daimler-Benz, and Chrysler's Robert J. Eaton: they became co-chairmen and co-chief executive officers. The press release announced that the merger would be '...uniquely positioned to exploit the growth opportunities of the global automotive market in terms of geographical and product segment coverage.' And Schrempp said, 'The two companies have skilled workforces and successful products, but in different markets, and different parts of the world.' For Chrysler, Eaton said: 'Both companies have product ranges with world-class brands that complement each other perfectly.'

In studying the product range, there is

The Cherokee Orvis interior has a wood-veneered dash, agate-grey leather seats and a sun roof as standard.

definitely a synergy: Chrysler occupies a mass market in the USA, whilst Daimler-Benz has the upper end. But there is also an obvious clash, in that the Jeep Grand Cherokee and Daimler-Benz's new 4x4 model, the ML Class, both occupy the same market sector. The Mercedes M Series 4x4 began production in the Daimler-Benz's own US factory in Alabama, and European versions of the Chrysler Voyager MPV are built in Graz, Austria. However, as from the year 2000, the new WJ Grand Cherokee and the Mercedes M-Class are scheduled for production in adjacent factories in Graz.

Daimler values the Jeep brand very highly, as it does its own image. A year after the announcement of the merger, the two partners were still working on the direction the company will take. New car platforms are extremely expensive to develop. DaimlerChrysler already plan the use of a new single platform to replace the Chrysler/Plymouth Voyager and the Mercedes V-Series MPVs. Furthermore, such co-operations in design as engine, transmission and floorpan-sharing are fully feasible for future generations.

THE WJ GRAND CHEROKEE

The new Grand Cherokee was announced in the USA in the summer of 1998. It was almost the same size as the ZJ, with an

---

Mahindra and Mahindra: The present day

After the American Motors' take-over of Kaiser-Jeep, Mahindra's move to total local manufacture continued, increasing to 97 per cent by 1967. In 1971 a new Research and Development Department was set up. Within a collaboration agreement with AMC, Mahindra introduced the CJ-4A, the 101in (2,565mm) wheelbase utility vehicle using CJ-3B-style front sheet metal and the Hurricane engine. The forward-control models continued to be popular, and 1975 saw a new version, the FC260, using a new chassis, and the MD 2350 diesel engine. There was also a new diesel utility, the CJ 500, based around the CJ-5.

The Mahindra Armada takes the CJ-5 concept further, meeting the Japanese competition head on. The front sheet metal is obviously CJ-5 derived, but the all-steel station-wagon body is Mahindra's own, and the bumpers, looking like composite items, are of a more practical steel construction. Using a 105in (2,667mm) wheelbase, the mechanical specifications are shared with the CL series.

Links with Peugeot resulted in the construction of an assembly plant in Ghatkopar in 1981, and another in Igatpuri two years later, to make both petrol and diesel engines for utility vehicles. Mahindra continued to develop their own range of vehicles based on CJ-3B, CJ-5 and FC Jeep designs. There are long and short wheelbase models, with hard and soft tops, single and double cabs, pickups, station wagons and a military version. The newest model is the 1997 Voyager, and the new Scorpio, aimed at the suburban market, is in the pipeline for 2000.

identical 105.9in (2,690mm) wheelbase, but 2.5in (63mm) longer and 1.6in (41mm) wider. As a wholly new vehicle, only a handful of components were carried over, most of which were fasteners and trim clips; the largest component was the oil filter of the 4.0 litre six! The drivetrain of the new Grand featured a 45RFE five-speed automatic transmission with a 'dual' second gear, with a ratio of either 1.67 or 1.5, depending on throttle setting, to improve low-speed acceleration. Improved brakes were fitted, and the coil-spring suspension was uprated, with an A-frame locating the centre of the rear axle. By giving firm lateral location, the A-frame reduces body roll and bump steer, an inherent characteristic of the solid axles, without hampering the axle articulation so important for serious off-road use.

The four-wheel-drive system developed for the WJ is Quadra-Drive. As in the ZJ, the Quadra-Trac centre differential feeds power in a variable ratio to each axle as demanded by the road conditions. The VariLock multi-plate clutch in the front differential comes into play as soon as a loss of traction is detected in any wheel. The drive is transferred from that wheel to any of the other three that can find grip, even if it is only one.

The 4.0-litre six was carried over, but in further refined form than it was in the TJ. It produced 188bhp and 218lb/ft of torque, thanks to a new cylinder head and manifolds. For the top of the range, a new V8 engine was introduced. A 4.7-litre single overhead cam per bank unit, its 217bhp (net) is ten more than the old 5.2-litre engine, and the torque figure of 288lb/ft is up by 3lb/ft. Remarkably, this engine is 54lb (24.5kg) lighter than the old 5.2. A 139bhp five-cylinder 3.1-litre VM diesel for the European market was designed into the WJ from the start. As the WJ was on

the verge of introduction when the merger was announced, it was far too late to engineer Mercedes diesel engines to fit it. Crucially, one in three export ZJs were diesels. For the first time a Jeep diesel will offer an automatic gearbox, the four-speed 44RE.

The Limited model has standard air-conditioning, dual air bags, one-touch electric windows, agate or camel leather trim depending on the choice of body colour, wood-veneered fascia and door cappings, power-adjustable front seats and 60/40 split rear seats, and the spare wheel is carried under the floor to make more luggage space. In the Orvis model a twelve-disc CD changer occupies one of the storage pockets in the rear.

WJ Grand Cherokee in the UK

The European-model WJ Grand Cherokee was scheduled to be built in the Graz factory in Austria, and British buyers were impatient to buy it. Some 1,300 advance orders were placed – 10 per cent of the total UK sales of the old model. In spite of the fact that the WJ was an all-new vehicle, the

The 4.7-litre Power Tech V8 engine of the WJ Grand Cherokee. This brand new engine replaces the ZJ's old 5.2-litre unit, which can trace its line back to the 273ci engine from the 1964 Plymouth Valiant.

introductory UK prices – £29,995 for the 4-litre Limited and £34,995 for the V8 Limited – were exactly the same as the equivalent ZJ models. The UK launch of the WJ was in March 1999 at the Loch Lomond Golf Club, Scotland. Motoring journalists were first presented with a line-up of WJs fitted with off-road tyres and optional-equipment under-body guards. They were taken round a mountain course which included driving over rocks, down slopes of one-in-three gradient, and along a stream. Two hours later not one of the WJs had put a wheel wrong.

The WJ's one-piece tail-gate lifts up, but the rear window can open separately. Air vents are built into the rear lights. Prices for 1999 ran from £29,995 for the 4-litre six, to £34,995 for the V8 Limited.

THE FUTURE

The XJ Cherokee is the next Jeep model for replacement – although surprisingly, sales of the old Cherokee still hold up well, especially in the UK. Also resale values for all models – the Cherokee, the ZJ Grand Cherokee and the Wrangler – remain buoyant. In fact by the end of the 1990s the ZJ was arguably the most sought-after luxury four-wheel-drive vehicle on the market, holding its value better than the Range Rover and the Mitsubishi Shogun.

At one time Jeep was supremely capable but very basic – tough but uncompromising. We are reminded once again of Barney Roos's comments that the Jeep was not a forerunner of a new type of automobile, and that although it might make concessions to art, it made none at all to comfort. On the contrary, the Cherokee, Grand Cherokee and Wrangler have shown the world that Jeep really *was* the forerunner of that new type of

The right-hand-drive UK version of the WJ Grand Cherokee was launched in May 1999 at the Loch Lomond Golf Club. The more rounded frontal appearance and the tapered grille give the WJ a forceful appearance. It is also more aerodynamic, enabling a top speed of 122mph (196kmph), and 22.4 mpg (12.6l / 100km) – in urban areas – for the 4.7-litre V8. The body sides of this model are more deeply sculptured.

automobile. In the Wrangler there *are* concessions to comfort, and in the XJ and WJ, to sheer luxury – yet none of the off-road capabilities are compromised in any way. Thus Jeep has been taken beyond the wildest imagination of anyone at Camp Holabird in 1940. So Barney Roos was right to build the jeep tough, but as regards saying that the jeep was not the forerunner of a new type of automobile, and that it gave no concessions to comfort, perhaps he might have been happy to admit that he was wrong.

As the new century begins, it would be interesting to know how the German part of DaimlerChrysler values the Jeep. Asked at a press conference: 'How will you [DaimlerChrysler] position the Grand Cherokee against the Mercedes ML320?' the answer was, 'We believe both vehicles are strong contenders in the SUV market. However, both also have their own place in the growing luxury sport-utility segment. While the ML320 is a new entry, it has a very strong brand recognition, and has been on the forefront of the SUV market, even before it was such a popular segment. We believe there is room for both models to do extremely well.'

But Jeep's future may be detected in four concept vehicles unveiled between 1997 and 1999. All except one, the TJ-based Dakar, have taken the concept begun with the ECCO, and moved it further.

The Icon

The Jeep Icon concept car was first shown at the 1997 Detroit Auto Show, and on this occasion a remark made by Trevor M. Creed, design director of Chrysler Corporation, showed that he obviously fully understood the Jeep philosophy: 'As we move closer to the next century, Jeep enthusiasts will be happy to know their Jeep will still look like a Jeep.' Designed by Robert Laster, the Icon takes part of the ECCO concept – namely the unitary construction and all-independent suspension – much further, whilst keeping the seven-slat grille and round headlights, both of which are Jeep signatures. Its power was a 2.4-litre four-cylinder petrol engine, making it a feasible vehicle for production. However, it would be superseded by something more exciting: the new Jeepster.

The 'Icon' concept vehicle takes some of the features of the ECCO, including the unequal length, wishbone all-independent suspension. It still has very strong Jeep looks, and in particular round headlights – the YJ treatment has never been repeated on a 'trad' Jeep – and a seven-slat grille echo the old MB across the decades.

The return of the Jeepster

Introduced to the press in mid-1998, a new concept vehicle brought back an old name: the Jeepster. AMC had revived the Jeepster name for another concept car in the early 1980s, but it went no further. Based on the 1997 ZJ Grand Cherokee platform, Chrysler's Jeepster took not only the idea of the Jeepster, but also that of its preceding concept cars, the ECCO and the Icon, to the limits. Designer Mike Moore is British-born, and his idea was to take the power and excitement of a true sports car, and put it into a genuine off-road package. A roll-back roof sits above a body that takes its styling cues from Kaiser's Jeepster, including a seven-slat grille and circular headlights. Even the Jeep's wartime heritage is recalled, with military-style instruments. Under the bonnet is the 4.7-litre V8 from the WJ Grand Cherokee, tuned to produce a maximum of 275bhp, put through the dual-range Quadra-Trac II four-wheel-drive system and a four-speed auto gearbox. Alloy wheels of 9x19in dimension give the Jeepster a purposeful look, and the ride height of its all-independent suspension can be adjusted by an electronically controlled screw-drive mechanism. For highway use there is a low clearance setting of 5.75in (146mm), and then there is a higher 9.75in (248mm) clearance for off-road work. DaimlerChrysler claimed no plans to put the Jeepster into production . . . but that is what was said about the Dodge Viper and the Plymouth Prowler. . .

The Dakar

Concept cars can be roughly divided into two groups: the extreme and the feasible, and the Dakar fits into the second category. Jeep people say that Dakar 'takes Wrangler's amazing versatility and extends it'. Essentially, Dakar is a TJ Wrangler built upon the 108in (2,743mm) wheelbase frame found on Venezuelan and Israeli YJs. The 4-litre in-line six engine, the four-speed automatic transmission, solid axles and coil-spring suspension were all TJ. And thanks to the longer wheelbase it showed all the highway manners of the

The Jeepster. The lowest point of any vehicle is the differential, and this dictates the ground clearance of an off-road car. On a solid axle Jeep, extra ground clearance is gained by first fitting larger tyres and wheels. The Jeepster's unequal length, wishbone front suspension – visible in this front end picture – can be raised 5in (127mm), lifting the differential higher without the need for bigger wheels, suspension lifts or body lifts. Whether the Jeepster will go into production is anyone's guess. . .

The Dakar. Based closely on the TJ, it could easily become a production vehicle if customer demand, and the will to make it, are there. Behind the front wheel is a folding shovel.

Wrangler, plus a better ride. The TJ Wrangler front sheet metal gives the 'separate wing' look in the old Jeep tradition, something that other makers of off-road vehicles try and emulate by fitting huge, flared wheel arches. But from the cowl back, the full four-door enclosed steel body was all new. There is a fixed windscreen and a full-width single rear door, and the roof has a slide-back canvas section, built-in tubular roofrack with rally lamps and the spare tyre. As a full four-seater station wagon, it was not only what it looked – a safari and adventure vehicle – but with running gear and dimensions equivalent to an XJ Cherokee, it was potentially a good family car, too.

The Commander

Chrysler continues to explore the future of automotive technology, and in particular, alternative fuels. The Jeep Commander concept vehicle was exhibited at the 1999 Los Angeles Auto Show. The Commander's designer, Trevor Creed, states on the very first page of the publicity brochure: 'This concept marries the industry's most advanced powertrain with one of the fastest growing market segments.'

The principle was to apply good fuel economy, a feature normally associated with small cars, to a much larger vehicle. Styled like the Grand Cherokee, the Commander is constructed entirely of carbon fibre, in just the same way as a Formula One Grand Prix car: this combines strength with lightness, and gives the sort of shapes that cannot be formed in pressed steel. It is claimed to be 50 per cent lighter, and it is said to save between 10 and 50 per cent in manufacturing costs, and to provide an almost 100 per cent recyclable body. Its shape is specifically designed to maximize the aerodynamics when the vehicle is travelling at speed, in particular the smooth underbelly pan and retractable roofrack and spoiler.

The most innovative part of the Commander is as yet not fully developed. In 1997, Chrysler engineers suggested that hydrogen could be extracted from petrol in a fuel cell, and could be used to generate electricity to drive a motor vehicle.

The huge Commander concept vehicle uses a fuel cell to generate electricity from liquid fuel. Styling is true Jeep station wagon, even down to the seven-slat grille. The graphics to the left of the picture refer to the built-in control features offered to the driver.

DaimlerChrysler's engineers planned to have the fuel cell fully functioning by the end of 1999, using methanol as its fuel; methanol does not require the same bulky fuel tanks that hydrogen needs, and it is as safe in use and storage as petrol. The merger of the two companies promises to help that development greatly. At the time of Commander's introduction, the drive is from electric motors on both axles, as you would expect on a Jeep. Voice-operated controls are another main feature of the Commander.

All existing Jeep vehicles follow the tried and tested formula of solid axles. With the exception of the Dakar, all Chrysler Jeep concept vehicles since the ECCO of 1993 have used unequal length independent suspension. Also, the Jeepster and the Commander use an electrically controlled mechanical jacking device to raise the ground clearance for off-road work.

All this clearly indicates that Jeep intends to keep its place as the premier on- and off-road performer. And if Chrysler engineers follow this path into production

vehicles, then whatever the motive power, the Jeep of the future will not only offer the best performance on the highway, but will continue to astound even its truest followers off-road. Thus Jeep will still be true to its roots.

The Commander's fascia is taken from the WJ, but is adapted to take blue LCD displays. The centre console can dock a lap-top computer, giving a GPS facility and internet access for traffic and weather reports. Voice activation operates the controls of both the vehicle and the add-on facilities. If the vehicle is stolen, a small camera photographs the thief and sends the picture to the police.

10 Owning and Using Jeeps

Jeeps were always meant to be used. Immediately following World War II, Jeeps were not only being used for any number of industrial and agricultural uses, but for sport as well. And so it has gone on, with Jeeps being taken off the road for competition or just for the sheer pleasure of getting away from it all. American Motors were extremely wise to move away from the workhorse image to the leisure market at home, for the growth in this sector was nothing short of amazing. The Jeep has also found its niche in the more modern phenomenon of the classic vehicle world, the military vehicle preservation movement – and of course in off-road work.

TRAILING

Enzo Ferrari was once quoted as saying that the Jeep was America's only true sports car, and there are plenty of people all over the world who spend their weekends and holidays trying to prove him right. Jeep trailing in America is almost as old as the Jeep itself. Some of the first, such as the DeAnza Jeep Cavalcade in the desert in Hemet, California, began in 1948. The great majority of the competing Jeeps were ex-military, but amongst the hundred plus that took part in the two-day event there were some new CJs. A number of these were trail-prepped with more powerful engines and uprated transmissions, and nearly all were towed to the venue behind family cars. The whole business grew. Now, Jeep jamborees in the US attract huge

numbers, and for many, going to one of the big events is the trip of a lifetime.

OFF-ROAD COMPETITION IN BRITAIN

It didn't take too long for British motor sport enthusiasts to discover the Jeep's abilities, and to start playing around with them. Trials, as opposed to trailing, has been a popular form of off-road motor sport in Britain for many years; competitions are held for both cars and motorcycles, but in essence they follow the same format. Trials are not speed events: they are tests of sheer driving skill in adverse conditions. The cars first used – and still used – are lightweight, rear-wheel drive, open two-seaters, based around the Austin Seven and small side-valve Fords. The object is to drive around a marked-out course, over steep gradients, mud, rocks or whatever can be found, without stopping or reversing. Either of these will incur penalties, and the competitor with the least penalties at the end of the day is the winner.

The All-Wheel Drive Club (The AWDC or 'All Wet and Dirty Club' as they became known) was a pioneer in introducing four-wheel-drive vehicles to trials. The club was started by Brian Bashall as a spin-off from the Rover Owners Club. Not surprisingly, the ROC was not interested in any other off-road vehicle than the Land Rover, but many Land Rover owners also had other makes of four-wheel-drive vehicles. Brian therefore felt that there could be an all-

Pat Willis on the trials course at Broxhead Common in the late 1960s. Mechanically this jeep is standard. Even the exhaust, which is re-routed around the front, is a late military optional item, designed to clear deep fords. The lights are removed for safety reasons, and a roll bar fitted. Mounting a roll bar too rigidly could prevent a jeep chassis from flexing too much, so care had to be taken to allow just a bit of 'give' without making it insecure.

sorts club for off-roaders, and in response to his advertisement in the magazine *Exchange and Mart*, some three dozen vehicles with their owners met in the summer of 1968 at Blacknest farm, Dunsfold, Surrey. The AWDC was born.

Most of those four-wheel-drive vehicles were either ex-military or had some military connection; they included Jeeps, Land Rovers, Austin Champs and Gypsys and Haflingers. All these found their way onto trials courses, though the flat-fender jeep was the best of the bunch. In first gear and low range four-wheel drive it could climb anything, its low profile keeping it stable where Haflingers and Champs were likely to topple over, and its flexible chassis enabling it almost to bend over uneven ground.

The club often had to prepare their own courses, sometimes cutting down trees – a practice which nowadays would create an outcry! – in the Camberley and Pirbright areas of Surrey, where most of the early members lived. The early competitions were very informal and were run for the fun of it – and according to all those who entered, that's just how they were.

At the Hungry Hill trial in summer 1970 a speed event was introduced. Whilst there were not many competitors at first, it grew in popularity and more powerful trials cars were built for the class. Some Jeeps were fitted with hotter engines, including American V8s, but specials began to rule the class and Jeeps were seen less and less.

The Welsh Hill Rally of 1971 was a turning point in the AWDC's history, and was a nemesis for the Jeep in UK off-road competition. It was a Rover whitewash. Land Rovers were far more plentiful, and as the seventies progressed, the Range Rover provided a ready-made V8 conversion. Spares were easy to get, and the Land Rover, the Range Rover and hybrids of the two got more popular, ousting Jeeps. Spares for the MB and those CJ-5s that were used began to get scarce, and the Jeep became the tool of the true enthusiast. Wranglers are seen today, as are CJ-5s and CJ-7s. In fact the rules have been amended to allow CJ-6s and CJ-8s to reverse just once on each section of the course without penalty, as despite their amazing ability, they are simply too big to get round the tighter turns. But many older UK-owned Jeeps are collectors' items, and often owners are not willing to risk these valuable vehicles on cross-country courses.

MILITARY JEEPS

If you love military vehicles, and want one for yourself, a jeep has to be one of the most practical types you can buy and run. If you are hardy enough, then they can even be used as a daily driver. Simply made, the jeep was designed to be serviced in the field – literally! The very early models, such as the MA, GP and Bantam, if you can find one, are the realm of the skilled specialist. On the other hand, an MB, GPW, MC or M38AI is a viable proposition. They will fit in the garage and don't demand huge lifting tackle when you come to work on them. A jeep's bodywork is extremely simple, and the mechanical components equally so in comparison with modern vehicles. Almost every spare part is available, some as a re-manufactured item and some, remarkably, as new old stock, and a number of specialist dealers supply them.

There are two very good options for the newcomer. One is an ex-French army Hotchkiss, whose 12v electrics spin the engine over faster than the heart-stopping chug of a 6v Willys! Hotchkiss models were carefully maintained, and during their service life were often upgraded with the addition of more modern equipment such as an alternator. In addition, a good many

1950s French-built Hotchkiss, the driver in a French uniform, giving a lift to two passengers dressed as German World War II officers, in mid Kent. It could only happen in a military rally like War and Peace.

MB spares will fit them. The second option is a Dutch-built M38A1. These were assembled in the Nekaf factory in Holland, and were used for a considerable time by the Dutch army. Just like the Hotchkiss, the Nekaf M38A1s were well maintained, and can be bought at a quite reasonable price.

Restoring and buying military Jeeps

When restoring any historic vehicle – one is tempted to use the over-worked word 'classic', although in every sense the jeep is a prime example of a classic – the question arises: to what degree do you restore? Jeeps were built as military vehicles, and never given a showroom shine. Thus we can coin a phrase 'service condition' – that is to say, as it would be found in military service: clean and fully roadworthy, with properly undertaken repairs and modifications made during its service life. A few genuinely acquired combat wounds such as dents or bullet holes add to the character and patina.

But what about that old chestnut, 'originality'? Many jeeps were built and rebuilt in the field and in the workshops and motor pools around the world, and modified by many units whilst in active service. Quite a lot of owners fit their jeeps out in the colours of particular regiments. Sourcing the right colours, and getting hold of the correct equipment to fit on a particular vehicle, is all part of the enjoyment of ownership.

You could also bring your jeep up to ex-factory condition. Although the MB and the GPW were intended to be identical, there are a great number of detail differences between the two. For instance Ford marked all of their bolt heads and many of their components with an F. Also, the Willys has a tubular front cross-member, whereas the Ford's is a square-section pressing. A lot of

the minor fittings are different, but are completely interchangeable. In the field they were almost certainly swapped, and parts taken from a wrecked jeep to keep another in service. So if you want to bring an MB back to how it left Toledo, you may have to do a lot of work to change every little detail. On your side is the fact that the Army would not allow Willys or Ford to make any improvements to the jeep during its wartime manufacture. But you could just leave a few parts different, on the premise that they might have been fitted in service because that was all there was to hand!

Some Hotchkiss models of 1950s vintage have been painted in World War II colours, and some flat-fender CJs have been converted to an MB look-alike. If you want a genuine MB or GPW, look to see that it has no tail-gate, or filler cap in the driver's side (the wartime jeeps had the filler cap under the driver's seat), and make sure that it does have a lower windscreen. (This can be misleading, as a number of CJ windscreens were fitted to MBs and GPWs in an earlier civilian existence to give more headroom.) And check the commission plate, although it is possible that this might have been changed. Also, many UK-owned Nekaf M38A1s have been 'Americanized': that is, painted in US Army markings. The owners of these are quite happy to say that this has been done, and they are often used as part of an American Army display.

But beware of what might be termed counterfeit vehicles. Within the law, everyone is entitled to do as they like with their own vehicle. If you know what you are buying and the vendor tells you what it is, then fine. However, if, for example, a Hotchkiss or a CJ were to be advertised as a wartime MB and the intending purchaser was unaware of the difference and the vendor had no intent of saying so, then that is a more serious matter.

It must be said that it is questionable as

The final prize-giving at the War and Peace show, Beltring. This is the largest military vehicle show in Europe. The line-up of class winners here is just a small percentage of the number of vehicles present. There were over 350 Jeeps entered alone!

to why flat-fender CJs are converted to wartime replicas. Whether the value of a wartime vehicle is more than that of the CJ is open to debate, but the CJ, especially the 2A, is very much the rarer beast, so it ought to be a good idea to keep CJs original, or to revert a converted one back to 'civvies'.

Military rallies

When you have got your military jeep on the road, take it to military rallies. Here you can make new friends and meet up with old ones, and discuss your pride and joy with the visiting public. The autojumble

and trade stalls make an ideal opportunity for finding that elusive part you've been hunting for for months or even years. The largest military rally in the UK is the War and Peace Show, held every July near Ashford in Kent, by the Invicta Military Vehicle Preservation Society (the IMPS). The proximity of the venue to the Channel Tunnel and ferry ports means that a great many continental owners visit the show, and it's not uncommon to see all kinds of military vehicles with French, Dutch, Belgian and German number plates.

The Military Vehicle Trust is a national organization but with many informally run branches, and its members have interests in all makes, ages and types of military vehicle. The Trust was formed in 1969 from a group of local enthusiasts. Today they hold shows around the country, and organize trips abroad, such as to Normandy for D-Day anniversaries. The clubs are run very well, and the atmosphere at the meetings is very informal and welcoming to a newcomer.

JEEP AND CLASSIC CAR SHOWS

Car shows, especially the ones for American cars, are a popular venue for Wagoneers, CJs and early Willys vehicles. Even though a CJ-7 might present a stark contrast to a 1959 Cadillac, there is no disputing that both are true American legends in their own right! At most car shows in the UK you will find, not surprisingly, British vehicles in the majority, but American cars have a smaller but very enthusiastic following, and there is no reason why Jeeps shouldn't be seen alongside Morris Minors and Triumph TR4s. Just be sure to check whether there is an age limit for entries: some car shows have one, sometimes excluding vehicles built before 1970, so your prized CJ-7 would sadly be excluded. However, many car shows have classes for military vehicles too, so an army jeep would be a welcome entry.

Nowadays there are shows exclusively for Jeep owners, and these are a new and welcome addition to their calendar. First there was the Jeep Show, and more recently the annual Sheffield-based Jeepfest, run by *Jeep World* magazine. Jeepfest gives the enthusiast a chance to meet other Jeep addicts, to test their toys on an off-road course, and to buy spares and accessories from a number of suppliers. Held over the August Bank Holiday weekend, on-site camping and evening entertainment make for a complete, exciting family event. Very welcome has been the support of Chrysler Jeep UK, who have given the chance for many people to ride in brand new Jeep vehicles over the off-road course.

New and old go through the cross-country course at the 1999 annual Jeep World *magazine Jeepfest. In the foreground is a TJ Wrangler, and behind, on a parallel course, is a CJ-6.*

Jeepfest offers the chance to get you and your Jeep just a bit muddy.

XJ Cherokees cope easily with off-road courses.

GREEN LANING

This is a subject that can cause controversy, but with common sense and respect for others it need not. Some walkers and horse riders may disapprove of large 4x4s of any sort being driven along unmade roads, but grass-roots countryside users have respect for each others' rights of way. After all, most farmers, and many people who both live and work in the countryside, own and use 4x4s themselves. The great majority of 4x4 owners – and it is appropriate to talk of enthusiasts of all makes here – do treat the countryside responsibly and are more considerate than some casual day-trippers on foot or in ordinary cars, who have little experience of the country code.

Rights of way are historical, and are often enshrined in common law rather than statute law – and herein lies the problem. There are, generally, three categories of rights of way in the countryside: footpaths, bridleways and byways. Footpaths are for walkers, bridleways are for walkers and horses (but not horse-drawn carriages), and byways are for all traffic. Motor vehi-

cles may not use bridleways or footpaths. There are also unclassified roads, which can be either 'made' (with a hard surface) or 'unmade'. Green lanes fall into the byways category, but the law concerning access to them by motor vehicles is something of a grey area, as rights of access in general are claimed by historical usage.

Establishing what constitutes historical use is the source of the conflict. Those ramblers and riders who would oppose the use of green lanes by motor vehicles may make a general claim that green lanes have been used by farm traffic, including cattle droves, for centuries, and that the rights of way over them are for non-motor traffic. Use by a motor vehicle over a period of, say, ten to twenty years on a regular basis may be considered fairly to be historical use, and this is the basis of off-roaders' arguments. But historical use has to start with one single occasion, and militant anti-motor vehicle campaigners would sooner prevent an off-roader using a by-way in the first place.

But how will a newcomer to green-laning know what routes can be used? Before the coming of the road makers Telford and

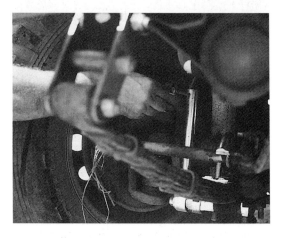

Going off-road. First, disconnect the anti-roll bar: doing this will allow full axle articulation.

Next, lock the free-wheel hubs, if your Jeep has them. For dry dirt, fat tyres like these are fine. For mud, you need something skinny to sink down to the more solid stuff. The winch on the front is not for show: there are times when it can be a life-saver for hauling a disabled Jeep or even pulling a rolled-over Jeep off a trapped occupant.

Grab handles are useful if you don't want your passenger in your lap. . . It's always best to go off-road in company, as you can never be sure of not getting into trouble. A CB radio is essential, and for excursions over big areas, GPS must be considered as something for the immediate future.

Selecting low-range four-wheel drive, we can set off to find some interesting going, like this drop. Keep it steady: first gear, foot off the clutch and let the engine do the braking. This Scrambler is actually an automatic, so even though it is in 'low', a touch of brake may be necessary.

MacAdam and the mail coaches that used the new turnpikes, ancient rights of way would be known locally. There was certainly no Ordnance Survey to supply maps to anyone who needed to know where they were going. Knowledge of drovers' roads was passed around the community, handed down from father to son, and from master to apprentice. Even then the route to take would change with the season: thus the high road, which would be perhaps a steeper or longer path, but dry, would be used when the low road might be impassable in winter. No sensible user would take his cart or livestock along the wetter, and therefore more difficult or impassable route.

The principle of local knowledge of byways is as valid today as it was a century or two ago, only nowadays, that knowledge is found with local members of such organizations as the All-Wheel Drive Club, and within local off-road groups. Anyone wishing to take their Jeep – or any other 4x4, for that matter – on green lanes should join such a club and get to know the people involved, because they will know what byways you can use, and which to avoid. Buy some up-to-date Ordnance Survey maps and a compass, and learn how to read them – but remember that not all unclassified roads are marked, so if you are in any doubt about your rights to use a route, leave well enough alone. It is far better to find out later at a club meeting that you could have used that route, than to find yourself confronted by an angry land owner who is well within his rights to order you off his property!

Clubs do stress that green laning is for observing and enjoying the countryside. There may be parts of a byway that require some skill in negotiation, and testing your driving skill is part of the enjoyment. However, green laning is not about high speed work. If you want to do that, go in for one of the competitions organized specifically for the purpose.

It cannot be stressed enough that off-roaders should act responsibly. Don't drive recklessly and churn up paths and roads. Leave farm gates as you found them, whether open or closed (remember, a farmer may have left his gate open deliberately to allow his livestock to move into a different field). Do not leave litter around, or make excessive noise, stick at all times to the tracks you are allowed to use, and don't trespass onto land where you shouldn't be.

The Cherokee and Wrangler Rubicon

Jeeps' off-road performance is inherent, but in the early years, comfort was not. These days Wranglers, Cherokees and Grand Cherokees can be driven in comfort over long distances to more remote countryside, taken over the most difficult terrain with no more alteration necessary than disconnecting the anti-roll bar if an attachment is fitted, and then driven home in the same comfort. Taking this ability further, and proving it to hard-bitten motoring writers, was the motive behind two remarkable Jeeps: the Cherokee Rubicon and the Wrangler Rubicon.

The story goes back to the mid-1980s. Chris Bashall, the son of AWDC founder Brian Bashall, was not happy with the sort of after-market service that off-road enthusiasts were getting, so he set up his own company, Surrey Off-Road; at first they were based in Cranleigh, Surrey, then in

The Cherokee 2.5 turbo-diesel Rubicon, built to demonstrate Jeep's total versatility, even with some degree of suspension lift. The Rubicon can be driven on the highway in complete comfort, yet the suspension modifications enable it to tackle some pretty rough country.

1995 they moved to nearby Dunsfold. The company supplies a full range of accessories for all Jeep models from CJ-5s through to TJ Wranglers, and also specializes in building high quality, custom off-road vehicles. The preparation of vehicles for major expeditions is also part of the company's business.

Then Barry Stallard of Chrysler Jeep UK asked Surrey Off-Road to build a special XJ Cherokee for a customer; it was christened the Rubicon after the famous trail that all new Jeep models have to be capable of driving. Later, he went to Surrey Off-Road with a very special request. French off-road events are very much tougher than those held in the UK, by virtue of some much more rugged countryside; moreover nearly all the competitors take their vehicles to and from the

With 7in (178mm) of axle articulation each side, the Wrangler Rubicon can ride over the most difficult ground. The standard-tune 4-litre six gives plenty of power, but at a comfortable cruising speed of 60mph (100kmph) the driver and passenger can still hear the radio.

competition on a trailer. Chrysler, however, were to put absolute faith in the TJ Wrangler: they wanted one that would be capable not only of taking part in the off-road event in the hands of motoring writers, but also of being driven the length of France both to and from the event in comfort similar to, or very close to a standard vehicle.

The result was the Rubicon II. The chassis modifications are in no way extreme: it has a Teraflex 3in (76mm) suspension lift, a 1in (25mm) body lift, Rancho 9000 shock absorbers and 33/9.0x15 Mud Terrain tyres. Everything else on the Rubicon II is necessary extra equipment, such as Warn winches front and rear, a Rokraider snorkel, an ARB air-operated differential lock, a windscreen protection frame and extra lights. Pioneer tools were fitted on the back as much as a joke as anything else, although they have proved useful in digging other vehicles out of trouble!

The Rubicon II was given to motoring writers, who were told they could take it from Chrysler Jeep UK's base in Dover, across the Channel, drive it down to one of Europe's toughest off-road events, the Trophée Cevenol in the South of France, and drive it back – in comfort. Where other competition vehicles were trailered to the event, the Rubicon II cruised down the autoroute at around 60mph (100kmph) (the diff. ratio is a low 4.56:1) with the radio playing (and still audible!). The writers com-

pleted the course, and came home again with no problems. This was surely a vindication not only of Chrysler's faith in the product, but of Surrey Off-Road's workmanship and Jeep's own engineering capabilities and dedication to the concept.

Chris Bashall has also built what must be the UK's ultimate YJ. It uses Warn Black Diamond coil-spring conversion, which does away with the original leaf spring set-up. Long radius arms, anchored close to the transfer box, locate each of the Dana axles – a 30 on the front and a 44 at the rear – and CVJ is fitted to the centre of the rear drive-shaft. The original 4.0-litre engine is basically unmodified, although there is a custom-built exhaust system with a dual cat-alytic converter and dual silencer. This YJ is right-hand drive, and the five-speed gearbox has a JB short-shift conversion. It has been tested on the Trophée Cevenol, and gave an outstanding performance.

Surrey Off-Road's YJ Wrangler. Clearly seen are the windscreen protection frame, and the snorkel, rising along the driver's side of the windscreen. The degree of axle articulation given by the Warn Black Diamond coil-spring suspension conversion is vividly shown – the body is at an angle of some 30° to the rear axle.

Furthermore there are plenty of other users, such as walkers, mountain bikers and horse riders, who have just as much right to the road as you. Be courteous to others on foot or on horseback. If you come across a horse and rider, give them right of way. Don't sound your horn or rev your engine, and be prepared to switch off your engine if the horse appears nervous. A horse has a mind of its own, which it can use unexpectedly against the will of others; your Jeep does not, much as you might think it has sometimes! The sight of a brightly painted CJ with wide wheels may well be an unfamiliar, terrifying sight to the animal, but a sensible rider will take the opportunity to accustom their horse to this strange sight: if the off-roader can accomodate this, then relationships between the two sports have a good chance of remaining amicable. Only by careful, responsible, considerate conduct can the

privilege of driving off-road be kept, and your enjoyment of it maintained.

RESTORING AND MAINTAINING JEEPS

Spares for civilian Jeep models imported from 1972 onwards are obtainable in the UK through specialist dealers, which can be traced through off-roading and jeep magazines. Parts for the older civilian models such as Station Wagons, Trucks, Jeepsters and FCs need to be traced in the USA. Parts for MBs and GPWs are the most readily available from specialist suppliers, and M38A1 parts are not too difficult to come by. Club and national magazines are the best place to find these suppliers, who not only sell remanufactured parts, but have a surprising amount of new old stock available.

Early XJ Cherokees, Comanches and Wagoneers are different in many respects from the post-1993 models, and parts cannot be obtained from main dealers. These must be sourced from specialists, but are readily obtainable. YJ and TJ Wranglers, XJ Cherokees and ZJ and WJ Grand Cherokees are modern vehicles. Spares for those models imported directly by Chrysler Jeep UK can be supplied from a local Chrysler Jeep dealer. Officially imported XJ, ZJ and Wranglers have been excellent sellers. They are tough and have a very long life. New, they are top value; good second-hand examples hold their value well; and there are over one hundred Chrysler Jeep dealers across the UK to keep them serviced.

MODIFIED JEEPS

There are a number of specialist dealers who sell and sometimes fit a huge variety

A Jeep half-breed

When Brooks Stevens and Achille Sampietro put their talents together to produce the Wagoneer and Gladiator, they built a station wagon and a truck with both highway comfort and top class off-road performance. Now what would you do if you wanted a jeep with the off-road ability of a trail-prepped CJ or Wrangler, but with the comfort, stability and power of the Wagoneer? One answer is to buy a Grand Cherokee, but that would not come cheap, despite the ZJ and WJ's undoubted value. So what if you had a rusting SJ Cherokee on your hands?

One of Richard Pickles' cut-down SJ Cherokee specials. That's not a Jeepster grille, but an eleven slatter, made up of two CJ items. The bonnet is widened by welding in the centre section from the Cherokee.

In 1993 Richard Pickles had a Cherokee Chief that was suffering more than the usual amount of rust, so he built a unique off-road Jeep special. He chopped off most of the body, shortened the chassis by 14in (356mm), moved the 360ci V8 back a bit and built a new open body using CJ and Cherokee bits. CJ front wings were grafted onto the Cherokee scuttle, and the bonnet was widened with the centre section of the Cherokee's. A new grille was made up by welding two sections of CJ grilles together. The rear body was built from scratch, as the Cherokee's was beyond practical repair.

Not satisfied with just one, Richard built three more, this time using rear bodies made from the donor Cherokees. And according to those who own and drive these vehicles, their performance is outstanding. The power of the 360ci V8 is no longer hampered by the weight of the SJ body, which is nearly a ton lighter. Each of the four specials – they have yet to be given any name – are automatics with Borg-Warner Quadra-Trac. Moreover the lighter weight, longer wheelbase, wider track, and the springing which was originally set for a big body all combine to give a ride far better than a CJ or a YJ. And so far as anyone knows, nothing like these have been built anywhere else but in England – even the Americans have not cottoned on to the idea.

of accessories to make your Jeep an even more impressive performer off-road. The most common modifications involve suspension and body lifts and bigger tyres. Suspension modifications, such as a detachable anti-roll bar, enable the axles to articulate to a greater extent, keeping all four wheels on the dirt on extreme ground. In doing this, the wheels risk fouling the body, so a suspension lift and a body lift give just that bit more room.

Roll bars are essential for off-road work. Sometimes an owner can become somewhat over-ambitious, and come tumbling down from a hill, or hit a hidden tree stump when driving at an angle of 45°, and roll over. That roll bar may save his life. 'Bull bars' sometimes suffer from a bad press, although this is generally in connection to their being fitted to suburban 4x4s whose only off-road work is a supermarket car park. Again, if a Jeep starts to slide down a slope in thick mud, that bull bar may save some expensive damage.

The correct choice of tyre is important, too. The type of countryside available to UK off-roaders is more often than not totally different from the terrain typically used in the USA. For instance, when tackling the huge rocks found in the wilds of America, huge tyres must be fitted in order to get any grip on them at all. The traction is often better than on a highway – and herein lies a danger, because if driving a Jeep without a centre differential over big, smooth rocks, putting on too much power can wind up and literally snap an axle. In the softer going found in the UK, wide tyres are fine in dry conditions; for mud, however, a thinner tyre with a more open tread is best because they allow the Jeep to sink right through the softer mud and find harder ground underneath.

Two trail-prepped CJs, both with Chevy V8 power, if a potential 120mph (190kmph) with no doors is your thing. Speed is not the real reason for fitting a big engine in a Jeep, but low down grunt for getting over big obstacles. It can't be stressed enough that fitting big brakes and strong axles go hand in hand with installing big, high-powered engines.

Tailpiece

Beware: Jeeps are addictive! If this isn't a window sticker, it should be. Once you have owned a Jeep, whether it is a military model, a CJ or a modern Cherokee, you'll buy another one, sometimes before you've sold the first! The Jeep brand engenders a great loyalty amongst its owners, a loyalty earned by the vehicles' inherent toughness and uncompromising off-road performance. The origins of the name 'Jeep' has been the subject of years of discussion and false information for as long as the Jeep has been in existence. At one time it was said to stand for 'Just Enough Essential Parts', but Chrysler Jeep UK's advertising people put things into perspective in the course of their campaign for the Cherokee. The slogan simply said 'Now you don't have to accept Jeep imitations'.

Index